Dancers as Diplomats

DANCERS AS DIPLOMATS

American Choreography in Cultural Exchange

Clare Croft

OXFORD
UNIVERSITY PRESS

OXFORD
UNIVERSITY PRESS

Oxford University Press is a department of the University of
Oxford. It furthers the University's objective of excellence in research,
scholarship, and education by publishing worldwide.

Oxford   New York
Auckland   Cape Town   Dar es Salaam   Hong Kong   Karachi
Kuala Lumpur   Madrid   Melbourne   Mexico City   Nairobi
New Delhi   Shanghai   Taipei   Toronto

With offices in
Argentina   Austria   Brazil   Chile   Czech Republic   France   Greece
Guatemala   Hungary   Italy   Japan   Poland   Portugal   Singapore
South Korea   Switzerland   Thailand   Turkey   Ukraine   Vietnam

Oxford is a registered trademark of Oxford University Press
in the UK and certain other countries.

Published in the United States of America by
Oxford University Press
198 Madison Avenue, New York, NY 10016

Library of Congress Cataloging-in-Publication Data
Croft, Clare.
Dancers as diplomats / Clare Croft.
    pages cm.
Includes bibliographical references and index.
ISBN 978-0-19-995819-1 (hardcover : alk. paper)—ISBN 978-0-19-995821-4 (pbk. : alk. paper)
1. Dance—Social aspects.   2. Dancers—Travel.   3. Diplomacy.   4. Cultural relations.
5. United States—Foreign relations.   I. Title.
GV1588.6.C75 2015
306.4'846—dc23
2014022835

CONTENTS

ACKNOWLEDGMENTS

I can scarcely believe the amount of kind, smart, generous support I have received throughout the years that have gone into this book.

Teachers have always shaped my life in important ways. Without the example, mentorship, and profound generosity and guidance of Jill Dolan, I am not sure where I would be. Thank you so much. Charlotte Canning has been a stalwart mentor and offered incredibly incisive comments about the performance of nation. Deborah Paredez, Michael Kackman, and Susan Foster have constantly reminded me that asking hard questions is the best form of mentorship. I am particularly grateful to Deborah for her work on divas, without which chapter 3 would not have been possible. Martha Norkunas taught me that listening could be a radical political practice, and set an example I will always try to model. I am also indebted to Jon McKenzie and Ann Daly, who saw the promise of this project before I did.

A number of teachers created the spaces where I first imagined dance could be a way of thinking about the world. I am grateful to Chrystelle Bond for introducing the very idea of dance scholarship to me. Mary Marchand guided me and listened with a generous ear as I first imagined what dance, theory, and politics might have to do with one another. Finally, my love for writing about dance has roots in a tiny dance studio in Andalusia, Alabama. I could never have written a book had Meryane Murphy not taught me through dance what it means to work in a rigorous, impassioned, and disciplined way.

I have also been lucky to be part of a network of dance studies scholars who have been wonderful interlocutors over the years. Kate Elswit, Hannah Kosstrin, Katherine Profeta, and Rebecca Rossen found time to read drafts and give me thoughtful feedback. I am grateful to all the participants in the Mellon Dance Studies in/and the Humanities 2013 Summer Seminar at Brown University. I am also grateful to all those who gave me feedback at a variety of conference presentations, including the conferences of the American Studies Association, Congress on Research in Dance, Society of Dance History Scholars, American Society for Theatre Research, Association for Theatre in Higher Education, and the Collegium for African Diaspora Dance.

A number of fellowships and organizations have generously supported my research. At the University of Texas at Austin, I received a Continuing Fellowship that allowed me to complete my dissertation. At the University of Michigan a number of sources have supported me: the Michigan Society of Fellows, a Faculty Seed Grant from the Institute for Research on Women and Gender, grants from the Center for Research on Learning and Teaching, and grants from the Nam Center for Korean Studies. Funding from the Nam Center was supported by the Academy of Korean Studies (KSPS) and a Grant funded by the Korean Government (MOE) (AKS-2011-BAA-2102.)

My research was also made possible through the generosity of friends who housed me many times over, including Erik and Lisa Oksala and Jonathan and Kate Eyler-Werve. Margaret Hanson, whose picture may well appear in the dictionary next to the word "generous," let me live with her in New York while I was visiting archives and chasing dancers across the city. Thank you, Margaret, Captain, and Chance Hanson.

Every historian knows that the secret to strong research is the people in libraries who help make it possible. For their assistance with archival work, I am particularly grateful to Vera Ekechukwu in Special Collections at the University of Arkansas and Pat Rader at the Jerome Robbins Dance Collection of the New York Public Library. While she is not officially an archivist, Tara Sheena has been a remarkable excavator of every photograph in this book, a tiring task I never could have done without her. I am also grateful to Michigan students Inae Chung, Andrea Davis, Nora Hauk, and Scott De Orio for their help with translation, and to Lisa Chippi, Willie Filkowski, Brian Garcia, Maddy Rager, and Nola Smith for their proofreading assistance.

Previous versions of portions of this work have appeared in academic journals. At *Theatre Journal*, I am grateful to Catherine Schuler's editorial guidance with the article, "Ballet Nations," which appears in part in chapter 1 of this book. At *Dance Research Journal*, I thank editor Mark Franko, who edited the article, "Dance Returns to American Cultural Diplomacy," portions of which appear in chapter 4. I am also grateful to *Dance Magazine* and Dance/USA's *From the Green Room* for giving me opportunities to write about dance and cultural diplomacy in popular venues.

At Oxford University Press, Norm Hirschy has shepherded this work for years, and I am grateful for his expert advice and boundless enthusiasm.

He also secured anonymous readers who provided insightful feedback on earlier versions of this book, and I thank them for their careful readings.

This book has now moved with me through a number of periods in my life, from the Austin heat to the Michigan winter. My sense that dance could transform the social and political was largely forged in the community of the Performance as Public Practice program at the University of Texas, where I had simply amazing colleagues who expanded my mind every day—often over the best fish tacos we could find. I am particularly grateful to those who read and commented on portions of this book: Michelle Dvoskin, Rebecca Hewett, Kelly Howe, Jenny Kokai, Patrick McKelvey, and Tamara Smith. My intellectual growth in Austin, and, indeed, much of this book, would never have been possible without Angie Ahlgren's brilliant support. In Austin and long before, I have been lucky to tread so many paths with Amanda Moulder, whose friendship challenges and sustains me always.

This book took its final form at the University of Michigan, where I was lucky enough to be part of two networks of intellectual and artistic support. I'd like to thank my students and colleagues in the Department of Dance who remind me every day that dancing is an intellectual, socially engaged, and beautiful action. Second, I'd like to thank the world's most stimulating community: everyone in the Michigan Society of Fellows, but particularly Don Lopez, Linda Turner, Roger Grant, Lily Cox-Richard, Beth Pringle, Sarah Quinn, and Brian Kapusta. And then there's Sara McClelland, my fellow among the fellows, who reminds me always to think big ideas with love, hope, and laughter. I'll see you on the boat soon.

Finally, no words could express my love and gratitude to Rozilyn, John, Johnny, and Harper Croft for their unending support and love. Mom and Dad, thank you for believing that dance scholarship was indeed a thing a person could do.

I'm grateful to *Theatre Journal* and *Dance Research Journal* for granting permission to use portions of the following previously published material: Copyright © 2009 The Johns Hopkins University Press. "Ballet Nations: The New York City Ballet's 1962 US State Department-Sponsored Tour of the Soviet Union" first appeared in *THEATRE JOURNAL*, Volume 61, Issue 3, October, 2009, pages 421–442.

"Dance Returns to American Cultural Diplomacy: The US State Department's 2003 Dance Residency Program and Its After Effects," by Clare Croft, *Dance Research Journal*, Volume 45, Issue 01 (April 2013), pp. 23–39 Copyright © 2013 Congress on Research in Dance. Reprinted with the permission of Cambridge University Press.

Dancers as Diplomats

Introduction

In 2009, the US State Department funded the construction of a theatrical stage in the country of Burma. While a special floor suitable for dancing in bare feet and theatrical lighting equipment might seem odd American foreign-policy budget line items, both expenditures made a lot of sense in a country where slow economic development and decades of military dictatorship rule meant that few people had Internet access or mobile phones. Live interactions through performance promised a connection where Facebook and Google could not reach. On a day in February 2010, San Francisco's ODC/Dance Company walked onto that newly built stage at the American Center in the northern Burmese city of Mandalay. (figure I.1) Under many watchful eyes, the contemporary dance company offered some of the first steps in a new State Department initiative: the international dance touring program called DanceMotion USA.

ODC, as well as the Brooklyn-based dance companies Urban Bush Women (UBW) and Ronald K. Brown's Evidence, represented the United States abroad in DanceMotion's inaugural year. The new dance touring program demonstrated a State Department investment in live engagement that seems almost quaint in a digitally-saturated twenty-first century context. The investment in performance, however, gave the dancers hope that art, particularly dance, still counted as a public good—an idea that had catalyzed the American dance boom of the 1960s and 1970s, when government funding helped American dance grow exponentially. As ODC dancer Dennis Adams put it, "It was nice to know that the US government was using dance to further its diplomatic endeavors. . . . It was nice to know that dance [is] still on the radar."[1] (Adams's choice of the

Figure I.1
Members of ODC/Dance in Rangoon, Burma, performing artistic director Brenda Way's
24 Exposures (2001). The dancers are (*left to right*) Elizabeth Farotte Heenan, Jeremy
Smith, Dennis Adams, Quilet Rarang, Anne Zivolich, and Daniel Santos.
Source: Photograph by U Kyi Saw.

word "still" references the precipitous drop in public arts funding in recent
decades, especially in comparison to the Cold War–era funding levels.)
The ODC dancers took to the Burmese stage as an example of government
investment in live, embodied engagement and with the personal sense
that dance mattered to the life of the nation and the world. State support
and public good might be mutually constitutive possibilities.[2]

Although the US government invested in ODC's performances, the
Burmese government, a military dictatorship resisting soon-to-come
democratic reform at the time of the 2010 tour, did not. The Burmese government could not cancel the ODC performance because the American
Center was technically US property. The Burmese government could,
however, make it extremely difficult for people to get to the performance,
and circulate misinformation about the performance's date and time so
that people interested in attending would miss the event. Dancer Yayoi
Kambara said that evidence of the government's misinformation campaign lay in plain sight: the local Burmese-published, English-language
newspaper printed an article before ODC even arrived in Mandalay that
claimed the performance had already happened.[3] Obstacles continued to

proliferate as the performance dates drew near. The government called a ten-day meditation, which included the broadcasting of prayers over loud-speakers across the city. The company feared the broadcasts would have a doubly negative effect on potential audiences. People might stay home feeling they had to abide by the government edict to meditate. If people came to the performance, the chants issuing from the loudspeakers out-side the compound would drown out the music.

Neither American officials nor the ODC dancers could have predicted what happened at the Mandalay performance space that night. ODC is a company known for its fresh, athletic dancing, qualities the State Department and the Brooklyn Academy of Music (BAM)—the State Department's private partner in the touring endeavor—highlighted in DanceMotion materials, which also note the company's "passion."[4] But that night it was the Burmese who demonstrated what passion for free-dom in the face of government oppression looked like. The Burmese locals did not just come to the performance. They came in droves. And when the conditions onstage grew difficult for the American dancers, the Burmese audience, quite literally, kept them going.

As soon as they stepped onstage that night, the ODC dancers saw ample evidence that state edicts do not always determine people's actions, even in the most extreme circumstances. Dancer Daniel Santos recalled that he had expected a "decent-sized" crowd at the show. He understood from American officials that the Burmese people who fre-quented the American Center were already accustomed to pushing the limits of governmental rules by just by coming to the center in the first place, so attending the performance would just be another instance of their choosing to disregard government guidelines. But attendance far surpassed expectations.

When the members of the ODC company told me the story of what they experienced in Mandalay, they spoke with such excitement that they physically enacted parts of the story and interrupted one another to inter-ject even more detail. Dancer Jeremy Smith remembered the scene:

> All the chairs were filled, and people were standing, wrapping around the stage as well. It was a regular proscenium stage without wings on the side, but people were just standing wherever they could. There were people standing outside the complex, peeping through the fence.[5]

The Burmese government's propaganda campaign seemingly had not deterred any audience members. Other dancers saw audience members perched in trees and in the stage rafters. The State Department estimated the crowd at about 1,400 for the one performance.[6] Dancer Dennis Adams said he knew something transformative was happening when even the Burmese police stationed around the complex—not so much to ensure safety as to intimidate potential concertgoers—dropped their vigilant stances and turned to watch the show.

With the ever-growing audience, the program proceeded without incident until the final piece, *24 Exposures* (2001), an upbeat number choreographed by the company's artistic director Brenda Way. Electric service in Burma is erratic, and the American Center staff had warned the dancers that the center might lose electricity during the show (likely another Burmese government obstructionist tactic). If this happened, the center could keep the lights on, but the technical crew would have to scramble to bring generators online to power the sound system. The company had agreed pre-performance on a backup plan. They decided that, if necessary, they would freeze until the music returned. When the company got to *24 Exposures*, the accompanying Appalachian bluegrass music began, but then suddenly cut out. The dancers froze, as planned, but as the silence continued, they realized the music might not be coming back at all. A substantial amount of *24 Exposures* remained. How could the dancers decide as a group, while still onstage, what to do?

As the silence grew interminable, Dennis Adams heard the sound of clapping from the back of the stage. Daniel Santos had begun clapping the rhythm of the piece. (As the group recounts the story, Adams begins clapping, creating a sound that echoes forcefully in ODC's small office but that must have been just a tiny noise in an outdoor theater filled with 1,400 people.) Suddenly, inexplicably, the clapping grew louder and louder. The entire audience had joined Santos, clapping along to the beat he set. Now there was music, but it was not the piece's usual music. It was the rhythmic sound of what dancer Quilet Rarang described as "5,000 hands working together."[7] Vanessa Thiessen danced the rest of *24 Exposures* with tears running down her face. She recalled, "It was amazing to hear all these people who d[id]n't know us, who d[id]n't know what we do, fully there and fully accepting. I seriously think that experience right there is what the program [DanceMotion] is all about."[8] ODC had arrived as a symbol—an American group performing for foreigners. Through live performance, a collaborative space emerged, exceeding the frames of national difference that were also present at the performance.

As DanceMotion performers, ODC was an agent of American cultural diplomacy, a branch of foreign policy that, among other things, presses art and artists into government service abroad—and that national service had clear political and economic goals in Burma.[9] ODC arrived in the country as an extension of a US government trying to expand US-Burma diplomatic relations. Burma, like Iran, was one of the first countries targeted by the administration of new president Barack Obama in its efforts to increase communication with countries the US had previously ostracized due to their repressive regimes. American dance and dancers came to Burma as the opening salvo of the new approach.[10] The American dancers' presence in Burma represented one node of international connection between the long-estranged American and Burmese governments, a mode of engagement less-charged than a partisan political visit. When ODC performed in 2010, it would still be more than a year before President Obama announced major shifts in US policy toward Burma, and three years before Obama and then Secretary of State Hillary Clinton would make a much-publicized visit to Burma.[11] The tour also happened amid changing economic concerns, since Burma represents a foothold in US foreign relations with China, the country increasingly appearing as the United States's counter global power in early twenty-first-century trade and politics.[12]

Considering these policy developments alongside the dancers' stories shows how the ODC appearances in Burma bolstered official national aims and exceeded those political strategies, too. The title *24 Exposures*, the piece for which the Burmese audience provided the impromptu musical accompaniment, references how photographs capture only one second within complex moments: motion, affect, and exchange always partially occur beyond what the frame holds. And the framing has as much to do with the photographer—the picture's author—as it does with the event itself. On the DanceMotion tour, ODC, as did all the dance companies featured in this book, appeared in frames crafted by the US State Department and its various public and private partners. (In 2010, the nonprofit arts presenter BAM and the arts management firm Lisa Booth Management, Inc. administrated DanceMotion.)

But these frames do not contain the full picture. Understanding ODC as "American," even on an official government-sponsored tour, addresses only one aspect of this multiply diverse, multinational company's identity and misses a number of other important identities and practices. And to see that night in Burma only as evidence of a successful campaign for the United States would miss the complicated feedback loops that make a live performance a dynamic event. In these tensions lives a fascinating possibility for cultural diplomacy, particularly as it is embodied in dance, to be simultaneously propaganda and something more than propaganda. Cultural diplomacy is full of opportunities for dancers to make their mark on ideas of "America." That is what this book is about.

Dancers as Diplomats examines the American government's harnessing of dance to export an idealized image of "America"—an image dance artists simultaneously fulfill, reimagine, and at times, critique. This book focuses on the early decades of the Cold War and of the twenty-first century, periods when the United States sent artists, as well as art objects, abroad as part of its cultural diplomacy programs. Dance artists' performances on stages, in nightclubs, and in everyday interactions amplify the paradoxical entanglement of dominant narratives of "America" with artistic and personal reimaginings of "America." Focusing on dancers' management of their "official" status on tour understands dancing as a strategy for negotiating the complications of national identity at the levels of individual, community, and nation. Investigating dancers' experiences as cultural ambassadors exposes on-the-ground tensions and possibilities within the often idealized category of American identity—a category seen as exciting or at least approachable by some, but threatening or uninhabitable by others.

While many important distinctions exist between the Cold War and the twenty-first-century programs, one almost mundane idea animates both eras of dance-in-diplomacy: all the State Department programs described in this book moved living artists through foreign countries as representatives of the United States. American forays into cultural diplomacy began in the 1930s and 1940s and centered on visual art;[13] the performing arts programs did not begin in earnest until the 1950s. As embassies no longer hosted only art objects (such as paintings and sculptures), presented without their makers, but instead presented dancers and musicians, the new emphasis on sending people abroad made cultural diplomacy particularly fertile ground for simultaneously functioning as propaganda and dissent. While art objects can raise questions or critiques about hegemonic national narratives, artists do so more publicly—a situation that, on one hand, government officials had to manage but, on the other, could act as proof of American democracy's promise: a government system that allowed individual dissent. As historian Penny Von Eschen has shown in her work on the State Department jazz tours, musician Louis Armstrong often blatantly spoke out from the stage, critiquing American civil-rights restrictions.[14] In chapter 3, I argue that Martha Graham's provocative onstage and offstage play with gender had a similar, if less blatant, critical function. Such public performances offered evidence of American individual freedom, even as these individual artists and groups of artists pressed back on the claims made by the nation they represented.

To track the shifting and often overlapping, even contradictory, ideas within the public staging of American national identity, I traveled from New York to California and from Minnesota to Texas to interview more than seventy dancers who participated in tours sponsored by the State Department. These interviews form the backbone of this book. I turned to dancers, not just choreographers, as figures who consistently interpret and reinterpret choreography and history. This book reckons with what dance theorist Susan Foster has called "choreographing history," taking seriously "the possibility of a body that is written upon but that also writes."[15] Dance is not just a repository of social ideas and contexts. Dancing produces meanings and contributes to larger cultural ideas. In the case of American diplomacy, dancers constantly reframe what it means to be "American." Taking embodiment seriously does not elevate dance, onstage or elsewhere, to the mythic status of universal communication. Instead, embodiment—in all its iterations: dances of a variety of artistic genres, as well as how people use their bodies in everyday situations—considers how people use their bodies (consciously or not) to express their desires and ideas, communicate with others, and make meaning within a specific time and place. With this frame in mind, I turn to the tours as diplomatic endeavors that unfolded, not just in spoken or written conversations, but in physical interactions between people.

Focusing on dancers as specific actors in these diplomatic dramas has important ramifications for dance history, too, because it is through the dancers' perspectives that we can see how choreography develops both over time and in time. Dancers have a particularly intimate experience of choreographic works shifting across performances, especially the repeated performances that happen over many weeks of touring. The dancers helped me chart how Wednesday's performance both replicated and differed from Tuesday's, rather than treat choreography as though it is frozen in time at a premiere date only to shift upon a major casting change. Place, as well as time, has a huge impact here, too, as sites on the tours infuse and recalibrate meanings within choreography. For instance, when the Alvin Ailey American Dance Theater performed Ailey's *Revelations* (1960) for Kenyan postcolonial leader Jomo Kenyatta in 1967, the dancers talked about their sense of the work as part of the African diaspora. Three years later, when several of the same dancers performed *Revelations* in the Soviet Union on tour as the first American modern dance company to enter the USSR, they discussed the work as particularly American. Anyone familiar with *Revelations* knows (as chapter 2 discusses) the work is very much both of the United States and of the African diaspora; these are not mutually exclusive categories, yet the dancers' stories help us see how one work takes on different inflections across time.

Dance and dancers are the heart of this book, but the book's structure centers on key policy events and shifts in dance-in-diplomacy programming. *Dancers as Diplomats* does not present an exhaustive history of all dance tours supported by the US State Department, but rather follows major shifts in American history and policy history that served as the catalysts for tour planning and execution. Chapter 1 presents the Cold War's most foundational policy frame: the US-Soviet standoff. Chapters 2 and 3 take a more global approach to the Cold War era, focusing on the American presence in Africa and Asia as the US-Soviet standoff intersected with postcolonial movements. Chapters 4 and 5 discuss what I call the "collaborative turn" in American cultural diplomacy, the hallmark of the twenty-first-century programs that focused on building international relationships rather than exporting American superiority.

The case studies selected for each chapter represent tours by full dance companies rather than the State Department programs that funded individual artist's work abroad. Traveling with companies, especially the kind of companies most often selected for the tours—those with long-standing histories that offered regular employment throughout a year, often over several years—made the dancers aware that they represented something bigger than themselves. They represented a community (the company) and a nation (the United States). The dancers often described this sense of layered identity in the interviews, saying that every day on the tour, they felt the weight and excitement of representing larger ideas. Dancer Bonnie Oda Homsey (figure I.2) recalled the preparations for the Martha Graham Dance Company's 1974 tour of Asia: "Martha did not allow any of us to wear jeans or bring jeans on [the] tour. It was [all] dresses [for the women]. . . . [She said] that we were really an extension of her and the United States. That was definitely drummed in."[16] Homsey described how Graham acted on her own behalf and on that of the nation—and then asked her dancers, as a group and as individuals, to do the same.

One of the key ideas of *Dancers as Diplomats* is that this self-consciousness about representation stems from artists being tapped as "official" representatives of the United States. *Dancers as Diplomats* asks, When people become aware of being marked as "official" Americans, how then do multiple layers of representation—of the nation, various communities, and the individual—either serve the construction of American identity or fall outside of that identity? The answers to this question vary greatly throughout the book, depending on the artists' and dance companies' social locations, but two ideas persist. First, the very constitution of the

Figure I.2
Bonnie Oda Homsey, a relatively new dancer with the Martha Graham Dance Company in 1974, greets a classical Thai performer on the company's 1974 State Department–sponsored tour of Asia.
Source: Photo reproduced courtesy of the Special Collections, University of Arkansas.

category of "official" Americanness implies that something exists beyond that officially recognized national identity—an excess that the government cannot fully control. Second, it is in the dancers' movement between that "official" identity and what lies beyond it that we see how the arts help us to recognize that national identity, especially American identity, is always in process. To be charged with representing a group implies that there is some essential quality to be represented. Dancers move between what has been counted as "official" and what exceeds the "official," demonstrating that "American" is truly a performative category—an identity created through "doing," to borrow philosopher J. L. Austin's conception of the "performative." Dance allows us to see how this complex, ever-unfolding process occurs in ways as mundane as dancers' choice of dress and as extraordinary as the public spectacles they pour their energy into onstage. They make these choices, often with their bodies, always with an awareness of being part of several types of groups.

Performance and national identity, especially in the context of the dance-in-diplomacy programs, share the attributes of being products of collective labor and negotiation. Groups of artists collectively embody and reinterpret what it means to represent "America." Seen this way, the funding programs emerging from the State Department over the last seventy years contest a common narrative of dance history and American history alike that seizes on the singular, exceptional (often male) figure as a source of paradigmatic social change. On the State Department programs, the responsibility for ensuring the tour's success and for conveying the conception of "America" was spread across, quite literally, many shoulders. By turning to dancers' roles in American cultural diplomacy, this book asks how dance sets American national identity and power in motion.

Why Dance?

On a 1962 State Department–sponsored tour, the dancers of the New York City Ballet (NYCB) pirouetted on a stage inside Moscow's Kremlin Complex as the Soviet leader Nikita Khruschev negotiated a resolution to the Cuban missile crisis with the American president John F. Kennedy. The two events, the performance and the nuclear crisis, did not directly affect one another (beyond elevating the dancers' anxiety), but their coincidence exemplifies the multiple levels on which diplomacy works. Soviet audiences went wild for the NYCB performances: tickets sold out weeks in advance, the audiences in five cities gave standing ovations, and the Soviet dancers remarked about the importance of seeing the 1962 performances in autobiographies written for decades thereafter. In verbal and written diplomatic exchanges, the American and Soviet governments posited an opposition so great that it fed the possibility of mutual destruction; while in the physical and affective sharings in the theater, diplomatic exchanges imagined connection and shared joy. Considered side-by-side, the two events and their respective outcomes serve as a reminder that verbal and written exchanges between leaders constitute much, but not all, of diplomatic exchange.

Dancers as Diplomats, with its specific focus on dance as a mode of international engagement, makes clear that diplomacy has always unfolded in embodied ways. This book looks at dance from three vantage points: as a cultural export that emphasizes the body as a representational force; as a form of social engagement in communal spaces, including both theaters and social-dance floors; and as a mode of analysis. To study dance over the course of a lifetime, as dancers and dance scholars do, is a way of training one's eyes and body to understand that the world is full of people making meaning with their bodies, even beyond the spaces where people are officially recognized as "dancing."

Dance and the various modes through which people engage in dance analysis, including the act of making dance as well as the act of writing about dance, foreground not only the effect bodies might have on one another, but also the institutional policies and practices that facilitate cultural diplomacy. How do people and their bodies come together, at what costs and with what gains? With its focus on relationships developed from physical, local interactions,[17] dance helps us see how people come together in social networks, a central concern for policy. In American foreign policy, dance is one of the most concrete couplings of the physical and the political. Considering policy and dance together creates space, in performance theorist Jean Graham-Jones's words, in which to explore those very real moments when individuals and communities—to cadge the clichéd phrase—"act locally" and "think globally."[18] One of the most concrete examples of this simultaneous local and global moment constituted through dance arose, not in my interviews with the dancers on the DanceMotion tour, but in my interviews with the dancers who worked together in a dance program partially funded by the State Department from 2003 to 2007 that was an immediate forerunner to DanceMotion. Over a number of years, the San Francisco modern dance company Margaret Jenkins Dance Company and the Kolkata-based Tanusree Shankar Dance Company collaborated on a new dance work, *A Slipping Glimpse* (2007). The State Department funded some aspects of the creation and also partially supported the two companies on a tour of India. While the companies often worked in studios on different continents, the dancers literally found themselves always thinking of their international counterparts. Varshaa Ghosh, a Shankar dancer, described rehearsals when the companies were apart: "We [the Shankar dancers] would be in the studio [in Kolkata] and say to each other, 'Ok, Steffany [one of the American dancers] is there. How do we go around her?' I never thought of the other dancers as a completely different aspect. It's not like we [we]'re existing in two different worlds."[19] As Ghosh told me this, all the dancers sitting around her, American and Indian, nodded enthusiastically. The American dancers, too, had been aware of the Indian dancers' bodies, even though those bodies were rehearsing thousands of miles away. The Americans had replaced abstract ideas of Indian people with more specific knowledge of the Shankar dancers. Americans and Indians had to move through their daily jobs constantly thinking about where the bodies of other people were and how the movements of their own bodies would affect others.

All these modes of interaction propagate intercultural sympathies, a fraught, but persistent goal since the incorporation of the performing arts into American cultural diplomacy. American studies scholar Christina Klein has shown that President Dwight Eisenhower's early cultural diplomacy initiatives in the 1950s made sympathy a central "structure of feeling" of the new performance programs.[20] Focusing primarily on the People-to-People program created by Eisenhower in 1956, Klein described sympathy, which she defined as "the ability to feel what another person feels," as the "double-edged sword" of American diplomacy.[21] Klein feared that sympathy has offered Americans an "emotionally satisfying bond" that imagined "access to another's subjectivity."[22] In the context of American attempts to gain global power,[23] cultural diplomacy, then, became a tool of American domination, one enacted through the encouragement of sympathy rather than through the use of force. Klein's suspicions of cultural diplomacy's aims are ones I share, and it is important to see how dance's entry into cultural diplomacy in 1954 was part of the emotional project of American Cold War politics.

Dance in cultural diplomacy relies upon an intercultural emotional appeal that extends into the physical as dance emphasizes the relationship among sympathy, representation, and the corporeal. Through dance, State Department efforts to use cultural diplomacy—to "win hearts and minds," as the saying goes—moves from an emotional appeal to a truly affective one as emotional, intercultural bonds manifest in and through bodies. The performing arts got their biggest consolidated push into the diplomatic arena in 1954 with Eisenhower's creation of the President's Special Emergency Fund. The fund sent $2,225,000 to the State Department to support dance, music, theater, and sports tours; and $157,000 to the United States Information Agency (USIA) to publicize the tours.[24] (Adjusted for inflation, that would be like President Obama in 2013 sending $20 million to the State Department to fund dance tours.)[25] The fund's first action sent the José Limón Dance Company to Latin America. The choice of dance as the best way to begin the program moved from sympathy as a structure of feeling to empathy, a structure of feeling with an explicitly corporeal manifestation. Dance theorist Susan

Foster has argued that the term "'empathy' was invented not to express a new capacity for fellow-feeling [sympathy], but to register a changing sense of physicality that, in turn, influenced how one felt another's feelings."[26] Foster, in a theoretical move parallel to Klein's, has demonstrated how dance can mobilize empathy "to rationalize operations of exclusions and othering": the feelings of less powerful groups are displaced by the feelings of those more powerful, as those in the more powerful groups focus on their own feelings *about* the less powerful, rather than actually caring what the other group feels and/or thinks.[27] Diplomacy programs tried to make Americans care about other people and, less progressively, also asked people in other countries to care about Americans. *Dancers as Diplomats* considers where physical connection falls into the dangerous exclusionary and domination practices Klein and Foster detail and when physical connection might have liberatory possibilities that exceed state edicts.

In the two eras featured in this book, the affective arguments made through dance took very particular historically constituted forms. During the Cold War, the government turned to dance to offer evidence that the United States excelled not just at capitalism but at culture, too. Dancers on the first dance-in-diplomacy tour, the Limón company's tour of Latin America, discussed the multiple representational burdens they experienced in 1954, naming art's relationship to industry as a particularly potent one at that time. A *Dance Magazine* article summarized the dancers' sense of themselves as scions of culture:

> The pressure to perform is at any time enough to rack one's nerves, but how much more so when you have to come across for an audience that (only too well aware of the wonderful automobiles and kitchen gadgets we Americans produce) is waiting eagerly on the other side of the curtain to see what kind of culture we are capable of.[28]

The dancers' task on tour was to represent *more* than American consumer culture.[29] Exporting only consumer goods threatened to foreground capitalism instead of democracy and freedom more broadly. During the Cold War, American cultural diplomacy ensured that US cultural exportation included not only cars, TVs, and refrigerators but also Robert Rauschenberg, the Paul Taylor Dance Company, and jazz improvisation.

Emphasis on live interaction gave dance a prominent role in another aspect of Cold War American cultural diplomacy as dance played a complicated part in the relationship between the federal government and the civil rights movement. Onstage, dancers and artists in other live performance mediums, such as jazz, presented images the US government could cite as evidence of racial tolerance. By the mid-twentieth century, what the black public intellectual W. E. B. Du Bois predicted would be the greatest American problem of the twentieth century—"the color line," the inequitable and divisive segregation of white Americans from Americans of color—had become, as Thomas Borstelmann and Mary Dudziak have shown, not just a domestic issue, but also an international one.[30] How could the US persuade the world to adopt American government models supposedly based on egalitarianism and individual rights when foreign publics saw daily images of violence against Americans of color protesting for rights they did not have, despite being American citizens? As Penny Von Eschen has shown in her work on the State Department's support of international jazz music tours, performances by African American artists offered a way to celebrate American modernist abstraction, which Cold War intellectuals saw as "synonymous with democracy," and also spoke to "America's Achilles heel of racism in ways that a painting . . . could not."[31] When black artists took the stage, in music or dance performances, they performed an image of racial inclusivity and an official embrace of African American culture.

Performers of color were not, however, merely shills for a government agenda. Von Eschen has described many black musicians' challenges to government structures as they criticized government policy, speaking from the stage or at other public events on tour. *Dancers as Diplomats* takes this possibility for critique a step further, assessing how African American, Asian American, and Latina/o performers did not just voice their criticism, but also choreographed and danced critiques of American policy, inserting embodied narratives of self-determination into American cultural diplomacy, which paradoxically served both to showcase American individual freedom and to disrupt the duplicitous staging of the United States as fully racially integrated.

If the rejection of consumerism and entanglement with the civil rights movement were primary structuring questions of dance-in-diplomacy during the Cold War, how the United States can be both a leader and a global partner has been the animating issue behind recent tours. Since the attacks on New York and Washington, DC in 2001, but even more so since international opinion of the United States turned overwhelmingly negative after the invasions of Afghanistan in 2001 and Iraq in 2003, the role of cultural diplomacy has been a topic of debate in Washington. Over more than a decade, these debates have centered on how the United States might project an image of being a global partner, listening to other countries' needs.[32] This directive crystallized in the early years of the Obama administration as a premise for diplomatic policy. As Obama said in a 2009 speech, the United States now "must not lead in the spirit of a patron, but the spirit of a partner."[33]

Dance has a particular route to considering what the United States as global partner, rather than just a dominant power, might look like. Dance's possibility, not only as a concert form, but as a way to create space for international collaboration, is a key rationale behind dance's inclusion in contemporary cultural diplomacy programs. DanceMotion USA, which has sent three to four dance companies of a variety of genres and styles abroad for month-long tours, centers primarily on community engagement, rather than concert performances. American dancers teach, but they also act as students learning from local dancers. Since 2012, DanceMotion has matched an American and a non-American company to collaboratively create a work that premieres in New York City at BAM. The logic behind this collaborative turn in dance-in-diplomacy seems to be that physical sharing, considered as less reliant on language, enacts intercultural exchange with US representatives as partners as well as leaders.[34]

Dance's impact on American cultural diplomacy has been a two-way street: the US government benefits from dance companies' work abroad, and the dance community benefits from the funding and international exposure. The State Department programs, created in 1954 (Eisenhower's Special Emergency Fund) and 1956 (the Cultural Presentations Program) along with the creation of the National Endowment for the Arts in 1965, fashioned the public institutional pillars of what dance historians and enthusiasts often term the American "dance boom," the exponential growth of American concert dance organizations in the 1960s and 1970s. While dance historians often tell the story of twentieth-century dance as one of individual genius—from George Balanchine to Martha Graham—what is less commented on is that these artists enjoyed tremendous institutional support, much of it from these newly created public sources. In the fifties, sixties, and seventies, the State Department supported almost every American dance company that now constitutes the twentieth-century American dance canon. Among those sponsored by the State Department on entirely government-funded or partially funded tours were the companies of Limón, Martha Graham, Alvin Ailey, Paul Taylor, Merce Cunningham, and Alwin Nikolais, as well as ballet companies, including the New York City Ballet, American Ballet Theatre, and the Joffrey Ballet. How DanceMotion funding will affect the contemporary American dance scene remains to be seen; however, the importance of public funding cannot be overstated, especially considering the role funding played in the longevity of specific twentieth-century artists, such as

Graham and Ailey. This serves as an important reminder that dance history must attend to the role economics plays in creating artistic hierarchies and canons. In addition, it is important to note the role that public support has played and continues to play in the arts. My commitment to the necessity for public funding for the arts (always importantly paired with a healthy suspicion about the exportation of empathy) animates the central questions of *Dancers as Diplomats*.

Examining the structural mechanisms that shaped State Department sponsorship of international dance tours exposes another popular myth in the dance community: the idea that modern dance, the genre of dance most frequently exported, is uniquely American. Looking at the tours from an institutional standpoint and from the levels of individuals and communities demonstrates the constructed nature of the category of "American" as it relates to both identity and dance. In identifying modern dance as a primary cultural export, the State Department claimed modern dance as quintessentially representative of and indigenous to the United States. The government's maneuver required ignoring modern dance's roots in other nations, for instance, Germany, and in cultures that included but extended beyond the United States, particularly those of the African diaspora. Ironically, the actual tours often made American dance's transnational ties evident. Touring Europe in 1957, José Limón and fellow American dance choreographer Doris Humphrey enthusiastically met the German modern dance matriarch, Mary Wigman (figure I.3), who had begun making what Americans would call "modern dance" years before Limón or Graham, the two choreographers most often put forward by the State Department as the "creators" of modern dance. Audiences in Berlin received the Limón company that year enthusiastically, in part, Limón dancer Pauline Koner felt, because work by German modern dance artists like Wigman, Harald Kreutzberg, and Gret Palucca had already taught German audiences "how to watch" modern dance.[35] The American government exported Limón's work as American even as the Germans received it well because of modern dance's roots outside of the United States.

What became part of the category of "American dance," too, had influences from beyond the United States, sometimes precisely because of the State Department tours (at least in part). The art and culture American dancers experienced while on tour often became highly influential in the work dancers and choreographers created upon returning to the United States. For instance, the Alvin Ailey American Dance Theater's 1967 tour of Africa, according to the dancers, inspired Ailey's subsequent work (see chapter 2). Notably, Ailey wrote a program note for *Masekela Langage* (1969), one of the pieces he made shortly after returning from the Africa

Figure I.3
José Limón, Doris Humphrey, and Mary Wigman dine together in Berlin, where the Limón company was appearing at the 1957 Berlin Festival, one of many instances the Limón company appeared abroad under the auspices of the State Department. The formal dinner was likely one of many dinners and receptions organized to introduce the visiting American artists to the locals, though this meeting did not bring together strangers but luminaries of the transatlantic modern dance community.
Source: Photograph courtesy of Charles Tomlinson, Pauline Lawrence Personal Collection, New York Public Library for the Performing Arts.

tour in which he described how the work intermingled American and South African racial politics. American modern dance, even if made in the United States by a soon-to-be iconic American artist, was a product of transnational influence. The project to claim modern dance as American was just that—a project, not a fact. Dance in cultural diplomacy, in practice, and as a metaphor illustrates that national identity is never stable or monolithic. *Dancers as Diplomats* aims to examine how these unstable national identities were experienced and interpreted through the lives of dancers who were a part of the larger international project of American cultural diplomacy.

THE POLITICS OF AMERICAN CULTURAL DIPLOMACY

It might seem obvious that American cultural diplomacy is a political endeavor: all the tours discussed in this book received the majority of their funding from the State Department, and even when private organizations selected artists or administered tours, a government presence was always nearby—through embassy officials to name but one example. Yet policy and legislation, particularly through careful language choices, frequently dissociate cultural diplomacy from politics. Policymakers' tenuous framing of cultural diplomacy as apolitical means that dancers must navigate meanings of "political" and "apolitical"—even when their artistic work is quite politically engaged.

How we talk about and define cultural diplomacy reveals its relationship to other forms of diplomacy. Two sets of terminology frequently used to discuss cultural diplomacy name tours and other cultural exchanges as distinct from political diplomacy. The first categorization is of cultural diplomacy as a special subcategory of what is known as public diplomacy. The second categorization is what is known as "soft" versus "hard power," which works to elevate all other forms of international engagement—namely, economic and military engagement—above cultural diplomacy.

The first binary, cultural versus public diplomacy, removes cultural diplomacy from the directness of politics—that is presumed to be the work of "public diplomacy." Political scientist Harvey Feigenbaum has offered the clearest description of how policymakers usually distinguish between cultural diplomacy and public diplomacy. "Cultural diplomacy," he writes, "allow[s] people from different cultures to get to know and understand each other;" whereas "public diplomacy" closely resembles propaganda, getting "America's word out—in a hopefully persuasive way to hopefully receptive publics in other nations."[36] State Department officials usually cast dance and other art and education programs as cultural diplomacy, imagining these programs as unsullied by politics. In practice there exists little distinction between cultural and public diplomacy. For instance, the USIA, originally established by the Eisenhower administration to oversee propaganda (public diplomacy), partnered with the State Department throughout the Cold War to administer the on-the-ground international aspect of the dance tours.

In the second binary, soft power versus hard power, cultural diplomacy's distance from the explicitly political diminishes its importance. Political scientist Joseph Nye famously conceptualized "hard power" versus "soft power," where the former (with all its masculinist connotations) refers to military and economic actions, and the latter (with all its feminized connotations) refers to public diplomacy, including cultural diplomacy.[37] Leaving aside for now these terms' gendered implications, what is crucial in Nye's formulation is the pretense that culture is separate from and perhaps less than political or economic diplomacy. Acting as though culture is somehow not political or is less political than other diplomatic means is itself a political choice as it veils the political agendas that are very much embedded in American cultural diplomacy. As Penny Von Eschen has argued about culture in Cold War politics, the "pervasive separation of 'culture' from 'political economy' in historical writing, further incarnated in . . . [Nye's] 'hard and soft power,' remains an obstacle to understanding American culture as well as the exercise of U.S. power in the world."[38] In effect, claiming that cultural diplomacy efforts like the State Department support for international dance tours are largely apolitical obscures how US power and influence move in the world.

This distancing of cultural diplomacy from the political is not just a scholarly comment on how the US government works; it is an argument built into cultural diplomacy legislation and organizational choices, too. American legislation displaces politics' role in cultural diplomacy in favor of more neutral language of "connection" and "understanding." In 1961, the Fulbright-Hays Act (officially known as the Mutual Educational and Cultural Exchange Act of 1961), the single most important piece of legislation in cultural diplomacy history, clarified the programs' aims: to be "non-political," represent "America," and promote "excellence in the arts."[39] These ideals remain foundational to today's cultural diplomacy programs. Yet representing "America" is political—only one of many contradictions inherent in the legislation. The contradiction between international connection and exporting the United States's supposedly "superior" art vibrates at the core of all the programs discussed in *Dancers as Diplomats*.

In some eras of American cultural diplomacy, the government has hidden not just its political agenda but also its role. The most publicly fraught moment in the relationship between politics and arts funding occurred when the CIA covertly sponsored cultural programs in Western Europe after World War II. The CIA designed the programs to diffuse cultural elites' passion for communism—an intellectual containment plan of sorts—and to assess how strongly various communities felt about communism. Historian Frances Stonor Saunders' book *The Cultural Cold War* (1999) describes how the CIA created shell foundations to funnel American government funding to literary magazines, conferences, and performing arts presentations, including arts festivals in Paris and Berlin, which both presented several dance companies.[40] The CIA ceased funding cultural initiatives in the mid-1960s after a series of news articles revealed their funding source.[41] Cultural diplomacy often catches the government in the gaps between rhetoric and practice: arguing for the benefits of openness while practicing the covert dissemination of ideas. Such covertness is only possible if cultural programs are presented as apolitical.

When State Department officials prepare the dancers for the tours, they sometimes explicitly instruct them to maintain that their work is apolitical. In these warnings, it seems apparent that "political" usually equals what artists say, not what they do as dancers. For example, when DanceMotion companies traveled to Washington for pre-tour briefings in 2010, many dancers reported that State Department desk officers gave them specific instructions to avoid all political conversations while abroad. (It was up to the dancers to determine what constituted a "political" conversation.) Dancers from the Cold War–era tours remembered being warned to avoid saying anything that could be construed as a political comment. On early tours, the State Department officials briefed the companies in their studios, and, according to most dancers, emphasized that everyone must remember that their actions represented the United States. As the Vietnam War became a hot-button issue in the late 1960s, the warnings turned explicit. Embassy officials at every single tour stop overtly warned the dancers to avoid talking about the war.

If the government eschewed anything that seemed too political at the micro, everyday level, there can be no doubt that at the macro level, particularly in the choice of tour destinations, politics had real influence in dance-in-diplomacy programs. In the early Cold War, the State Department targeted regions thought to be susceptible to Sino-Soviet Communism. Even though dance companies frequently expressed greater desire to travel to Europe than elsewhere, the State Department rarely routed tours there. Instead tours generally went to Eastern Europe, Latin America, sub-Saharan Africa, and southeast Asia. More recently, countries with significant Muslim populations have been chosen for DanceMotion tours, and the first four years of funding also suggest that Asia is the most important region for American cultural diplomacy. Tour destinations are also important choices because that is the area where the State Department has clearest power. Other decisions about tours—the artists chosen, the choreography presented, and community partners tapped—have often been made outside the State Department and, in some cases, outside of government agencies entirely.

To be fair, it is not true that every era of diplomacy or every governmental official or agency involved in cultural diplomacy has obscured programs' political agendas. Most notably, since 2009, former secretary of state Hillary Clinton has adopted Nye's newer term, "smart power," to advocate for a foreign policy agenda that uses any tools necessary—cultural, economic, and military—to advance American government goals in the world.[42] The more capacious term puts the three strains of diplomacy previously put into a hierarchy by Nye on the same level, although there might be another political strategy inherent in Clinton's vocabulary: elevating cultural interventions to the same level as economic and military interventions potentially raised the cachet of the State Department, which Clinton led at the time.

Clinton's expansive understanding of diplomacy, though it does explicitly pull from Nye's recent work, also hails back to very early Cold War foreign policy, which took an "any means necessary" approach to containing Communism. As theater historian Charlotte Canning has noted, NSC-68, the 1949 document that defined the United States's policies for the containment of Communism, named "image, prestige, and credibility," not just military and economic efforts, as key to winning the Cold War.[43] These broader conceptions of diplomacy undoubtedly facilitate more roles for the arts and culture in diplomacy, even if that role is still sometimes suspiciously framed as apolitical.

These broader understandings of how culture and politics might be interrelated also invite questions about the relationship between cultural diplomacy and economics, particularly since a hallmark of American cultural diplomacy in comparison to almost all other countries' cultural diplomacy efforts, is the United States's hybrid public-private funding structure.[44] *Dancers as Diplomats* focuses solely on international tours primarily funded by the US government, though few tours (if any) traveled abroad with only State Department funding and almost none happened without input from private partners. Private investment in the tours continues to be key to their breadth and reach. For example, in the 2010 DanceMotion pilot program, the pharmaceutical company Pfizer financed the tours' educational efforts, providing funds for the distribution of dance books and DVDs to libraries in the countries visited. This would not have been possible without private funding, but it also raises questions about the influence private companies could have on program choices.[45] There is no way to extricate American politics from American commerce; thus the market, represented by the private sector, always, often explicitly, factors in American cultural diplomacy.

WHO MAKES DECISIONS AND WHY

The entanglement of the private and public, often framed as fully public, makes it necessary to denote what have been the various organizations playing a role in the history of American cultural diplomacy. It is important to avoid treating the US government, or the US State Department, as monolithic institutions; it is also key to recognize how public-private divides structure American cultural diplomacy. Four organizations are most important in *Dancers as Diplomats*: the State Department's Bureau of Educational and Cultural Affairs (ECA), the USIA, the American National Theatre and Academy (ANTA), and BAM. The ECA has been (although sometimes under slightly different names) the US State Department's central artistic and educational hub. Government employees in this bureau helped administer and shape all the tours described in this book. While the State Department employees worked on the tours from Washington, the USIA officers, known abroad as USIS representatives, facilitated the artists' travel. Created in 1953 by the Eisenhower administration (and closed in 1999 as part of the Clinton administration's National Partnership for Reinventing Government), the USIA is best understood as the agency responsible for American propaganda efforts abroad. The agency, like the Special Emergency Fund that first sent the Limón company abroad in 1954, grew out of President Eisenhower's Communist-fighting foreign-policy efforts.[46] During the Cold War era, the ECA and the USIA ostensibly handled the political aspects of the tours, leaving most artistic decisions to the New York–based ANTA. ANTA ran three selection panels—for dance, theater, and music—composed of arts administrators, critics, and, less often, artists.[47] The government, in Washington and at posts abroad, designated what parts of the world would see the chosen American artists.[48] ANTA, however, usually knew the countries the State Department planned to target, so the panel conversations often included considerations of the match between artist and locale, even though that fell outside of ANTA's official charge.[49] When the State Department ended its contract with ANTA in 1963, the panel system continued under the auspices of the State Department's Advisory Committee on the Arts, though significant overlap remained between the ANTA administration, former ANTA panelists, and the advisory panel membership.[50]

Much as the State Department did with ANTA during the Cold War, DanceMotion relies on its private partner BAM for artistic guidance and for logistical support around arts presenting. The partnership makes BAM an even greater gatekeeper than was ANTA, since, rather than gathering experts from the field-at-large to choose the artists for the tours, BAM, with minimal outside input, selects the artists. (Artists from previous DanceMotion tours sometimes contribute to the current selection process, as do some State Department employees.) Although American cultural diplomacy promotes ideas of egalitarianism and partnership abroad, the selection process for the tours is anything but egalitarian and open. During the Cold War, dance companies could approach ANTA or the State Department to be considered, though few made it into the discussion. There was no official avenue through which artists could apply. Today there is still no application process. The DanceMotion website states: "Please note that there is no application for this program. Dance companies and countries are selected by a panel of dance experts, as well as representatives from the Bureau of Educational and Cultural Affairs and the grantee organization."[51]

In part, the tight grip on the selection process stems from the often small, often unstable history of cultural diplomacy funding in the United States. The early infusion of funds into performing arts diplomacy, first with the 1954 inaugural program, and then with Congress's 1956 vote for long-term institutional support, were exceptional increases in the budget. From the late fifties through the early sixties, Congress kept the program's budget flat, and then slowly decreased funding through the 1960s. Shifting global politics in the late 1960s, largely tied to US involvement in Vietnam, further reduced program support in Washington. By the late 1970s, funding for large dance company tours had mostly disappeared.

The Cold War's end in the 1980s precipitated American cultural diplomacy's major decline, although smaller groups and individuals continued to tour through the eighties and early nineties. Three factors eventually decimated American funding for cultural and public diplomacy: the end of the Cold War, the Clinton-Gore administration's reinventing government initiative, and the communications and information revolution. That said, it was the State Department's decades-long reliance on the Cold War to justify cultural programming that truly foretold the program's demise: no more Cold War, no more funding for cultural diplomacy. [52] On a broader level, the end of the Cold War also facilitated a turn in attention from the international to the domestic, which contributed to the downsizing and then closing of the USIA in 1999.[53] The State Department's Bureau of Educational and Cultural Affairs remained, but the programs were small and staffing was minimal.

Less than a month after the September 11, 2001 attacks, Congress convened hearings about cultural diplomacy. After later hearings that circled around the negative international opinion of the United States following the 2003 invasion of Iraq, public diplomacy again became a priority.[54] From this resurgent interest, the State Department created, first, Rhythm Road, a program that sent musicians, mostly jazz musicians, abroad, and then, in 2010, DanceMotion USA.

SPEAKING WITH DANCERS, SPEAKING THROUGH DANCE

This book brings together the cultural recognition of physical action, writing, and orality as mutually constitutive of dance practice and dance history and, indeed, American history. Although policymakers principally think of dance as a nonverbal art form, dance practice and creation are, as dance theorist Judith Hamera has noted, always enmeshed in language. Hamera writes, "Relationships between corporeality and language are sometimes represented as especially, even uniquely fraught, with dance serving as a special limit case. But this line of reasoning ignores the practical reality that all performance, including dance, is enmeshed in language, in reading, writing, rhetoric, and voice."[55] Dance is a practice that is always, at least partially, transmitted through oral history. Older generations of dancers pass technique, choreography, and dance history onto the next through discussions in the studio. As dance theorist and oral historian Jeff Friedman writes, "Both the teaching and creative practices of the profession rely on orality during the transmission of kinesthetic knowledge."[56]

I tap the practice of dancers telling their stories to one another in my interviews for this book. *Dancers as Diplomats* brings those dancerly conversations to a larger readership. Over the last eight years, I have interviewed more than seventy dancers who traveled on tours sponsored by the State Department (as well as several of the administrators associated with the tours). These dancers represent a broad sample, ranging from those who traveled on ballet tours in the early 1960s to those who toured through DanceMotion in 2012. Some are now household names—stars like New York City ballerina Allegra Kent and Alvin Ailey American Dance Theater soloist and former artistic director Judith Jamison. But most are known primarily within the dance world—many of them journeyman members of ensembles. Dancers of all types, from those who danced in the corps to those who danced the solos, contribute to the creation and reinterpretation of dance history.

Talking with the dancers about multiple performances across multiple countries and tours reckons with the insufficiency of what performance theorist Diana Taylor describes as the "archive," the more officially recognized, often text-based historical record.[57] Following Taylor's argument for expanding the notion of "archive" and "repertoire"—the embodied acts that often resist cultural practices' hegemonic constrictions and documentation—I examine dance and the dancers' stories as additional forms that support, exceed, and, sometimes, critique the written word. Indeed, I argue that through dancers' repeated performances of their dancing—onstage across months of touring and as they recalled their experiences in the oral histories that inform this book—that they reenact, in performance theorist Rebecca Schneider's terms, the fleshy "histories of body-to-body transmission of affect and enactment."[58] Their memories demonstrate that physical performance both has impact and remains with us across time. The book pairs information and perspectives gathered through interviews and performance analysis with archival material, government memos, and meeting minutes, as well as newspaper articles and reviews. Looking at archive and repertoire together opens dance history to various acts of transmission, as the dancers share knowledge and ideas among bodies, with one another, and across time, rather than imagining knowledge as happening only in one moment, one body, or one iteration of a choreographic work.[59]

Interviews also allow me to unsettle dance history's singular emphasis on the choreographer, undoing a familiar narrative that focuses on a choreographer (often a man) as the genius who guides and shapes a group of dancers (often primarily women). In this way, approaching dance as a collective process does more than provide multiple perspectives; it also marks larger cultural, gendered power dynamics that have too often been transferred unmarked from dance organizations into dance history. For instance, autobiographies and biographies of NYCB artistic director and choreographer George Balanchine usually relegate the NYCB dancers, particularly the company's women, to the status of choreographer's "muse," refusing to acknowledge their impact on the choreography in creation, in performance, and in cultural diplomacy efforts. In chapter 1, my focus on dancers disrupts the hagiographic literature about Balanchine. The 1962 tour was Balanchine's first return to his homeland. While the complications of the Russian émigré's role as American ambassador make a compelling story, that narrative ignores the enormity of the tour, on which eighty-seven people traveled, including sixty-six dancers who danced eight performances per week for two months.

Some of the dancers I interviewed have written about the tours in their autobiographies,[60] but this project seeks to bring together multiple voices from the tours in ways that a single person's perspective—particularly a star dancer's, rather than a dancer who performed mainly in a company's ensemble—cannot. I bring the dancers' voices and experiences to the center of the historical record in an effort to expand a dancer's role beyond that of a muse or mute object, and, in fact, to understand dancers as acting as national mouthpieces and politically astute respondents to the nation.

In each of the interviews, I asked the dancers about the reasons they felt cultural diplomacy was important (or not). I wanted my narrators to discuss how they understood and valued cultural diplomacy, rather than to position myself as the sole interpreter of the information they provided. In this choice, I follow oral historian Michael Frisch's exhortation to oral historians to ask all narrators, not just those in leadership positions, to discuss the broader implications of everyday actions.[61] This intermingling of voices from a variety of positions in the hierarchies within dance companies and between government officials and artists results in an account that intertwines micro and macro political histories. Taking an oral-history approach to the interviews allowed me to traffic in the specificity of individual experiences and, with my narrators' assistance, to tie those experiences to larger historical and cultural issues.

Though oral history offers a multilayered, dancer-centered approach to the history of dance in cultural diplomacy, the interview format has its limits. Many dancers from the early tours had passed away or, often because of their age, did not want to be interviewed. In writing about the Ailey company, for instance, I feel the absence of Miguel Godreau (figure I.4), the company's leading dancer on the 1967 Africa tour. (Godreau passed away decades ago, while only in his early forties.)

Several of the Ailey dancers I interviewed spoke about Godreau's importance on the tour and their fear that he has been left out of Ailey history (and as a result, American history). Other gaps in the interviews speak to larger trends in dance: some of the absent voices are those of gay men lost in the eighties when AIDS ravaged the ballet and modern dance communities, especially in New York City, where most of the companies selected for diplomatic tours were based.

Most, but not all the interviews were done one-on-one. When interviewing dancers involved in the DanceMotion tours—interviews that often took place during rehearsal breaks—time constraints often meant interviewing them in small groups. On the one hand, this meant that individuals spoke less and probably curtailed comments that they might have made in a more intimate exchange. On the other hand, the group format often prompted back-and-forth exchanges among the dancers that simulated the studio conversations that often animate the creation and restaging of choreography. Another limiting but important factor in the more recent interviews has been that many of the companies who have traveled on the DanceMotion tours hope to be chosen for the program again. And, given my own investment in dance, I hope many of these companies, especially those committed to rigorously investigating what it means to use dance to engage with multiple audiences, are chosen again for the tours. The financial reality of future funding must have shaped how artists talked to me about their experiences, leaving me to hypothesize not just about what the dancers said but also about the absences and silences within their comments.

My emphasis on returning dancers to dance history offers many opportunities for complex historiography, but the danger of my approach lies

Figure I.4
Miguel Godreau in Alvin Ailey's signature masterpiece *Revelations* in 1966.
Source: Photo by Jack Mitchell. Courtesy of the Alvin Ailey Dance Foundation, Inc.

in the potential overvaluation of the voices of narrators, what Frisch calls the placement of "unquestioned authority on direct experience."[62] I mitigate this effect through archival work, gleaning information about governmental mandates and agendas, and the companies' institutional structures. These documents, mostly collected from government archives and dance company archives, along with press material from American and foreign newspapers, create a fuller picture of the tours and their impact and help me discern how various government agencies and individuals had different, even competing goals. The USIA officers situated abroad often had different conceptions of the tours' value than did those based in Washington, DC, for instance.

In addition to the USIA officer reports, press coverage offered a primary link to audience reactions abroad. Companies gave me access to their collections of tour reviews, usually from foreign newspapers, and embassy reports in government archives contained foreign press clippings, too. Both sources have limits: the government and companies valued positive reviews over negative ones; hence negative reviews have often disappeared from archives. Too, the relationship between the press and the tours unfolded differently for each company. The New York City Ballet received much more attention abroad, and, since *New York Times* dance critic John Martin traveled with the company for the entire 1962 Soviet tour, the NYCB also received extensive coverage in the United States. A wide variety of African newspapers wrote about the 1967 Ailey performances, though many of these reviews speak very cursorily about the company's actual dancing onstage, making the reviews better for assessing the general response, not the specificities of dancing. There was copious news coverage of all the tours by the Graham company, in part because Graham was famous well before State Department programs began in the 1950s. The dearth of contemporary dance criticism in print journalism has translated into less coverage of the DanceMotion tours and the choreographic works they featured. The twenty-first-century rise of the Internet, however, means that blogs figure prevalently in the documentation of recent tours. Notably, the State Department maintains a blog on all the DanceMotion tours, so I had some access to dancers' reflections while they were still on tour, rather than only relying on their memories of past events. Given the blogs' "official" nature, however, these mini-essays likely offer only a slice of the dancers' thoughts.

Written documentation of the tours offers insight into the governmental agendas behind international, state-sponsored dance tours. Those agendas, however, are most fully realized *and* most clearly subverted from the stage, as American dancers, sometimes joined by dancers from other nations, perform. All the dance company tours, in the Cold War and more recently, raise questions about why national identity might be productively considered as performative. I use the term "performative," not in its lay definition as a mere synonym for "performance," but as an evocation of an act/action that has impact in a social sphere: to name dance as "American" does not just describe the choreography or the dancing, but the "issuing of the utterance is the performance of an action . . . not just saying something."[63] While J. L. Austin coined the term "performative" as a form of linguistic or written speech, I, following Rebekah Kowal, consider dancing as a form of utterance, too, capable of *doing*.[64] Considering American identity as performative reckons with nationalism, as theorist Paul Gilbert writes, as "not so much a system of beliefs but as a set of practices, through which national loyalty is cultivated and nations sustained."[65] Gilbert's definition connects representation and embodiment, pointing to how people construct and enact national affiliations, and how these constructions and actions change over time and in different contexts. Even when governments sponsor artists in hopes of promoting what dance historian Anthony Shay calls "highly essentialist portraits" of national identity, choreography and dancers' experiences point to the performances of national identity as "multilayered political and ethnographic statements."[66] Performances always exceed government guidelines and intentions, even as they also enact and sustain the nation.

The dance companies at the center of this book do not serve official government edicts nearly as closely as arts groups entirely funded by the government might. These companies, I argue, simultaneously maintain and contest the politics of the nation-state they represent. In the formal performances foregrounded in the Cold War era and in the more informal workshops foregrounded in DanceMotion, dance functions, as David Román has argued, as a "a form of counterpublicity to the dominant discourses of the nation-state, . . . put[ting] forward alternative viewpoints, showcase[ing] emerging perspectives, and allow[ing] for cultural dissent."[67] Performing official American identity on tour, dance companies *both* represent the nation *and* resist essentialist notions of "America."

Dance is the link between the dancers and the government in this project. The choreographic works considered at length in this book include George Balanchine's *Agon* (1957), *Serenade* (1934), and *Western Symphony* (1954); Jerome Robbins' *Interplay* (1945); Alvin Ailey's *Revelations* (1960); Martha Graham's *Diversion of Angels* (1948), *Night Journey* (1947), and *Phaedra* (1962); Jawole Willa Jo Zollar's *Walking with Pearl* (2005); Ronald K. Brown's *Ife/My Heart* (2005); Brenda Way's *24 Exposures* (2001); and Trey McIntyre's *The Unkindness of Ravens* (2012). Choreographic analysis helps me find evidence of the ways representation cohered on the tours and of the artistic loopholes in the official ideas of representation the dancers and choreographers exploited. Movement phrases and performance choices, as well as scenic, lighting, and musical contributions, built and displaced pictures of national identity.

Choreographic analysis is always, and certainly is in this project, an approximation of the performances that occurred onstage. I have drawn composite pictures of what a dance might have been through studying videos and from watching live performances of a piece years, sometimes decades, after the its premiere. The dances in chapters 1, 2, and 3 rely heavily on the available commercial videos, PBS documentaries, and the archives of the Jerome Robbins Dance Collection at the New York Public Library. When possible, I watched videos made as close to the date of the tours as possible, recognizing that dancers' technique and performance styles shift as companies' leadership and guiding ideologies change. Small shifts can easily transform a work's meaning. Watching portions of

Revelations recorded in the USIA film about Ailey that was screened during the company's 1967 tour, I was surprised to hear the musical accompaniment to the dance "Sinner Man" done with what sounds like banjos. Today, all the *Revelations'* music has a faster tempo and the orchestration for "Sinner Man" has a driving, electric sound—very different from the banjo twang in the 1960s. Only for chapter 5 was I able to see all the performances I describe live, since I followed the Trey McIntyre Project and the Korea National Contemporary Dance Company on their 2012 national tour. (Although even then, the line between live and recorded performance is murky, since I watched the New York performances with an online audience via a simulcast of the event.)

I enmesh my choreographic analysis in thick movement description because, as dance historian Thomas DeFrantz writes, detailed description allows a degree of accessibility to dances long gone, while also providing a sense of how the dances I studied resonate with me.[68] Movement description is not an objective practice, but rather must be understood as a subjective rendering of my experience of a dance. In all my writing about dance, I try to be aware of my own subjectivity and that of the dancers. The latter arises particularly in movement description as I try to capture movement in terms of people and not just bodies. For instance, a hip does not "jut forward" in McIntyre's *The Unkindness of Ravens*; instead dancer Lee So-jin juts her hip forward. Writing about dance should display people's agency over their bodies' movements, a key idea to understanding artists as active participants in cultural diplomacy. Both of these writing choices—acknowledging the subjectivity of movement description and the control dancers exercise over their bodies—stem from feminist imperatives, recognizing how personal choices about how we use our bodies resonate with and are influenced by larger cultural fields.

My emphasis on choreography and dancers clearly situates me within the field of dance studies, but my work also operates in the realm of performance studies. I explore the dancers' full experience of touring, engaging with Richard Schechner's concept of a "whole performance sequence: training, workshop, rehearsal, warm-up, performance, cool-down, and aftermath."[69] Performance studies enables me to write about dancers' experience of the tours onstage and off, assessing the role of everything from their trips to dance clubs to formal dinners as part of the embodied experience of cultural diplomacy.

Examining choreography and the dancer interviews from a performance studies perspective also enables me to write an embodied history of the entirety of the tours, understanding how daily, often mundane, practices make up history, rather than seeing political events like the

Cuban missile crisis or American race riots as the dominant determining factors in people's daily lives. With a focus on everyday activities and individual actors, I have written a history in the manner described by theorist Michel de Certeau, as a story that "begins on [the] ground level, with footsteps. They are myriad, but do not compose a series. . . . [A] swarming mass is an innumerable collection of singularities."[70] Seeing the messiness of histories, and thus seeing the way individual stories do not add up to a single representative image or narrative, makes it easier to see how multiple agendas unfold at once.

IMAGINING A NATION, IMAGINING A WORLD

Dancers as Diplomats tells the story of the roles dance and dancers play as official representatives of the United States to consider how national identity is both embodied and performative. Performance theorist Elin Diamond defines "performance" as always a "doing" and a "thing done," a framing that can help us see how "America" is both a category with already attached meaning and cultural, military, economic, and political weight, as well as a category that is constantly being refashioned and redeployed.[71] The dance-in-diplomacy programs constantly perform a hegemonic, state-sponsored version of "America," even as the individuals and communities involved in the programs critique and reimagine "America," too.

These constant reshapings of "nation" are particularly visible in the Cold War and the early decades of the so-called War on Terror, the two periods at the center of this book. Both periods share a heightened awareness of American identity as produced in relationship to a global sphere. Despite the many differences between post–World War II and post-9/11 United States, both eras functioned within a dominant narrative that painted the United States, to borrow theater historian Bruce McConachie's description of Cold War containment discourse, as a "virtuous 'us'" distinct from "an evil 'them' without ambiguity."[72] This rhetoric's very force and repetition points to its constructed nature. Dancers traveling on the State Department tours danced and lived in the space between this forceful rhetoric of American exceptionalism and cultural hybridities produced by many forces, including migration, diaspora, and globalization.

Dancers as Diplomats first chapter focuses on New York City Ballet's tour of the Soviet Union in 1962 and its overlap with perhaps the most iconic US-Soviet standoff of the Cold War: the Cuban missile crisis. In the same months that the United States and USSR teetered on the brink of nuclear war, company dancers, led by NYCB founding choreographer and Russian émigré George Balanchine, walked through the schools of the famous Russian ballet academies and saw Soviet dancers execute dance technique the Americans performed onstage as "American." They heard Balanchine strategically describe his national identity, sometimes as American, sometimes as Georgian, claiming the identity that best suited his agenda in a given setting. The dancers also listened to American and Soviet officials argue over whether Balanchine should or even could be claimed as a Soviet. National identity reigned as the key identity marker on the tour, but that category only captured partial aspects of artists' lives and techniques.

Chapters 2 and 3 place the State Department Cold War touring programs in a global context, expanding beyond the US-Soviet standoff. Both chapters consider how tours to Africa and Asia, sites chosen specifically because of the postcolonial movements in each region, impacted Cold War policy and history. The State Department and, indeed, everyone supporting the early dance-in-diplomacy tours also saw Latin America as a key site in the US-Soviet struggle to shape the future of newly decolonized countries—so much so that the President's Special Emergency Fund sent the first dance tour, the tour of the Limón Company in 1954, to Latin America.[73]

Both chapters 2 and 3 also consider how American domestic events shaped international politics. Chapter 2 focuses on the relationship among American identity, race, and sexuality, primarily by examining performances by African American dancers: Arthur Mitchell of the New York City Ballet and the dancers of the predominantly African American Alvin Ailey American Dance Theater. I focus on these dancers' choices, onstage and offstage, building upon Penny Von Eschen's important work on jazz music and American cultural diplomacy to consider how modernist aesthetics contained, obscured, and exported racialized meanings. For many artists on tour, their races and sexualities created a double minoritarian status, which I consider in light of homophobic State Department policies, now known collectively as the Lavender Scare.[74]

As artists of minoritarian status well knew, American ideals—freedom and individualism among them—so eagerly exported by the United States during the Cold War were not without limits. Chapter 3 considers how the rhetoric of "freedom" became a double-edged tool on the State Department tours, and argues that the Martha Graham Dance Company became one of the companies most frequently supported by the State Department, in part, because the company and its well-known, provocative female leader performed the possibilities of freedom for women, particularly sexual freedom, onstage and off. At the same time, however, Graham's work rarely pushed boundaries too far by Cold War standards—as would have been the case had the sexuality in question been male homosexuality. Graham represented the apex of American dance modernism and its claim to universal communication, especially to the ANTA panelists choosing artists for tours. She became the indomitable female choreographer of State Department tours because she, unlike her female contemporaries, the African American choreographers and anthropologists Katherine Dunham and Pearl Primus, performed "American freedom" in the "correct" contexts.

This is not to say that Graham only benefited from the system. She also challenged the system, particularly through her use of the body in what I call a "diva stance." With her body, she crossed the boundaries of what women could and should do in the public sphere at mid-century, navigating first a congressional scandal about her work in 1963 and the sensitive tour of war-torn Vietnam in 1974.

Chapters 4 and 5 examine dance-in-diplomacy programs in the early twenty-first century. By focusing primarily on DanceMotion USA, I track the shift from the Cold War export-based model of cultural diplomacy, bringing "America" to the world, to the partnership-based model of cultural diplomacy. DanceMotion tours supported American efforts to work *with* other nations, an outgrowth of a twenty-first-century globally networked world.

Chapter 4 discusses how DanceMotion emerged from a post-9/11, post–US-invasion-of-Iraq political landscape. Principally, the chapter considers how the program's emphasis on American companies—Urban Bush Women, Ronald K. Brown's Evidence, and ODC/Dance—working with foreign audiences and artists has shifted the focus away from theatrical presentations and toward community engagement, usually in the form of lecture-demonstrations and workshops. In the 2010 pilot program, DanceMotion's embrace of partnership was extended to include the African diaspora as part of American culture, a diasporic formulation that was used but often backgrounded in the Cold War era.

Dancers as Diplomats concludes with a meditation on the concept of exchange with an ethnographic essay about my time following the Korean National Contemporary Dance Company and the Trey McIntyre Project on their US tour. In 2012 the State Department introduced a two-way exchange program into DanceMotion, bringing Americans abroad and, later, non-American dancers to the United States. Although "exchange" had been a fantasy of the dance programs since their inception, the State Department did not fully finance back-and-forth relationships until 2012. The Boise-based contemporary Trey McIntyre Project was one of four that traveled on the 2012 DanceMotion USA tour. Months later the Korea

National Contemporary Dance Company, with State Department support, came to Boise to make a work with the McIntyre group, and the two company then toured that work across the United States.

Chapter 5 presses against the assumption that two-way exchange is possible in relationships characterized by an immensely asymmetrical power imbalance, as is the case between the United States and virtually any other nation. How do asymmetrical power relationships curtail, but perhaps not entirely block, exchange? And, really, what is being exchanged? Money? An approach to movement? Dance itself? And finally, who or what is "changing" in the space of State Department-sponsored exchange, in the past and in the present?

Dancers as Diplomats argues that dance and dancers, in part because of their understanding of representation and social change as always embodied, have shaped and re-shaped American identity. It is clear to me, after living with this material for over a decade, that by thinking about performance—and specifically dance—much can be learned about how national identity is formed and reformed with and through bodies. When the State Department funded dance companies to travel around the world on behalf of the US, it funded footprints that left impressions on individual artists' political consciousness, on other countries' sense of the United States and themselves, and on domestic life in the United States.

CHAPTER 1

Ballet Nations

The New York City Ballet on Tour in the

Soviet Union in 1962

When the dancers of George Balanchine's ballet *Western Symphony* (1954) run, they bounce—a choice accentuated by the women's short, lacy, barmaidesque tutus. Generally, when dancers run in classical ballet they stay close to the ground, feet slightly turned out, knees bent. They look as though they are skimming across the stage. In *Western Symphony*, the women kick up their heels, almost hitting their flouncing skirts. This stylized, buoyant run fills the stage in the ballet's finale, when the entire cast, over twenty-five men and women, lace through one another's arms, square dancing in pointe shoes. The group then moves into a classical step, *sissonne à la seconde* (a jump to the side in which the dancer opens both legs in the air, and then lands in fifth position), followed by a *pas de chat* (a quick jump in which the dancer raises one leg and then the other—the English translation, "step of the cat," might help with the visual). Bounce, *sissone, pas de chat, sissonne, pas de chat*, run, run, kick up those heels! The ballet concludes with the cast's women on their knees, arms open, chins up. The men bookend the kneeling women, and then leap into the air, bending their knees and tucking their feet behind them. Cowboy hats go flying.[1]

When the New York City Ballet performed *Western Symphony* in Moscow's Bolshoi Theatre in October 1962, there was no doubt the Americans had arrived in the Soviet Union (figure 1.1). It was not just the American and then Soviet national anthems played just before the curtain rose that marked that night as an international affair, but also the way the dancers moved that marked them as American. These dancers, led by the Russian émigré Balanchine, were quickly refashioning ballet as it had been known in Europe and the Soviet Union into an American form—still working with the classical vocabulary familiar to the Soviet balletomanes but with a twist or, in the case of *Western Symphony*, a swagger. When the women in the corps de ballet rip through a series of fast *pas de bourrées*, usually a transitional ballet step, they match their piercing steps to the syncopated rhythm of Hershy Kay's arrangement of "My Old Kentucky Home." The women's legs move through classical positions, *passes* and tight fifth positions, but they also resemble fingers picking a banjo. The women's short phrase holds at least three historical references: ballet's classical history in Europe and Russia; an American balletic sensibility of speed and "folksiness;" and, through the musical choice, African American culture, which famously fascinated Balanchine (see chapter 2). Even a few seconds of a dance can hold a multitude of meanings.

Yet many histories tell a reductive version of the tour: one that over-emphasizes American and Soviet culture as starkly different. In these

Figure 1.1
The New York City Ballet takes a bow in Moscow in 1962 after a program that ended with Balanchine's *Western Symphony. Left to right*: Violette Verdy, a male dancer (likely Nicholas Magallanes), Gloria Govrin, George Balanchine, Melissa Hayden, and Arthur Mitchell.
Source: Photograph by A. Batanov. BALANCHINE is a Trademark of the George Balanchine Trust.

narratives, the NYCB's American style and Balanchine's choreography were not just new approaches to ballet, but the absolute opposite of Soviet ballet and the Imperial Russian technique Soviet ballet still drew on heavily. The *New York Times* dance critic John Martin, who traveled with the company on the entire tour, reported that the company's first performance in Moscow "introduced a completely new style of ballet" to the Soviets.[2] *Western Symphony* and the other ballets on that first Moscow program, Balanchine's *Serenade* (1934) and *Agon* (1957) and Jerome Robbins's *Interplay* (1945), are largely plotless, bare-stage productions. These ballets and many others chosen for the tour did contrast sharply with the Bolshoi Ballet's 1960s repertory, a mix of nineteenth-century classics, such as *Giselle* (1841) and *Swan Lake* (1877), reimagined as postrevolution Soviet narratives, and newer works, such as the heroic, spectacle-driven *Spartacus* (1956).[3] Form may have divided the two nations' approaches to ballet, but shared affection for ballet brought the two national cultures together.

By sending the NYCB to the Soviet Union as part of mid-twentieth-century American diplomacy, the US State Department and the American National Theatre and Academy (ANTA), the group that selected the artists for the State Department tours, pierced the Iron Curtain with one of Russia's best-loved art forms. Soviet audiences loved the American dancers; Balanchine's choreography; and the fast, rhythmically complex American performance style. Performances sold out before the company arrived in Moscow,[4] including opening night at the Bolshoi, ten days at the 6000-seat Palace of Congresses Theatre in the Kremlin, and a return to the Bolshoi for the final performances. All the dancers remember ovations lasting long after the curtain fell, a scenario that was repeated throughout the eight-week tour, which went on to Leningrad, Kiev, Tbilisi, and Baku after Moscow.

The NYCB did not just enthrall audiences; it also affected Soviet cultural institutional leaders. After the NYCB tour, at the 1963 Soviet choreographic summit, the All-Union Choreographic Conference, the head of the Bolshoi, Mikhail Chulaki, hailed Soviet ballet as "carrier of great ideas, distinguished by its unique capacity to express complex topics." But Chulaki also focused on "a poverty of dance and dance inventiveness in Soviet ballets," a critique that seems likely to have been influenced by the NYCB's recent visit.[5] Chulaki's celebratory but also critical comments cannot be entirely attributed to the influence of the NYCB's performances—the previous summit, held in 1960, had also included debates about the purpose of Soviet ballet—but Chulaki's critique of Soviet ballet's impoverished vocabulary and his yearning for "dance inventiveness" must have been influenced by the landmark NYCB tour and by Balanchine (though the Soviet ballet officials at the conference still described Balanchine as a personally repugnant figure).[6]

The Soviets' relative openness to the NYCB seems surprising, not because of the aesthetic differences between the two countries' ballet styles, but because the 1962 tour overlapped with one of the Cold War's most tense incidents: the Cuban missile crisis. State Department–sponsored dance programs usually have some tie to governmental politics, but the missile crisis made it impossible to overlook the connections between politics and the arts on the NYCB tour. Even though City Ballet was the second American ballet company to dance in the Soviet Union (the American Ballet Theatre [ABT] was the first, performing there two years earlier), the coincidence of the NYCB tour with the Cuban missile crisis makes it more prominent in State Department history.

Although Americans had tremendous access to news of the crisis, the NYCB dancers, busy with rehearsals and performances, had little. Embassy staff warned them to expect hostile audiences at the theater. Dancer Sally Leland remembered their instructions: "They said, 'You're in no danger, but you may—when you perform tonight or in the following nights—you may hear some boos, but that's all.'"[7] Precisely the opposite happened. The Soviet audience loved the NYCB that night. The crowds chanted "Bis! Bis! Encore! Encore!" so enthusiastically that principal dancer Edward Villella returned to the stage, ignoring Balanchine's tacit policy forbidding encores. To constant cheers, Villella repeated his solo from Balanchine's *Donizetti Variations* (1960).[8] Dancer Gloria Govrin said, "We had never experienced the kind of reaction that the audience had before anywhere; there were like twenty to twenty-five minute ovations."[9] As Govrin watched Villella and his partner Violette Verdy dance for the thrilled Soviet audience, Soviet officials sat in nearby Kremlin offices negotiating with their American counterparts, both sets of political leaders acting on the belief that Soviet and American ways of life were absolutely incompatible.[10]

This chapter locates the NYCB tour within the larger field of Cold War history, considering how dance history can contribute to a reconsideration of the Cold War that challenges the idea of the United States and the USSR as diametrically different societies. The image of a Soviet audience leaping to their feet as American dancers fly through Balanchine's high-speed choreography suggests that the performances created a "counterpublic," a group composed (mostly) of strangers who come together to offer alternative views to those promoted by the state.[11] Examining the NYCB Soviet tour offers a narrative of an American-Soviet encounter premised on a shared, transnational passion that glimpses, not a future, but a Cold War present in which the American and the Soviet people are not solely enemies. The creation of a binational public through embodiment does not imply that dance serves as a universal language, capable of uniting audiences and artists regardless of cultural difference. It does, however, suggest that, at least temporarily, ballet forged a connective tissue between distinct, but not entirely opposite, national cultures. In the theater and in everyday life, the Soviet response led the American dancers to question the conventional Cold War narratives of how the braiding of nation, community, and self manifested for the Soviet and American people.

Recognizing the role of the dancers, not just Balanchine's choreography, in this process is crucial to locating the 1962 tour in the everyday realities of the Cold War. The high caliber of both the company's dancers and Balanchine's choreography bolstered the tour's success. The cast lists from the 1962 tour include many of the NYCB's greatest dancers: Diana Adams, Jacques d'Amboise, Suzanne Farrell, Melissa Hayden, Allegra Kent, Patricia McBride, Arthur Mitchell, Violette Verdy, Edward Villella, and Patricia Wilde, among others. Some, such as Adams and d'Amboise, were at the height of their careers; others were just emerging. Kent became one of the tour's unexpected stars: a new mother, she had joined the tour late, eventually stepping into principal roles after Adams injured her ankle. Mitchell, the company's only African American dancer and the tour's breakout soloist, astounded Soviet audiences, who chanted "Arthur! Arthur!" when he came onstage. This chapter focuses on the tour repertory from the perspectives of these dancers. It highlights three of the four ballets that appeared on the program the NYCB performed on opening night in each of the five cities visited on the tour. That program began with *Serenade* (1934), followed by Jerome Robbins's *Interplay* (1945) then Balanchine's *Agon* (1957), and finally closed with *Western Symphony*. *Western Symphony*, *Interplay*, and *Serenade* animate this chapter; *Agon* plays a central role in the discussion of race and modernism in chapter 2.

Cultural diplomacy was shifting at the time of the NYCB tour. The company was among the last dance organizations contracted to go abroad before the State Department declared a temporary moratorium on performing arts programs in which to study and refocus its policy efforts.[12] This first era of dance-in-diplomacy revolved around the goal of exporting American dance, displaying "us" to "them," a goal that relied on a premise of absolute and recognizable difference between American art and that of other nations, particularly Soviet-influenced art. The State Department and the ANTA Dance Panel considered the NYCB's Balanchine repertory to be the opposite of twentieth-century Soviet ballet. Balanchine created fast, abstract, and music-driven pieces. Soviet work used spectacle to tell heroic narratives. The brief period of ballet exchanges, beginning with the Bolshoi Ballet's 1959 tour to the United States and including the simultaneous 1962 tours of the NYCB to the USSR and the Bolshoi to the United States, was one of the few moments when each side of the cultural stand-off saw the other country's artistic offerings in live performance.

The choreographic distinctions between Balanchine's primarily American work and Soviet realism, known in Soviet ballet circles as "drambalet,"[13] supported the official differentiation between American and Soviet culture.[14] But the NYCB dancers' experiences abroad and the classical ballet vocabulary manipulated in the NYCB repertory did not split Soviet and American culture so clearly. The City Ballet dancers had physical connections to Russian culture, having trained with many Russian teachers in New York and throughout the United States. The dancers' and ballet's debt to Russia blurred the stark distinction between American and Soviet ballet imagined, but never fully defined, by the ANTA Dance Panel who advised the State Department to send City Ballet abroad.

Even though the Dance Panel never arrived at an exact definition of American identity, and the City Ballet dancers felt themselves sliding in and out of the official category of "American," the ballet tour persistently revolved around the idea of "American" dance. The dancers felt their national identity form and re-form on a daily basis, even during the missile crisis. They represented the United States at a time of political turmoil, but they still had to decide how to do their jobs and how to care for themselves and others.

This chapter captures how much of the negotiation of an "official" national status in State Department tours happens offstage, in the mundane daily lives of dancers. The dancers' youth and their everyday needs as artists (overworked, physically focused artists on a long international tour) distracted them from the looming specter of nuclear war. By writing a history saturated with both the political and personal aspects of the dancers' time in Moscow—a history that includes the Cuban missile crisis, but does not impose it as the only or even primary event that structured the dancers' time—I shift the emphases in the historical records of the tour. I do not attempt to carve the tour into what theorist Michel de Certeau calls "events" situated around "substantial landmarks,"[15] seemingly making a time, place, and people clear and understandable. The political and cultural impact of the crisis on the NYCB tour is better understood as a layered, even messy, series of moments regulated equally by global events, daily life, and the demands of getting ballets onto the stage. Bodies in motion seem a fitting metaphor for a national identity constantly in the process of negotiation.

HIGH-STAKES CULTURAL DIPLOMACY: BALLET IN THE SOVIET UNION

Sending dance to the Soviet Union, the heir to the Russian classical ballet legacy, was a high-stakes affair, especially to the ANTA panelists who advised the State Department. Even though the arts tours' complicated logistics had been settled by recent treaty agreements with the Soviet Union, choosing dance companies to represent the United States' young ballet scene meant that the State Department and ANTA had to agree on characteristics that would make ballet legible as American. ANTA panel discussions eventually settled on citizenship and repertory as the primary categories to consider. But no clear consensus emerged as to what constituted the right ensemble or choreographic roster to definitively mark a group as American enough. In the case of the City Ballet tour, the panelists eventually settled on innovation and excellence as their criteria, qualities associated with American cultural diplomacy since its inception in the early twentieth-century. The panelists thought these qualities would be legible to Soviet audiences, too.

While the ANTA panelists mainly guessed at what Soviet audiences might think, the State Department officials had almost a decade of intelligence about Soviet culture. The creation of Eisenhower's Emergency Fund in 1954, the predecessor to the State Department's long-standing Cultural Presentations Program, followed a shift in Soviet society after Joseph Stalin's death in 1953. Increased travel (and intelligence gathering) between the United States and the USSR became possible during the period of "thaw" initiated by Nikita Khrushchev after the 1955 Geneva Convention.

Even though the State Department had charged the ANTA panel with the task of suggesting artists for engagements around the world, the Soviet Union loomed large as a destination. The first American theatrical production toured the USSR in 1955, when the Soviet government invited a group already performing in Western Europe to bring their *Porgy and Bess* to Moscow, Leningrad, and Stalingrad.[16] The newly formed ANTA Dance Panel discussed *Porgy and Bess*'s success at one of its first meetings in 1955.[17] The newly open Soviet Union proved to be a large target for dance advisers and State Department officials alike.

Porgy and Bess's success on Soviet stages did not necessarily prompt smooth passage for subsequent efforts. The 1956 Soviet invasion of Hungary appalled many Americans, including members of the ANTA panel, who became reticent to work with the Soviet government. Possibly the single largest logistical barrier to American-Soviet exchanges, however, was rooted in American law. The efforts by the impresario Sol Hurok and ANTA to bring larger Soviet groups—namely, the Bolshoi Ballet—to the United States would have been impossible before 1957, when US immigration authorities relaxed the fingerprinting laws for foreign visitors. Until then, the Soviet Union had refused to allow its artists to be fingerprinted en masse, meaning that a huge group like the Bolshoi could not enter the country.[18] The Soviets had also insisted all American-Soviet exchanges occur in equal numbers, so the Bolshoi not being able to come to the United States meant that no large American dance company could go to the USSR.

The first of several Soviet-American treaty exchange agreements, signed in 1958, finally addressed the demand for equal exchanges. The agreement outlined three tenets for the exchanges: "equality, reciprocity, and mutual benefit."[19] According to former State Department, USIA, and Moscow embassy–based diplomat Yale Richmond, the Soviet government favored these principles because, at least on paper, they figured the United States and the USSR as equals. (Over time, the agreements also shielded the State Department from criticism that it was too open to Soviet propaganda.[20]) From the very beginning of performing arts diplomacy, the US government had always envisioned a public-private funding structure, and the agreement established a unique plan for cost-sharing by both governments and private American donors.[21]

Although the agreements outlined exchanges in educational, cultural, and scientific fields, dance became one of the most public examples of the exchanges. Hurok and ANTA's plan for a Bolshoi Ballet tour was named in the initial 1958 agreement.[22] Hurok thus became the first of many private presenters to benefit from public policy, and his interest in Soviet-American exchanges increased their frequency and capacity. Hurok's on-the-ground negotiating abilities in the Soviet Union often proved to be the grease that kept the Soviet-to-America side of the tours running. In the late fifties, American audiences saw performances by Soviet folk groups, including the Moiseyev Dance Company, which made an appearance on *The Ed Sullivan Show*, and the all-female Berozhka troupe.[23] The 1959 arrival of the Bolshoi Ballet on its first American tour, under joint sponsorship by Hurok and ANTA, eclipsed the early folk-company tours. The Bolshoi and the Soviet Union's other main ballet company, the Kirov, made several trips to the United States in the follow-ing two decades, including the Bolshoi's 1962 tour, which coincided with the NYCB's appearances in the USSR.

The ANTA Dance Panel had to decide how the United States should counter the Soviet guests. At first, the strategy was a defensive one: what-ever the Soviets sent, the United States sent something of a similar genre. If the Soviet Union sent folk dance, as it did when the Moiseyev toured the United States in 1958, the panel looked for American folk dance com-panies. When the Soviets began using the Bolshoi and Kirov companies as cultural ambassadors, the panel agonized over how—or whether—an American ballet company could counter big, flashy Soviet ballet.

The Dance Panel worried constantly that the Russians, who were justi-fiably proud of a ballet tradition rooted in the country's Imperial period, would scrutinize American efforts in ballet. In a 1957 discussion about a possible ABT tour to the Soviet Union, one panel member remarked, "Bringing a ballet company to Russia is like bringing a report card. It is of greater import than just having the company there."[24] Other panel members referred to the dilemma over how to present ballet in the Soviet Union as a "national emergency."[25] The United States could not just show that it had ballet companies; it had to demonstrate their superior quality.

The panel decided that Jerome Robbins's small troupe, Ballets: U.S.A, should be the first dance company to go to the Soviet Union because its repertory, a collection of Robbins's ballets and Broadway numbers, would not directly compete with the Soviet ballets and would "show something America does well"— lighthearted, flashier fare.[26] The panel also thought that sending Robbins's company first with a major ballet company to follow soon after paralleled the Soviet programming, which often sent a smaller, more popular company like Moiseyev, and then a larger "high-brow" company like the Bolshoi.[27] The Gostkoncert, the Soviet cultural agency, eventually rejected Ballets: U.S.A for touring,[28] forcing the panel to shift their focus to ABT, even though the panelists doubted the company could remain stable long enough for the important tour.[29]

In the late 1950s, the New York City Ballet had substantial institutional stability compared to ABT, but the company's executive director, Lincoln Kirstein, had kept City Ballet out of the conversations about the Soviet tours. Both Kirstein and ABT artistic director Lucia Chase served on the ANTA Dance Panel, and the force of their opinions about artist selection is one of many examples of individuals exerting tremendous influence over the State Department programming. Kirstein thought no American com-pany, including the NYCB, could compete with Soviet dance tours—their spectacle or their funding. Chase thought ABT would just be too tiny in the Soviet Union's huge theaters.[30] But no concern could prevent the conversation from circling back to the problem of ballet and the Soviet Union. Eventually, at a May 1960 panel meeting, the Dance Panel approved ABT as the first American ballet company to go behind the Iron Curtain.[31]

Once the panel (and subsequently the State Department) chose ABT for the USSR, two concerns (which would persist in panel conversations for years to come) dominated the panel's conversation: the dancers' citizenship and the repertory. The panel had often discussed the importance of dancers' national origins, but no consensus emerged about whether American citizenship was necessary. The panel worried sending ABT's non-American principal dancers, such as the French Violette Verdy and the Danish Erik Bruhn, would indicate a lack of American talent. In the same conversation, however, the panel encouraged ABT to hire Melissa Hayden from the NYCB, even though she was Canadian.[32]

Panel discussions about repertory yielded a clearer picture of what the panel considered representative of American ballet: a mix of Americana-themed ballets and at least one Balanchine ballet, although discussions also suggested that layers of theme, form, and personnel obscured the national identity of a given dance. Some ballets offered more palatable combinations than others. The panel approved ABT's tour with the provision that Agnes de Mille's Western-themed ballet *Rodeo* (1942) be part of the tour. They deemed the freewheeling, romantic cowboy ballet crucial to Soviet audiences receiving ABT's performances as explicitly American.[33] Following the lead of ANTA's Music Panel, which had passed a resolution encouraging touring groups to program music by American composers, the Dance Panel considered works choreographed to music by American composers as more thoroughly "American."[34] This further bolstered *Rodeo*'s importance since American composer Aaron Copland wrote the music. Important pieces in American ballet history, such as *Theme and Variations* (1947), Balanchine's first ballet for ABT, also warranted inclusion.[35] In the negotiations for the NYCB 1962 tour, the Dance Panel continued to focus on ballets they thought Soviet audiences would easily understand as American, while the NYCB was focused on taking care of its dancers and making the best possible artistic impression. The company had three major concerns about the State Department tours: first, the duration of the tours exhausted dancers, a concern Kirstein frequently expressed in panel meetings; second, the company wanted to tour Western Europe before the Soviet Union; and third, it wanted to open the Moscow and Leningrad programs in the cities' most historic ballet houses rather than the lesser-known theaters the Soviet government was offering.[36] The tipping point in negotiations came when Hurok invested his own money in the tour, after realizing that without a City Ballet tour to Russia, the Bolshoi Ballet's tour to the United States would be canceled.

The repertory chosen for the NYCB tour largely emerged through a process predicated on selecting pieces that were stylistically different from Soviet ballet. Therefore ballets deemed heavy on spectacle or story were not chosen, but ballets with a loose sense of narrative, such as *Apollo* (1928) and *La Sonnambula* (1946), were. The NYCB also decided to take abstract, musically dissonant ballets, such as *Agon* and *Episodes* (1959), even though it could not predict how Soviet audiences, unaccustomed to the combination of dissonant music and nonnarrative choreography, would respond. (Both ballets were very successful on the tour.)

To arrive at the final list, many layers of financial and logistical issues had to be negotiated among the company, the ANTA Dance Panel, the State Department, and Gostkoncert. Suggestions by ANTA and State Department officials reflected the belief that to represent American ballet NYCB aesthetics should be easily distinguished from Russian classicism, which meant excluding Balanchine's versions of *Swan Lake* (1951) and *Firebird* (1949). The panel also argued that the NYCB should not suggest violence as an American concern, which excluded Jerome Robbins's *The Cage* (1946). The panel wanted accessible ballets, so they excluded Balanchine's *Episodes*, performed to Anton Webern's dissonant score. The panel also thought logistically complicated ballets, such as *The Nutcracker* (1954) and *A Midsummer Night's Dream* (1962), both of which required children, should be excluded.[37] Taken as a group, the panel's recommendations primarily consisted of Balanchine's "greatest hits" up to 1962, including *Agon, Apollo, Serenade, Symphony in C* (1948), *Prodigal Son* (1929), *Allegro Brillante* (1956), *Concerto Barocco* (1941), and *Theme and Variations*.[38]

The panel believed Balanchine's ballets represented American ballet as innovative and excellent, despite the irony of a Russian-born choreographer representing the United States in the USSR—an irony the panel discussed surprisingly little. American studies scholar Catherine Gunther Kodat describes Kirstein as having used his ties to cultural and governmental gatekeepers and his role on the Dance Panel to position Balanchine "as the man destined to give ballet a new life in the New World but also of cementing that claim with US government approval."[39] By 1962, the NYCB also had an extensive track record with the American government, dating back more than two decades. In 1941, its predecessor, the American Ballet Caravan, had toured South America for six months through the Office of Inter-American Affairs, whose cultural diplomacy program headed by Kirstein's friend Nelson Rockefeller, was a forerunner of the State Department exchange programs.[40] The NYCB had also benefited from covertly funded CIA programs in Europe when City Ballet performed at the 1952 Masterpieces of the Twentieth Century Festival in Paris.[41] In that festival, composer Igor Stravinsky conducted the orchestra for Balanchine's *Orpheus* (1948) in one of many well-known collaborations between the two Russian émigrés.[42] Both Stravinsky and Balanchine were friends of festival coordinator Nicolas Nabokov, one of many Russian émigrés (Hurok was another) involved in American cultural diplomacy.

Balanchine and Gostkoncert, whose representatives visited the United States in the spring of 1962 to watch the company, also weighed in on programs' aesthetics, politics, and logistics. Balanchine removed *Figure in the Carpet* from the selection pool because he, too, did not want to compete with Soviet spectacle,[43] but he overrode the panel's desire to exclude *Episodes*.[44] On a more political note, Gostkoncert wanted *Prodigal Son* purged from the repertory because of its biblical association.[45] In a mix of logistics and politics, Gostkoncert also rejected *A Midsummer Night's Dream*, which Balanchine had wanted to include despite the panel's objections, because the Soviet officials did not want Russian children to work with American dancers.[46] By August 1962, just before the company left for Europe, all the parties had agreed on a final list of ballets.[47]

Compared to the sparse, form-focused NYCB fare of quintessential neoclassical Balanchine ballets, such as *Agon* and *Episodes*, the works the Bolshoi brought to the United States in 1962 looked astonishing. The Bolshoi program mixed classical ballets like *Swan Lake* and *Giselle* with the world premiere of *Ballet School* (1962), a look at the techniques and sequences of Russian ballet training, and the American premiere of *Spartacus*. All the Bolshoi ballets were generally well received by American critics and audiences, who, in many cases, had stood in line for hours—even days—to purchase tickets (much as the Soviets did to see the NYCB). The only exception to the positive critical acclaim was the spectacle of *Spartacus*, which Allen Hughes, the *New York Times* music critic who was covering the Bolshoi tour because John Martin was in the Soviet Union with the NYCB, described as "the most preposterous theatrical exercises . . . ever seen."[48]

If critics had issues with some of the Bolshoi's choreography, there was no similar concern about the dancing. As had happened on the Bolshoi's 1959 tour, critics raved over the company's dancers. In 1959, Maya Plisetskaya, known for her explosive jumps and turns—best showcased in her performance as the Black Swan in the company's many offerings of *Swan Lake*—wowed balletomanes and critics alike.[49] When she returned on the 1962 tour, Plisetskaya was surrounded by a strong cast, including

Ekaterina Maximova, whom critics hailed as the heir to the recently retired Bolshoi star Galina Ulanova's legacy.

Given the accepted wisdom about the technical brilliance of the Bolshoi company across all ranks, the NYCB's repertory seems to have also been chosen with the goal of showcasing as much of the company as possible, thereby demonstrating to Europe and the Soviet Union that the United States had many talented ballet dancers, too. The ballets *Symphony in C*, *Allegro Brillante*, *Western Symphony*, *Concerto Barocco* and *La Valse* (1951) require large casts and conclude with the stage full of dancers moving with precision at high speeds.

The NYCB arrived in the Soviet Union on October 6, 1962, after six weeks in Western Europe, traveling with eighty-two people on the eight-week Soviet tour: sixty-six dancers; nine company staff members, including Balanchine and executive director Kirstein; four musicians and conductors (Russian orchestras played on all of the tour's stops); and three people from the Paris office of the tour manager, L. Leonidoff.[50] *Times* critic John Martin was there, too, but the State Department removed him from its manifest and did not help him get into the Soviet Union because of his status as a journalist.[51] The company performed in five Soviet cities, spending three weeks in Moscow, ten days in Leningrad,[52] and one week each in Kiev, Tbilisi, and Baku.

CUBA, CULTURAL DIFFERENCE, EVERYDAY PRACTICES

Jerome Robbins's *Interplay*, the only ballet included on both ABT's and the NYCB's first Soviet tours, climaxes as the cast of four men and four women compete with each other technically and energetically. The last movement begins playfully with cartwheels and games, and the dancers physically banter with one another as though playing a game of Red Rover. Then they shift into a more daring competition. The four men form a straight line: the first does one *tour en l'air*, a jump that involves rotating once in the air and landing in fifth position. The second man does two *tours*; the third does three. The fourth man does four *tours* in a row, a feat that requires mechanical precision and daring.

Dancer Robert Maiorano remembered admiring *Interplay*'s men in the 1960s as they increased the choreography's difficulty to display their technical prowess: "I remember Kent Stowell doing six consecutive double *tours* when he's only supposed to do four. . . . Frank Ulman, Kent Stowell could do [so much]—that was just their training. They just practiced everyday."[53] The choreography demanded that the dancers show off, and the dancers found ways to exceed the choreography's invitation through intense, daily, physical preparation.

Interplay offered dancers a perfect vehicle to showcase their virility and competitiveness, making the ballet emblematic of themes of American Cold War identity. Dance critic and historian Deborah Jowitt has described *Interplay* as the quintessential American postwar ballet: "The swinging ponytails, leapfrogging boys, and considerate bumptiousness suited the war years' optimistic vision of American culture."[54] Though City Ballet did not adopt the ballet's original set, a backdrop of swings and slides, the choreography still referenced youthful exuberance in its movement vocabulary, which includes the leapfrog, the Charleston, hopscotch, and cartwheels arranged in an energetic setting both playful and intense.[55]

Interplay's twin themes of youth and competition parallel the affective structures most prevalent during the NYCB's time in Moscow, the portion of the tour that overlapped with the missile crisis. Politics loomed nearby, threatening to overwhelm the artistic, mostly amiable encounters the dancers had with the Soviet audiences. In retrospect, the crisis seems the clearest reminder of the larger global political situation surrounding the tour. At the time, daily life was more complicated than a history focused solely on political events suggests.

The Cuban Missile Crisis figured within a layered landscape in which the dancers experienced differences between American and Soviet culture and between everyday life and political rhetoric. The political competition between the United States and the USSR clearly influenced the American dancers' attitudes about the Cold War, but other factors weighed on them, too, sometimes more so than did political developments. These factors included the demands of performing, the dancers' ages coupled with the singular focus ballet training requires, and the pedestrian concerns of everyday life.

Isolating the missile crisis as an event of singular importance, as historians have often done, distracts from politics' effects on people's personal lives throughout the Cold War. As historian David Caute has noted, Edward Villella performed his solo encore in *Donizetti Variations* to a packed audience at the Kremlin's Palace of Congresses Theatre on the same night Soviet foreign minister Andrei Gromyko denied the existence of Soviet missiles in Cuba.[56] In a similar parallel of political and artistic events, the NYCB enjoyed an enthusiastic reception at one of their final Moscow performances at the Bolshoi on October 26, the day Khrushchev admitted that there were Soviet missiles in Cuba.[57] These factual details are accurate: Villella did dance on the same day Gromyko made his denial, and the NYCB was met with acclaim on the same day Khrushchev made his admission.[58] The relationship between the ballet fanfare and the global crisis, however, was not so clear in the moment.

Previous histories of the tour have belittled the dancers', particularly the women's, inattention to the crisis. Richard Buckle, a Balanchine biographer, wrote: "Principal dancer Violette Verdy admitted that she and most of her colleagues were too concerned with their work to think much about politics; perhaps the men worried more."[59] Buckle's dismissive, sexist assessment denies the complexity of the dancers' lives. The Cuban missile crisis was one of many factors that shaped the dancers' perceptions of performing and politics. From the dancers' perspectives, a different history emerges—a history of what theorist Michel de Certeau describes as a chronicling of "tactile apprehension and kinesthetic appropriation."[60] The dancers negotiated the political and the personal in ways that bumped and rubbed against each other. Writing history from their perspectives brings the fluidity and everyday-ness of Cold War attitudes and life into wider view.

During the tour's Moscow leg, the company knew a bit about the events in Cuba, but information was scarce. The American embassy's daily newspaper and occasional embassy briefings offered the most accessible news. Bettijane Sills said that most of the dancers assumed that as long as the NYCB and the Bolshoi tours continued, war was not imminent.[61] Minimal access to news inevitably fostered gossip. When Kay Mazzo recalled the rumors years later, with the benefit of age and experience as an administrator, she laughed, "The rumors going around the company were 'Don't worry. They have a way of us all escaping from here. We'll get out. We know we'll be able to get out,' which was the most ridiculous thing I've ever heard of. Here we were in Moscow; that wasn't going to happen."[62] The dancers maintained a naïve faith in the company management, but management was at the mercy of the embassy staff. When Kirstein presented embassy officials with a potential escape plan, the American cultural officer said simply: "You don't have plans. You leave when we tell you to leave."[63] Had the crisis not been resolved and resulted in war, who knows what would actually have happened to the company.

Being in the heart of enemy territory, so to speak, actually distanced the dancers from the missile crisis because they could not feel the anxiety rushing through the American public and lacked sufficient language skills to discern Soviet opinion. Dancer Gloria Govrin said her knowledge of the crisis did not extend beyond what she could pick up from the Soviet radio piped into her hotel room. She recalled, "All you could hear was 'Cuba, Cuba, Cuba, and Amerinkinsky.' If you didn't speak Russian, you didn't know what was going on."[64] Meanwhile, in the United States, Americans saw headlines like "Big Force Masses to Blockade Cuba: Armada is under Orders to Open Fire, if Necessary—All Troops are Alerted" on the front page of the *New York Times*.[65] Daily reports of imminent war increased Americans' fear so greatly that the *Times* soon ran an article asking people to stop calling the newspaper for information: fifteen thousand calls in nine hours had jammed the newspaper's telephone lines.[66] Dancer Mimi Paul only realized the gravity of the situation when she talked to her father in Washington, DC: "He was very nervous about the situation because . . . from where he was in DC, he was hearing much more than we were. And we were so preoccupied and working so hard that I don't think we understood, really, what was really happening." Even after Paul's father explained what he knew of the situation, she "just thought he was being a nervous father." [67] Not speaking Russian fluently, and performing eight times a week, the dancers had little ability or time to gauge the level of danger.

It was not the crisis so much as everyday life, though, that made the dancers aware of the concrete differences between Soviet culture and American culture. They found the constant presence of police and hotel matrons disconcerting. On at least two occasions, they recalled late-night socializing ending abruptly with the appearance of or a phone call from a matron.[68] The dancers had little freedom to move about the cities, though some of the older dancers reportedly traveled on their own sometimes. (All the dancers perceived that the others were moving more freely than they were.) Dancers who separated from the larger group often encountered the Soviet police. A walk to the theater with Allegra Kent reminded Mimi Paul of her vulnerability: "We were in Red Square and we decided to cross on the diagonal, and there was no one around. And as we walked, we got to the middle of Red Square, and . . . two officers came up, pulled their whistles out, and told us that we had to walk around the square."[69] The dancers presumed the police had approached them because they were foreigners, but the incident could have resulted from their inability to read Russian, which might have caused them to miss signs prohibiting crossing the square. Though the incident might have stemmed from lack of familiarity with cultural codes, for the dancers it felt like a reminder of the Soviet state's seeming omnipresence.

The constant Soviet military presence also unsettled the dancers, especially because no one explained the contexts in which the military appeared. Bettijane Sills remembered a dinner interrupted by tanks "rumbling through the streets—tanks coming with guns—coming down the street as if in a parade almost, but it was nighttime."[70] During the crisis,

Arthur Mitchell and some of the other dancers awoke one morning to the sight of "guns and planes and tanks and people marching" outside the hotel, which prompted, as Mitchell remembers, "hysteria, [dancers were saying], 'Oh my God. We are at war, and how are we going to get out of Russia?'" Mitchell chuckled as he recalled learning at breakfast that morning that there was no war: the USSR was celebrating the Russian armistice. Nonetheless, Mitchell said the Soviet capital felt like the "end of the road [where] there was no more communication."[71]

For all their anxiety, the dancers recall only two genuinely dangerous incidents. The most serious occurred in Kiev when police arrested Shaun O'Brien for filming with an eight millimeter movie camera in a Moscow park. Suki Schorer and other dancers remembered that he was arrested because he had accidentally filmed a military jeep. Three hours passed before a Gostkoncert officer confirmed O'Brien's identity as an American ballet dancer. Soviet police released him two hours later and returned his film the next day. In retrospect, O'Brien's relatively quick release and the return of his film unmarred made the incident largely innocuous.[72]

The second incident troubled the dancers less but did turn physically dangerous. Several dancers recalled passing ongoing demonstrations at the American embassy or being asked to leave the embassy quickly to avoid an imminent public protest. These warnings were sufficiently reliable that the dancers were only caught in one protest. Kay Mazzo and the other teenage girls on the trip, Suzanne Farrell and Marnee Morris, had to walk through a demonstration to exit the embassy, and a protester put a cigarette out on Mazzo's arm. Although she was hurt, and says in retrospect that the incident was "not a big deal," Mazzo remembers being very scared.[73]

For the most part, however, the demands of elite ballet life allowed the dancers to ignore the crisis's possible ramifications. Keeping their bodies in peak condition on the tour was just one chapter in a lifetime of rigorous demands going back to being groomed to be a professional ballet dancer from an early age. Many of the dancers had joined the company instead of formally finishing high school and had experienced little of life outside the ballet bubble. The New York City Ballet dancers were, for the most part, quite young and absolutely singular in their focus. They were in Moscow to dance.

Performance and training were not just at the center of the dancers' lives; ballet practically constituted their entire existence. Ballet dancers are generally young, but Balanchine's love of youth meant the 1962 City Ballet was a group of exceptionally young dancers. At age twenty-five,

Allegra Kent was a group elder. This is not to say that young people cannot comprehend politics. Kent Stowell compared his State Department tours to his son's time studying abroad during college, a rite of passage during which many American youth grapple with international politics and the United States' place in the larger world.[74] Elite ballet dancers, however, are not typical youth. Sills, who later became a dance professor at Purchase College, described herself at college-age (she was twenty on the Soviet tour) as having little in common with the life experience of her students. She said, "I had a very sheltered life. I didn't date when I was in high school; I just danced, and I sang, and I took drama lessons. And I went to auditions."[75] The ballet world demanded that dancers focus on their rigorous physical training rather than consider how that training might be infused with larger political and social agendas.

The dancers worked diligently to maintain that intense physical regimen. Touring in the Soviet Union, regardless of the political events, meant grappling with less than ideal conditions in the theater and beyond. Sills carried the cleanser Ajax to clean theaters' dressing rooms and bathrooms.[76] Food in the Soviet Union was a genuine problem for the dancers, and would continue to be an issue for every State Department–sponsored dance tour to the USSR. The small meals included few fruits, vegetables, or palatable proteins. The dancers had brought nonperishable items, such as canned tuna and peanut butter, with them in their trunks, and most wished they had brought more. Carol Sumner remembered coming down with what the dancers called "Moscow tummy." During her recovery, she was ecstatic over her cooking invention: she found a discarded sterno and used it to cook Spam in its aluminum can.[77]

Many dancers got sick or were injured. The company arrived in Moscow already depleted; corps dancer Victoria Simon and male principal dancer Jacques d'Amboise had been hit by a tram in Hamburg while standing too close to the tracks.[78] Simon was able to dance in the Soviet Union, but d'Amboise could dance little. The expected female star of the tour, Diana Adams, also could not dance because of an ankle injury.

Physical trials wore on the dancers, and life back home in the United States also wore on them emotionally. Allegra Kent had almost skipped the tour because of her one-year-old child. She eventually decided to join the tour, meeting the company for their final European performances. When I asked Kent about her memories of the Cuban missile crisis, she responded that she was "frightened to death because it looked like we were going to have an atomic war. My baby was in New York City, and politics were what they were." She continued, "I did call home a little bit, and my marriage was falling apart at many points. . . . But I guess I heard that everything was all right with my baby, but, of course, I didn't know politically what was going on."[79] Kent's words show that her ongoing concern about her family in New York was intertwined with the events surrounding Cuba. Like many people during the Cold War, the dancers negotiated their knowledge of politics within and through their personal lives: caring for family members, careers, and their own health.

A story told by Robert Maiorano demonstrates just how intimate the national and the personal became on tour. Maiorano, who at sixteen was the company's youngest dancer, remembered performing in Tbilisi, not because of the roles he danced or because of Georgia's relationship to Soviet politics, but because he learned to shave there. One day, Maiorano arrived at the Tbilisi opera house at intermission to prepare for dancing in the evening's last ballet only to find Georgians practically rioting at the theater door because more tickets had been sold than the theater had seats. Maiorano remembered, "They wouldn't let me into the theater. Of course they're blocking anyone from coming in, so finally after yelling—I started cursing at them in Brooklyn-eese [sic] and that still didn't work." He was finally rescued and let inside when a company member vouched for him. Shortly thereafter, Maiorano realized why he had not been recognized as an American dancer: his newly present facial hair meant he looked "just like the Georgians, so one of the guys in the company said, 'Maybe we better get you some shaving cream.'"[80] Dancer Kent Stowell, one of the men Maiorano admired for his virtuosic abilities in *Interplay*, showed him how to shave. Maiorano, like all the still-healthy company dancers on the trip, danced a great deal in Tbilisi, but the movements he remembered best are those he learned from Stowell: how to stick his tongue into his cheek and then his upper lip to avoid cutting himself when shaving his adolescent beard.

Understanding the tour's intersection with the crisis demands understanding what it meant to keep working during the intense tour: meeting balletic and life challenges took as much time, if not more, than did global politics. Dancers were performing in poor conditions, with less than adequate food; and many were literally growing up on tour—learning for the first time how to live apart from parents and travel in a foreign country. To understand these challenges is not to apologize for the dancers' lack of political savvy. In the interviews, many admitted they gained interest in politics only later in life, often when the rigorous demands of their lives as professional dancers had ended. A history saturated with personal lives, professional necessities, and political exigencies produces a more detailed picture of how Cold War politics were embedded within the personal and even private narratives of dancers' lives.

As mentioned earlier, the first night the NYCB appeared in each of the five cities on the Soviet tour, the company always performed the ballet that might be considered American ballet's home: Balanchine's *Serenade*. The ballet begins with seventeen women onstage. They stand, right arms lofting up and forward, palms barely flexed. Blue light bathes their long, white tutus as the lush opening bars of Tchaikovsky's *Serenade for Strings in C Major* pour over them. Suddenly, simultaneously, the group moves. The women's wrists first bend, and then seventeen arms slowly trace an arc overhead. Once the women rest their wrists delicately on their left shoulders, they turn their heads. All of this happens with a hushed sensibility—felt more than seen. Still moving with a sort of nighttime reverence, they all lower both arms into a low circle, and then, in one sharp count, pop their feet open into first position. The women exhale, extend one leg to the side, and slide into tight fifth positions. As their lower bodies assume this bound shape, their arms float up and open. They lift their chests, sending their heads slightly behind them, gazing just over the horizon as though drinking in the moonlight.[81] This opening phrase for *Serenade's* ensemble—one of the best-known examples of Balanchine's choreography—gave many Soviet audiences their first glimpse of the NYCB. The combination of classical ballet's symmetry with the speed and angularity of American neoclassical ballet exemplifies some of the most frequently cited formal attributes of Balanchine's choreography.

Serenade provides a frame and a metaphor for the artistic mélange of US and Soviet culture in the midst of a political situation defined by the superpowers' supposedly polar opposition. The first ballet Balanchine created in the United States, *Serenade* was made for students. With *Serenade*, Balanchine taught American dancers what the future could hold for ballet in the United States and what the art form's past looked like in Europe and Russia. Tchaikovsky's music and the large group of female dancers in white tutus reference Imperial Russian classicism (and French romanticism), but *Serenade's* egalitarianism gives it an American sensibility, too. The ballet has soloist roles, but the seventeen women of the ensemble are its primary focus. Dance historian Nancy Goldner contends that early versions of *Serenade* barely distinguished between the soloists and the ensemble, contributing to the ballet's "feelings of community and sisterhood."[82] Most, if not all, NYCB women perform in *Serenade* many times during their careers, leaving the ballet emblazoned in their kinesthetic memories. These memories become part of the way dancers think about their place in Balanchine's company and in the larger ballet world.

Through *Serenade*, the NYCB dancers experienced their bodies as composites of Russian and American technique. The State Department and the ANTA Dance Panel imagined the NYCB as representing the best of American art abroad. But ballet, with its European and Russian roots, refuses national boundaries. The national amalgam present in the technique that guided every one of the City Ballet dancers' pirouettes points to the ways national identity is never stable or cohesive, but is instead a constant negotiation between individuals and the larger groups individuals comprise. The dancers felt this fluidity of national identity in their bodies, and performing on behalf of the United States in Soviet theaters made the complications of national identity legible. These theater spaces, particularly Moscow's Bolshoi Theatre and Leningrad's Mariinsky Theatre, heightened the dancers' sense of Russia as part of their artistic genealogy. Experiences of multiple, overlapping national identities, too, helped the dancers recognize that national identity can be shaped strategically. On a microcosmic level, the dancers watched as Balanchine refashioned his national identity for different contexts, while on a macrocosmic level, they saw American media representing Soviet culture as homogenous—a representation that did not correspond to the diverse Soviet landscape they encountered on the tour.

In their personal reminiscences of performing *Serenade* on the tour, the dancers revealed how they physically negotiated identities, simultaneously recognizing and exceeding their status as official representatives of the American government. Suki Schorer recalled the moments before performing *Serenade* as some of the most "moving" of the company's Soviet appearances. The stage manager called the *Serenade* corps to their places, and then, first the Russian and then the American anthems played as the corps stood, "hands across our chests," pledging allegiance to an imagined flag. When the American anthem ended, the women raised their arms to the high diagonal, *Serenade's* opening pose, only to pass moments later through almost the same "hands across our chests" position they had held during the national anthem—though now they were dancing *Serenade* (figure 1.2). [83]

The women's movements represented the United States, but they were not *only* representations of the United States. The first time the women hit the arm position they honored the United States; the second time they moved through this position, they represented not just the United States, but also ballet, and, more specifically, New York City Ballet dancers in a Balanchine ballet.[84] The women did not simply reproduce a homogenous or essentialized conception of official American identity, but instead marked multiple layers of affiliation through physical expression.

Figure 1.2
Members of the New York City Ballet, circa 1962, in the opening pose of George Balanchine's *Serenade*. From left to right: (*first row*) Diana Adams, Niema Zweili, Carole Fields; (*second row*) Janet Greschler Villella; (*third row*) Victoria Simon, Una Kai, Francia Russell, Marlene Mesavage; (*fourth row*) Diane Conossuer, Joan Van Orden.
Source: Photograph by Fred Fehl. Courtesy of Gabriel Pinski. Choreography by George Balanchine © The George Balanchine Trust.

The dancers used ballet technique to negotiate these identities. Dance theorist Judith Hamera defines technique as the mode by which dancers forge "a common 'mother tongue' to be shared and redeployed by its participants."[85] Through technique dancers become not individual moving bodies, but a community. Over several centuries, ballet technique has traveled across national boundaries, giving dancers a common language, a "mother tongue," composed of Danish, French, Italian, Russian, and American styles.

On the tour, the dancers recognized the differences and similarities between the American and Russian approaches to technique, especially during their encounters with the Soviet Union's two great ballet institutions, the Bolshoi School in Moscow and the Imperial Theatre School in Leningrad, where Balanchine had studied.[86] Suki Schorer was a dancer on the 1962 tour, and has since taught at the School of American Ballet and written the book *Suki Schorer on Balanchine Technique*, which discusses the details of Balanchine's approach to ballet. When recalling the tour, she listed what she felt were the characteristics that distinguished Balanchine's style from Russian approaches to ballet training. She said: "He [Balanchine] had the technique so we could dance the ballets . . . [with] speed, lightness, a freer *port de bras* [carriage of the arms] in a way. The landings from jumps are lighter. . . . The pirouettes are done usually from a large extended fourth [position], rather than from a much smaller one."[87] Elaborating on how dancers use these physical tools, she continued, "I want to say the movements are maybe bigger . . . The weight [is] on the balls of the feet, not on the heels. . . . And I guess the *plié* [the bend of the knees] is a more elasticized *plié*, . . . juicier, more continuous."

Because of the Soviet tour, many of the City Ballet dancers understood the intricate relationship between Balanchine's "American" technique and the Russian technique in which he had trained—they saw that these qualities specific to Balanchine were not completely removed from his background. Victoria Simon remembered walking through the school in Leningrad and seeing the long fourth position of the feet she knew as "the Balanchine preparation for pirouettes" (one of the qualities Schorer referenced in her list of Balanchine's stylistic inventions).[88] Simon thought, "Mr. B didn't make that up. . . . It came from his training somewhere." Later in the trip, Simon watched Balanchine teach a class for Soviet dancers and again noticed small similarities. She thought, "It's [Balanchine's style, but it's] based on his Russian training. . . . It's gone off on a different branch."[89] Simon recognized that every time the City Ballet dancers stepped into the preparation for a pirouette or moved their arms, there was a little bit of Russia in their American way of moving.

What the American ballet dancers saw as Russian technique was also an amalgam of several nations' ballet styles. The grace of the French school, the footwork of the Danish school, and the technical prowess of the Italian school informed the creation of nineteenth-century Russian ballet, which then formed the basis on which Soviet training was built. More expansive movement in the upper body, especially in comparison to the square body positions of the dominant French school, was one of Russia's primary contributions to ballet's development.[90] The technical carriage of the arms then had traces of French and Russian training, and then in NYCB, American influence, too.

Technique is, however, only one aspect of ballet culture. For young, elite ballet students and professional dancers, ballet is a lifestyle, and a physically intense one that often breeds an intense loyalty to one's peers and teachers. Balanchine and other Russian émigré teachers imparted their reverence for ballet as a discipline worthy of great personal sacrifice to their American students. Balanchine biographer Bernard Taper says Balanchine not only "did not feel abused" by his Russian teachers (though he talked about them as physically punishing); he thought he was "extremely fortunate" to have had them.[91] The NYCB dancers spoke with similar reverence about Balanchine. Gloria Govrin, who joined the company at age sixteen, repeatedly referred to Balanchine as a "father figure": "How many people have a genius in their life? Balanchine shaped my entire life. I'm the person I am because of him."[92] Govrin and other company members adored Balanchine even more than Balanchine adored his teachers.

Ballet technique and the intense ballet lifestyle created the possibility of a community of Americans and Russians completely committed to ballet. Violette Verdy's description of *Serenade*, a ballet she describes as "just so universal," becomes a fitting metaphor for an imaginary community of ballet dancers who transcend their national identities through technique and choreography.[93] *Serenade* is "universal" to Verdy because it is "a quite fantastic corps of anonymous people functioning in every possible way together and with absolute . . . passion and expertise." In using the word "universal," Verdy was not implying that ballet technique lacked cultural codes. Instead, she imagined technique as crossing borders of difference. Learning a cohesive physical technique pulls a group together, and through physical synchronicity the group achieves a common identity. Recognizing the Russian roots of the techniques they had learned from Balanchine provided the NYCB dancers with an intimate connection to one another and to their Soviet counterparts.

Many NYCB dancers felt further connected to Russian culture through their many Russian émigré teachers. Verdy, who trained in her native France, studied with Russian émigrés who had left Russia during or immediately after the 1917 revolution.[94] The NYCB's School of American Ballet (SAB) also had many Russian teachers.[95] Robert Maiorano remembered realizing that as an SAB student he could communicate with his Russian teachers in ways that American nondancers could not. He recalled a parents' visiting day at SAB:

> And she'd [Madame Tumkovsky would] talk, "Make me this. Make me this." And so we just do our steps, and of course she was speaking French with a Russian accent. And none of our mothers could understand how we could understand, when they didn't understand a word. [And I would say to my mother,] "What do you mean you can't understand her? She's easy." But so as I grew up, I always felt an affinity to Russians.[96]

Ballet training with Russian teachers gave the SAB students access to Russian people and culture.

Young American dancers, unlike many Americans mid-century, were taught to revere Russian culture, people, and discipline, which brought them to the Cold War with a different perspective than most. American ballet students who did not study at SAB also discovered Russia through ballet, since many Russian émigrés taught ballet throughout the United States. Before joining the NYCB, Nadine Revene, for example, studied with the popular New York–based Russian teacher, Helene Platova. Like many Russian teachers in New York, Platova taught in a mixture of Russian and English and had a Russian pianist. Having studied extensively with Platova and other Russian teachers who taught character dance classes, when Ravine walked into the Bolshoi School and started watching the dancers, the dancing "looked very familiar" to her.[97]

Platova was a Russian Jew sent abroad by her family during the 1917 Revolution to escape the pogroms.[98] Many of the City Ballet dancers had family members with similar personal histories. Simon and Govrin had Russian grandparents.[99] For the dancers of Russian-Jewish descent, the sense of familiarity they encountered in the Soviet Union must have been mixed with fear. Mimi Paul's father, a Russian Jew from Odessa who lived in Washington, DC, constantly reminded his daughter to always make sure she knew where the American embassy was when she was on tour.[100] Whereas dissent from, even hatred of, the Soviet Union drove some Russian émigrés to, like Balanchine, serve as American cultural diplomats, the dancers from Russian immigrant families reported complicated feelings standing in their families' homeland while representing earlier generations' adopted nation. Through family, through institutional affiliations, and through the technique that drove so many of the dancers' movements, the Soviet Union—or, more accurately, its Russian Imperial history and culture—felt familiar and personal to some of the City Ballet dancers.

Russian theater spaces made the dancers' complicated national affiliations more affectively legible. The NYCB dancers described feeling magnetically attracted to the Russian theaters that were so important to ballet history. While touring offered tidbits of ballet history, performances in Moscow's Bolshoi Theatre and in Leningrad's Mariinsky Theatre had such impact that the experiences remained firmly lodged in dancers' memories more than forty years later.

The Bolshoi and the Mariinsky theaters have synecdochic relationships to Russian ballet, standing as symbols of the longevity and passion of the country's ballet tradition. Because the sixteen-year-old Maiorano did not require supervision by parental chaperones as did the teenage girls on the trip (whose mothers came on the tour), he frequently escaped to explore

Soviet cities alone, especially the famous theaters. He remembered, "It's just that the first place I went when we got off the plane—I went to the Bolshoi Theatre and I did the same thing at the Mariinsky because this is where my teachers [were from]. . . . I didn't even unpack my bags. I threw them on the bed. I went to the theater and stood and absorbed it all." [101] Even during the Soviet era, the Bolshoi and the Mariinsky pulsed with ballet history. The Kirov had performed at the Mariinsky since 1885, and Petipa's ballets, including *Swan Lake* and *Sleeping Beauty*, premiered there.[102] The Mariinsky was, in dance historian Tim Scholl's words, "Russian ballet's Mecca" in the nineteenth century.[103] In the Soviet era, the Bolshoi Theatre, home to the Bolshoi Ballet and where NYCB gave their first Soviet performance, eclipsed the Mariinsky. From Stalin's regime forward, the theater hosted "innumerable" *Swan Lakes* for Soviet leaders and state guests.[104]

These legendary theaters impressed the NYCB dancers. Forty-six years later, many could still describe the spaces in detail, remembering the Bolshoi's lush gold and red and the blue and white of the much smaller Mariinsky. Some mentioned other theaters, particularly the cavernous Palace of Congresses, but the Mariinsky and Bolshoi came up in almost every interview I conducted. Given their significance in ballet lore, it is not surprising that so many dancers recalled them by name and visual detail.

Having trained at the Imperial Theatre School and performed at the Mariinsky, Balanchine understood the importance of institutions and buildings to ballet history. When Gostkoncert initially scheduled the NYCB's opening at the Palace of Congresses rather than at the Bolshoi Theatre, Balanchine protested.[105] Watching a performance in a historic theater could affect audience response. By inserting the NYCB into the ballet world alongside the greatest Russian, now Soviet, companies that performed there, Balanchine hoped to exploit the "clear and not easily dislodged generic expectations" that theater historian Marvin Carlson says audiences bring to spaces associated with particular artistic genres and histories.[106] If the NYCB opened at the Bolshoi, audiences would have higher expectations than if the company performed in a newer theater; but if the company met those expectations, its reputation would rise at home and abroad. The Soviet officials eventually relented.

The dancers connected to other tour stops in more personal ways. Few of the dancers I interviewed recalled Kiev and Baku, cities with lesser ballet traditions. They did, however, remember Tbilisi because it was Balanchine's cultural home. While in Georgia, the NYCB dancers met Georgian dancer and former Kirov Ballet star Vakhtang Chabukiani and watched him perform in Tbilisi, where he directed the Paliavili Opera House and the Tbilisi

Choreographic School.[107] Although the dancers found Tbilisi more interesting than Baku and Kiev, they still tended to gauge the country's culture through its ballet landscape, and they felt themselves part of a Russian ballet lineage.

The dancers' recognition of the hybridity of their artistic identities helped them achieve a broader understanding of Cold War culture. In the United States, mass culture and political rhetoric represented the 1950s and early 1960s as a time of broad public consensus: Americans supposedly wanted the same material goods, experienced similar social conditions, and accepted the same ideas—primarily fear of the Soviet Union and abhorrence of Communism. Many scholars have described the ways in which consensus culture functioned as a guiding myth in American Cold War rhetoric, obscuring the diversity of people and lived experience throughout the United States. Historian Alan Brinkley, who calls Cold War culture's emphasis on consensus "the illusion of unity," argues that the notion of consensus detracted from the economic and social inequities that affected working-class Americans, creating a "smooth surface" that covered the "cultural, economic, and demographic forces of a rapidly evolving industrial society."[108] Going further in the critique of consensus culture mythology, historian Peter Filene writes that the Cold War was primarily fought at "an elite level," disregarding how women and people of color did not fit, feel, or act within the national narrative of anti-Communism.[109] Claims of a singular, homogenous national identity obscured alternative points of view. There was no unified national culture in the United States in the 1950s, and by the late 1950s, as the civil rights and then women's rights movements burst into national view, American diversity could no longer be ignored.

Balanchine, who had enormous influence on his dancers, exemplified national cultural hybridity as he moved strategically among American, Russian, and Georgian identities. Many dancers recalled Balanchine's infamous retort to an interviewer for Radio Moscow, who greeted Balanchine on air by saying: "Welcome to Moscow, home of classic ballet!"[110] Balanchine replied, "I beg your pardon. . . . Russia is the home of romantic ballet. The home of classic ballet is now America."[111] In the context of a Russian tour sponsored by the State Department, Balanchine claimed the present and future of the ballet world for the United States. As a representative of the US government and American ballet, Balanchine proclaimed that his choreography and company most fully represented ballet's newest innovations. This is key to understanding national identity as performative—claiming an identity superseded any essential notion of one's national affiliation or what counted as representing a nation.

In fact, Balanchine's national origins were a complicated construction. Born in 1904 to Georgian parents living in St. Petersburg, he grew up in St. Petersburg, and his parents returned to Georgia when the revolution began.[112] (Balanchine's mother had German roots, too, adding another national identity to the mix.[113]) His original citizenship figured him as Russian, but Balanchine often claimed Georgia as his national home, and during the tour, he insisted on his Georgian roots to counter assertions by the Soviet press of his Russian—or worse, his Soviet—identity.[114] Arthur Mitchell remembers one occasion on which Balanchine used his Georgian identity against reporters. Mitchell said, "I remember we arrived at the airport and they said, 'Oh this wonderful son of Russia.' And he [Balanchine] said, 'I'm not Russian; I'm Georgian.' And I said, 'Mr. Balanchine, we just got here now. Take it easy.'"[115] By claiming a Georgian identity, Balanchine renounced Soviet communism and the Soviet empire. During the tour, Balanchine's dancers watched, heard, and sometimes intervened, as Mitchell did, in their leader's assertion that national cultural identity could be chosen, accepted, or asserted when the need arose.

Experiencing cities and peoples outside European Russia gave the dancers a better sense of the Soviet Union's multiple cultures and political affiliations. When the company opened in Kiev, the first stop in a non-Russian republic, the Ukrainian flag hung alongside the Soviet and American flags, and the orchestra played all three national anthems, acknowledging that Soviet power did not erase previously independent national identities.[116] Kent Stowell said that before the tour, his principal source of information about Soviet culture and society was *Time* magazine, which described the USSR as a homogenous society—entirely dedicated to Communism, which was simply "bad and dangerous." Although Stowell understood at the time that this was reductive American media spin, the *Time* genre of reportage was still the only thing he knew. Moving through Soviet cities altered Stowell's thinking. He said,

> Going from Moscow to Leningrad was a completely different culture: what a difference it was in the people. And then from Leningrad to Kiev, realizing that Ukraine is its own country and its own state and that they had certainly a different take on the political environment. And then being in Tbilisi of course where Balanchine was born [sic] . . . I remember going into a restaurant and being welcomed by a table. And of course the Georgians like to drink, so we sat there for hours drinking, and then castigating the Russians. [The Georgians said], "Americans we like. Russians, no!" So it made us aware that in this large Soviet conglomeration, that there was [sic], first of all, different cultures and different political agendas and ideas. And realizing that this Communist

environment was not all in agreement of what's going on. And being aware of the differences that were in that country—being there you could see it and hear it and feel it. [117]

Stowell's mistake about Balanchine's birthplace not only suggests that the choreographer shaped the dancers' view that Georgia was separate from Russia, but also reveals Stowell's assumption that an emotional connection to place and culture can trump place of birth and legal citizenship. Stowell's impression of Soviet culture points to an even more complex notion of nationhood. After that night in the Georgian bar, he saw neither the Soviet Union nor Communism as monolithic. Soviet national unity around Communism was largely imagined. Both the American and the Soviet notions of national consensus were political strategies not representations of the experience of all people.

The interviews with the NYCB dancers, however, quickly unraveled when I introduced the word "political." Suki Schorer was one of many who, when asked about the potential political impact of the tour, stated emphatically, "We weren't political."[118] When asked to explain her statement, Schorer said, "We weren't President Bush or [Condoleezza] Rice. . . . [T]hat was not our agenda. Our agenda was just to present dance and make [dance]—be friendly, if it was possible." To Schorer, it was not her national affiliation but her occupation as a dancer for the NYCB that determined her role on the tour. In the context of the dancers' sense of themselves as American, but not exclusively so, the language of politics felt too restrictive. For Schorer and other dancers, being "political" connoted a direct, public, even partisan, tie to US government policies and to American cultural identity. That was not the work she saw ballet or ballet dancers doing, even if they were being paid by the State Department.

Given the fluidity of the idea of nationality, Schorer and other dancers' disavowal of the term "political" may say more about their negotiations of American national identity than it does about their feelings about politics more broadly. As artists, particularly ballet artists in the Soviet Union, the NYCB dancers' bonds with their audiences and artistic colleagues transcended an international political scene grounded in a firm belief that the United States and the USSR were opposites and enemies. Nationally, absolute consensus was a fantasy. Internationally, absolute difference was a myth.

The City Ballet dancers' accounts of the tour provide us with a glimpse of their awareness of slipping in and out of "official" American identity even as they were representing the nation in an official capacity. The dancers' embodied experience of hybridity reveals the degree to which American ballet could not be separated from its Russian roots, no matter how often the American national anthem preceded the call to places for *Serenade*. But as the dancers knew from their training in the United States under Russian teachers, an art form does not have to disavow its association with other nations and national traditions to represent "America."

LASTING IMPACT

USIA officer Hans Tuchs filed the formal evaluation of the NYCB tour. Writing to the State Department, Tuchs hailed the tour as a success, saying that it "made a deep and long-lasting impression on Soviet artists and intelligentsia."[119] Although Tuchs mentioned the tour's effect on the Soviet elite several times, two scenes he described in detail suggest the tour's broader reach. Tuchs described the audience reception when "the real ballet enthusiasts" came to the theater (as opposed to the government bureaucrats who attended the opening night performances). He said, "The warmth of the reception and the volume and length of ovations immediately increased to reach its zenith at the final performance in Leningrad when a rain of flowers showered onto the stage and the audience continued its applause for over fifteen minutes after the final curtain." In Tbilisi, Tuchs reported that "the street from the opera house to the hotel was completely blocked with well-wishers who left a narrow path for the members of the company to pass through amidst congratulations and handclasps."[120] Across the Soviet Union, in Moscow, in the more European Leningrad, and in the empire's outer reaches, support for the NYCB was overwhelming and, though most of the Americans and Soviets could not speak to one another, the Soviets demonstrated their affection physically—throwing flowers, giving standing ovations, and lining the streets as the City Ballet dancers passed.

The dancers remembered mobs outside theaters and sold-out audiences. Mitchell recalled that they would sometimes try to predict ticket sales based on how many subway stops away from the theater people were lined up in hopes of claiming a ticket for company performances in Moscow.[121] Decades later, in his memoirs, former Kirov Ballet star and well-known Soviet dissenter, Valery Panov, would be one of many Russian émigrés to recall the NYCB tour as a landmark event for Soviet ballet. After the NYCB left, Panov said, "[T]he New York style would come to my mind every time I tried to work out a choreographic pattern."[122] After 1962 there was a bit of the United States in Soviet pirouettes and phrasing.

The NYCB returned to the Soviet Union in 1972 on another State Department tour, and the Bolshoi and Kirov would travel to the United States several times in the sixties and seventies, until Soviet criticism of the Vietnam War and contract complications with American theaters brought the American-Soviet exchanges to a halt. But the 1962 tour remained special. It was Balanchine's first trip home, and no one—not the government officials or the company artists—could have imagined the success the company would have. In the middle of global political turmoil a ballet company brought nations together in complicated, layered, embodied publics. ANTA never defined exactly what constituted American ballet, but, by sending the NYCB, ANTA and the State Department showed that the United States had its own ballet tradition. The NYCB dancers, however, recognized the debt their American work owed Russia, even as the structure of Soviet society demonstrated why artistic innovation might be better served by American society rather than the strict Soviet Communist culture.

CHAPTER 2

Refusing Modernist Formulas of Second-Class Citizenship

Arthur Mitchell and the Alvin Ailey American Dance Theater

What might make choreography—a term most broadly defined as the organization of motion—look "American"? This might be the most persistent question throughout American dance-in-diplomacy programs. While no answer ever satisfied the query, one artistic movement dominated the work sent abroad during the Cold War era: dance modernism, an approach to dance that spans both ballet and modern dance genres.

Dance modernism, like much of American modernism, strongly emphasized abstraction as a key—often the key—aesthetic element. As visual arts critic Clement Greenberg famously said of modernism, the "use of art [should be] to call attention to art."[1] In dance, this meant framing bodies as forms in motion, not necessarily as people, and, even more so, not as people who came to the stage to share movements from specific historical, cultural, or geographic contexts. In dance's modernist formula, codified by dance critic John Martin, dance was to strive for universal accessibility, which meant avoiding marking any element as from a particular culture.[2] As dance historian Rebekah Kowal has shown, the pairing then of universalist abstraction with American cultural diplomacy was a paradox, even contradiction.[3] Yet the pairing was also a brilliant move in political rhetoric: if dance modernism could be universally accessible around the globe *and* be marked as American, that would help establish an argument that indeed what was American was possible for—even good for—the rest of the world. This circular logic made dance modernism an ideal fit for an American cultural diplomacy working to persuade foreign publics of American superiority and the global adaptability of American ideals.

Any attempt to argue that American society is superior and capable of including all kinds of people, as a universalist proposal requires, had a huge public relations obstacle at mid-century: American race relations. In the early twentieth century, the black intellectual W. E. B. Du Bois had predicted that what he called the "color line," the strict segregation of white Americans from all other Americans, would be the great problem of the American twentieth century. By the 1950s, Du Bois's prediction had come painfully true, and the world knew it. As historian Thomas Borstelmann has shown, what was once an American domestic policy problem became, by mid-century, a foreign-policy problem.[4] Black Americans had, at best, second-class citizenship in the United States, and when they protested this status they were met with more oppression and violence. Soviet-financed newspapers and increasingly available televisions relayed this reality to people in the strategically important, newly decolonized countries of Africa, Asia, and Latin America,[5] as they read about and saw the horrible actions white Americans and government officials took against civil rights activists.[6]

At mid-century, then, the State Department faced competing challenges: arguing for American social and government systems as the best while also somehow framing the ongoing violence toward nonwhite Americans as not entirely negative. The wide dissemination of information about the civil rights movement and the violence against black Americans meant that denying their systematic disenfranchisement was not possible. Polls conducted by the State Department's partner in cultural diplomacy, the USIA, confirmed worldwide knowledge and disapproval of the United States for its racial politics in the late 1950s and throughout much of the 1960s.[7] Given this, the strategy of arguing for American democracy as superior despite the country's racism required framing American ideals as capable of addressing dissenting groups—those who felt disenfranchised could, over time, be brought into the American fold. American democracy could, at least eventually, offer everyone the possibility of inclusion.[8]

Black artists performing onstage in modernist art forms became the perfect vehicle for exporting this idea. Modernist abstraction offered a universalizing veneer for the performances. As historian Penny Von Eschen has shown in her work on jazz music, the presence of black performers onstage simultaneously highlighted racial difference and absorbed that difference, through abstraction, into a color-blind American vision.[9]

Modernist aesthetics perfectly fit this political campaign. Modernism had a long history of incorporating Africanist elements but then reducing them to unnamed, merely formal choices.[10] Think, for instance, of Picasso's use of the lines of African sculptures in Cubism, heralded only as evidence of white European genius.[11] Or, as dance historian Brenda Dixon Gottschild brilliantly revealed in dance, George Balanchine's incorporation of jazz music's rhythms and an Africanist "aesthetics of the cool."[12] Susan Manning has detailed a similar pattern of appropriation and re-categorization among white choreographers in American modern dance throughout much of the twentieth century, and she has also discussed the implications of this normalized racial appropriation for black artists.[13]

What, then, did black artists do in the face of modernism's legacy when they were tapped as official representatives for the United States in a moment when they were quite visibly second-class citizens of the country they represented? This chapter focuses on black artists' performances and the politics of self-determination within this aesthetic and political maelstrom, describing how black dancers, onstage and off, used modernism and American diplomacy for their own ends—at times exploiting their relationship with the idea of universalism and at other times claiming space for a performance of blackness *as* blackness.

These twin paths of strategic redeployment of universal rhetoric and black self-determination are illustrated in the stories of two artists associated with the Alvin Ailey American Dance Theater, the predominantly black company often sent abroad by the US State Department (figure 2.1). The first story comes from Alvin Ailey, company founder and choreographer, and the second from Sharron Miller, a company dancer in the late 1960s. Miller's is about her work on a 1967 State Department–sponsored tour of ten African countries. Ailey's story comes from the company's 1970 Soviet Union tour, when the Ailey company became the first American modern dance group to perform in the Soviet Union.

After returning from the high-profile Soviet tour, Alvin Ailey gave an interview to *New York Times* dance critic Anna Kisselgoff in which he adamantly refused her suggestion that the tour had anything to do with race. The Ailey company represented "American dance," he said, not blackness. The *Times* quoted Ailey as saying, "There was no special attention paid to the interracial nature of the company or its predominantly black membership . . . it wasn't a black thing: The posters said we were

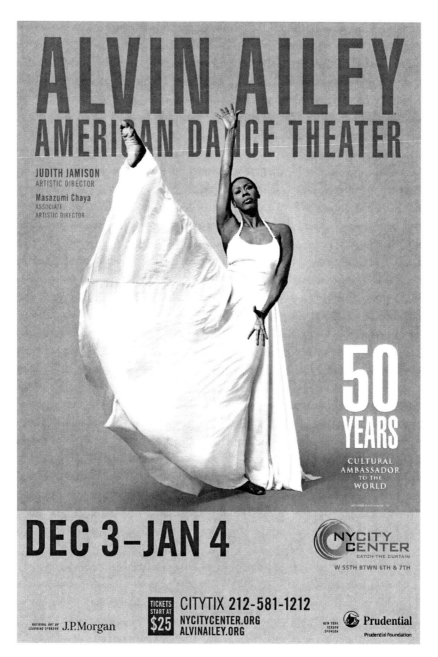

Figure 2.1
Judith Jamison of the Alvin Ailey American Dance Theater on the company's 50th anniversary poster, 2008, including the company's advertising of itself as "Cultural Ambassador to the World."
Source: Photo by Jack Mitchell. Courtesy of Alvin Ailey Dance Foundation, Inc.

an American dance company. There was no feeling of race whatsoever."[14] Ailey rejected being pigeonholed as a black company and insisted that all his work, including the State Department tour, represented American dance more broadly. In essence, Ailey used the intertwined logic of Americanness and universalism to his own ends. As a company touring on behalf of the State Department—especially as a company being presented to the Soviet Union as an example of American modern dance—Ailey was absolutely an American company. This was a hard-fought claim in modern dance at the time: for a predominantly black company to have not just entrée to the mainstream dance world but access to significant mainstream funding was rare. As will become clear, Ailey was not unaware of the racism, and also the homophobia, institutionalized within the American government. But he found ways to use these structures to benefit his company—most strategically when he manipulated the State Department into providing the company with crucial funding during its 1969 financial crisis. Ailey had always said that his work was capable of reaching a broad audience, regardless of race or ethnicity.[15] The State Department gave him further justification for this claim and access to money to build his young company—funding that would have been less available in the 1960s had his work been, as he put it, "a black thing."

Ailey's strategic use of universalizing rhetoric did not foreclose the presentation of blackness onstage. Sharron Miller remembered dancing Ailey's *Revelations* (1960)—the piece that chronicles American black life, remains Ailey's most celebrated choreography, and that closed every Ailey program on the State Department tours—as a public performance of a blackness that Miller felt she had been taught to repress in her community and, importantly, in dance classes. Miller found great possibility for the embodiment of African American culture and history through dancing *Revelations*:

> As an African American growing up, part of what you did back then was to try and rise above all the stigma, all the stereotypes, particularly if you wanted to dance. The idea of "Rocka My Soul" [*Revelations'* last section] was what my grandmother was and that was something I had tried to rise above. . . . All of that [Miller gestures with her hand as though waving a fan while pumping her chin and darting her eyes]. So it [*Revelations*] was like going deeper into my heritage and my culture to bring that part back to my own personal sensibilities.[16]

Miller's gesture was a direct physical quotation from *Revelations'* choreography—choreography that allowed her to access the attitude and black feminine swagger of her grandmother. Miller said *Revelations* allowed her to publicly embody part of her familial racial history that she had learned to suppress, partially through her ballet training in predominantly white Montclair, New Jersey. *Revelations* welcomed Miller's entire identity onto the public stage, and in the context of the State Department tour, gave her the opportunity to perform as an American black woman all over the world. Being part of a government-sanctioned official tour that hoped to present blackness as ripe for assimilation into American identity did not mean that something else could not happen, too. Onstage performance always has the potential to exceed officially-sanctioned narratives.

This chapter focuses on how black artists, through the act of dancing, made some of their most significant statements about the peculiar bond among modernist abstraction, American cultural diplomacy, and race at mid-century. The chapter begins with a short history of modernism's entanglement with American cultural diplomacy, including the shift from an initial object-based format in the visual arts to a focus on modernism as an embodied practice. Then I return to the tour that was at the center of chapter 1, the New York City Ballet's 1962 tour of the Soviet Union, to examine black dancer Arthur Mitchell's breakout performances within George Balanchine's coding of race in the ballet *Agon* (1957), among other works. The Ailey company anchors the second half of the chapter: first through a discussion of *Revelations* as the pinnacle of African American self-determination in American cultural diplomacy, particularly when the company appeared on the African continent, and then, as the company, particularly Ailey himself, battled not just the racist but also the homophobic practices institutionalized within the State Department. This final section moves beyond questions of race alone to consider how modernism in American cultural diplomacy circumscribed both sexual and racial minoritarian identities.

MODERNISM AND AMERICAN IDENTITY: THE PROBLEMS AND POSSIBILITIES OF PEOPLE

Dance theorist Mark Franko has described the animating force of modernism as being "a continuous reduction to essentials culminating in irreducible 'qualities'" that facilitates the creation of a "depersonalized ('universal') embodiment of subjectivity."[17] This possibility—that a set of aesthetic choices can allow the fashioning of a universal subject that references nothing outside of itself—fit perfectly with the early goals of American cultural diplomacy: choosing and then sending into the world art that could have universal reach. Post–World War II cultural elites, for instance visual arts supporter Nelson Rockefeller and dance leader Lincoln Kirstein, saw modernism's potential as American export, believing it could be an aesthetic route through which the United States could reach the world. These efforts began in the visual arts and, later, included the performing arts, too.

Historian Frances Stonor Saunders has argued that it was this generation of cultural gatekeepers who saw the possibility of modernism when it was linked with American identity. Modern art's brash, stripped-down aesthetic depicted the United States as "independent [and] self reliant" and distinguished American art from "European influence" and "Soviet realism."[18] Abstract expressionism, for instance, Jackson Pollock's huge canvases slashed with color, offer the best image of the tone American cultural diplomacy sought to export, and indeed abstract expressionism was one of the strains of modernist art exported through American cultural diplomacy before and after World War II.[19] With modernist art, the United States got an identity distinct from that of other countries but also could fantasize itself as elemental and bare—a palette others could (and should) imagine themselves into.

Even as modernist canvases seemed best for inviting others into the American experience, questions often arose about the relationship between people and objects in modernist visual art, either because the objects seemed too far removed from popular experience or because the people who made such art might not be of the American mainstream. High modernism, virtually antithetical in its aesthetics to American popular culture post–World War II, truly confused some audiences, and that confusion led to suspicion. In 1952, Congressman George Dondero famously pronounced on the floor of the House of Representatives that "all modern art [was] Communistic."[20] Modernism's abstraction offered no way in for many American audiences—no narrative to track as familiar. Later in the fifties, congressional challenges grew more specific as both the objects and the people who made them came under attack. These issues arose largely around abstract expressionism, peaking in 1959 when the USIA included paintings by Pollock and Mark Rothko in a Moscow exhibit as rumors of the two men's leftist political sympathies circulated in Washington. Congressional outrage reached such heights that only a public intervention by President Dwight Eisenhower prevented the show from being censored, even though the paintings were already hanging in Moscow at the time.[21] Public censorship would be antithetical to what anyone wanted to export as "American" (a theme to which I return in chapter 3's discussion of congressional controversy around Martha Graham). It is surprising after the controversies of the fifties that modernism would receive some of its greatest international circulation through American cultural diplomacy's then-just-beginning presentation of the performing arts, such as jazz music and modern dance. Yet it seems that the State Department's need to publicly embrace African American culture outstripped concerns about modernism because of modernist abstraction's complex presentation/non-presentation of blackness, especially in the performing arts. Having black performers onstage enacting modernist aesthetics in jazz or dance performances simultaneously championed and backgrounded African American culture.

The introduction of people, rather than art objects, created an even greater space in which diplomatic tours could simultaneously support the government's motives and challenge them. People, unlike art objects, can (literally) speak—speaking their minds and sometimes changing others' minds (or their own). Von Eschen offers many examples of black musicians, most famously Louis Armstrong, using the public stages provided by State Department tours to eloquently critique American civil rights policy.[22] Dancers of color, like the musicians Von Eschen discusses, were also outspoken about policy.

Dancing itself, though, is also a way of communicating a critique. In the moment of performance, dancers make choices (of timing and focus, among others) that literally reshape and comment on the choreography they enact. For instance, in the *Revelations* solo "I Wanna Be Ready" (performed on Ailey's State Department tours in the 1960s and 1970s by James Truitte and Dudley Williams) the soloist moves through a seated exercise from Horton dance technique known as the "coccyx balance." In the exercise choreographer Ailey transformed into performance choreography, the dancer balances on the back of his pelvis, his knees bent and feet raised off the floor, while his arms move through a series of poses (figure 2.2). The dancer's measured exhalations and his sometimes open-eyed, sometimes prayerful gaze elevates the movements from an abs-strengthening exercise to a spiritual offering, a man signaling his willingness to give up the self, to give up the body.

Such performance choices infuse intention into a choreographic work that, like much of dance modernism, offers few clues to its larger cultural context. The male dancer in "I Wanna Be Ready" wears a white shirt and pants, (usually) does not appear in *Revelations'* preceding pieces, and dances in almost no light. The audience does not know where he came from, in what world he moves, or where he is going. The absence of contextual markers allows dancers to conjure multiple worlds for the solo depending on the moment of performance. Dudley Williams said that when he

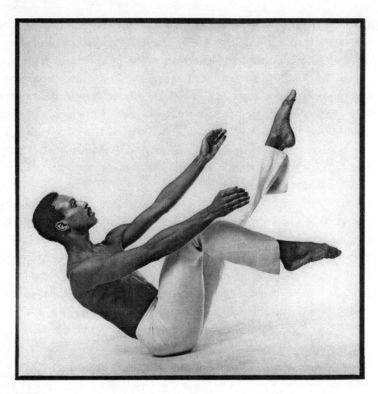

Figure 2.2
Dudley Williams in Alvin Ailey's signature masterpiece *Revelations*, 1969.
Source: Photo by Jack Mitchell. Courtesy of the Alvin Ailey Dance Foundation, Inc.

performed "I Wanna Be Ready" during the AIDS crisis of the 1980s and 1990s, which hit the New York ballet and modern dance communities especially hard, the piece became a memorial for his friends who had died or were dying. When the solo was performed in the late sixties on State Department tours, it is imaginable that for some—performers or audience members—the image of a lone black man struggling against physical limitations and oppressive darkness might have evoked those widely circulated images of black Americans pressing forward despite violent backlash from white supremacists and federal, state, and local governments—images such as that of African American activist James Meredith pulling himself across a road after being shot at a protest in Mississippi. Through performance, dancers speak with their voices and with their bodies, potentially connecting with the social contexts modernism pretended did not exist. The remainder of this chapter focuses on these people, these embodied performances, and how bodies and motion became conduits for championing American modernism while resisting it, too.

MAKING RACE VISIBLE TO EVERYONE: *AGON* AND
ARTHUR MITCHELL IN THE SOVIET UNION

George Balanchine's central *pas de deux* in the ballet *Agon*, created for Diana Adams and Arthur Mitchell in 1957, was an intensely physical, even sensuous embodied exchange between a black man and a white woman. The 1989 film *Dancing for Mr. B* includes archival footage from the 1960s featuring Allegra Kent and Mitchell, the couple that performed the piece on the 1962 Soviet tour, dancing an excerpt from the *pas de deux*. The dance's first long partnered phrase begins with Mitchell standing in a lunge, as Kent rests on his back and arms, her back touching his. Beginning to move, Kent wraps her leg around Mitchell's torso, nestling her pointed foot against his lower back. He steadies her with his arms and hands, and then slides his hands around her back. His biceps bulge slightly as he squeezes her—a squeeze that appears to be the catalyst for Kent to straighten her leg, circle it to the side and back, and lead the couple into their next partnered phrase (figure 2.3).[23]

When Mitchell, a black man, and Kent, a white woman, performed the *pas de deux* on NYCB's Soviet tour, the choreography was potentially extremely controversial. Balanchine is known for partnering that intertwines women and men like vines climbing up tree trunks, and *Agon* may be one of his most entangled duets. The man and woman in *Agon*'s central *pas de deux* constantly wrap around one another, their physical relationship intensified by its contrast with partnering done in the ballet's preceding sections, where men and women touch only one another's hands and arms. In the *Agon pas de deux* the man and woman press against one another's entire bodies, stomach to back, pelvis to pelvis. The sensuality between the two dancers is clear.

Agon's interplay of race and form, Mitchell's memories of the Soviet tour, and other dancers' memories of Soviet interest in Mitchell illustrate how choreography and performance exploded the modernist formula of using formal abstraction to obscure but not erase racial identity. State Department officials and members of the ANTA Dance Panel considered race and formal innovation together, seeking African American representation, while also stripping African American artists of their individual identities. Under the guise of modernism, *Agon*'s interplay of race and form can be reduced to "color and form" when necessary or convenient, just as the State Department could abstract the specifics of African American individual and community histories into symbolic racial harmony. Considering how the ANTA panel discussed Mitchell's presence in the New York City Ballet, how Balanchine's choreography

Figure 2.3
Allegra Kent and Arthur Mitchell in one of many physically intertwined moments in
George Balanchine's *Agon*.
Source: Photograph by Martha Swope. Courtesy of the New York Public Library for the Performing Arts.
Choreography by George Balanchine © The George Balanchine Trust.

framed Africanist elements, how Mitchell physically manipulated his
presentation of race, and how newspaper coverage of the tour discussed
(and often ignored) race demonstrates how physical performance—even
by one black dancer—revealed and challenged the over-valuation of choreographic formalism and whiteness that shored up modernism's value to
American cultural diplomacy.

Agon is a supposedly abstract dance performed in practice clothes: black
leotards and pink tights for the women and black tights and white t-shirts
for the men. Mitchell and Balanchine made the male role a signature
one for Mitchell in the City Ballet repertory, though a black dancer does
not always perform it. As Brenda Dixon Gottschild has illustrated,[24]
Balanchine's formalism was always entangled with race through its
Africanist elements—elements made more visible when Mitchell danced
Balanchine ballets.

On the 1962 Soviet tour, Mitchell was highly visible to Soviet balletomanes onstage and off because he danced a large number of principal

roles, including in *Agon*, and was the company's lone black dancer. Like all the dancers on the tour, Mitchell remembered the difficult conditions and enthusiastic audiences, but he also remembered feeling an intense personal burden. Returning from the tour, Mitchell's body forced him to reckon with the toll the tour had taken on him. Mitchell recalled the 1962 tour to me while sitting in his office at Dance Theatre of Harlem, the predominantly black ballet company he founded in 1968 in response to Martin Luther King Jr.'s assassination. Mitchell sat behind his large wooden desk describing his experiences on the tour: the strain of performing in substandard conditions, fear about the Cuban missile crisis, and worry over how the company would represent Balanchine in his first return to the USSR. He recalled conversations with friends once he returned to New York:

> They said, "Arthur, you're losing your hair." I said, "What do you mean?" [They said,] "You have this big bald spot in the middle of your head." I said, "What?" I didn't know that. And so I went to the doctor, and he said, "Oh, Arthur, you're having a nervous breakdown." . . . The pressure of all that was taking its toll on me, but I didn't even realize it at the time. Because, you know, artists can put themselves into a state where they can get through anything, but the pressure of it is something that you can't imagine.[25]

The tour had, almost literally, undone Mitchell because he had the multiple responsibilities of performing as a representative of the United States, of Balanchine, and of African American culture—a third layer no other dancer on the tour experienced.

As Mitchell spoke, a photograph behind his desk reminded me of the larger discourse of modernism within which he danced. The photograph featured a young Mitchell, dressed in *Agon*'s male costume of white t-shirt and black tights, floating against a solid off-white background (figure 2.4). He soars, his knees pulled up in a ballet jump named *Cecchetti changement*. Mitchell's head is turned to the left, his chin high, arms open. Energy streams from his fingertips, exemplifying the gorgeous, open dancing spirit I recognize from films of Mitchell dancing. He is recognizable even though the photograph, with its blank background and unseen floor, which gives few contextual clues to the dancer's identity or location.

The picture exemplifies the modernist formalism that structures Balanchine's most abstract ballets, emphasizing the shape Mitchell makes with his body rather than the social forces within which he moves. Mitchell's performance style, however, refuses anonymity. As a performer and as a person, he interceded in a nationally sanctioned, color-blind

Figure 2.4
Arthur Mitchell leaps in an example of the physical freedom and modernist abstraction in George Balanchine's *Agon*.
Source: Photograph by Martha Swope. Courtesy of the New York Public Library for the Performing Arts. Choreography by George Balanchine © The George Balanchine Trust.

narrative, keeping blackness clearly within the public view and refusing the largely white image of the United States offered by most American ballet companies at the time.

Balanchine's incorporation of Africanist aesthetics made his choreography well-suited for American cultural diplomacy's modernist project and ripe for Mitchell's danced critique of balletic modernism's overwhelming whiteness. Characteristics frequently used to describe Balanchine's work— speed, dense phrasing, articulation through the torso, and off-center movements—are also attributes of Africanist dance.[26] Yet, the discourse around Balanchine often camouflages the Africanist elements, rarely fully acknowledging debts to African American culture. Dixon Gottschild notes that formally oriented descriptions of Balanchine's choreography frequently displace blackness; for instance, the word "jazz" replaces "African American."[27] It is not as though "jazz" does not signal African American culture at all, but making that connection requires more knowledge of black culture than would, of course, the descriptor "African American." The category "American," another label often affixed to Balanchine's work, then subsumes racial specificity—race, particularly blackness, is still present but unnamed.

In *Agon*, however, blackness cannot be so easily obscured. African American and Africanist elements are not subtext in *Agon*; they are the ballet's primary visual, musical, and energetic elements. According to Mitchell, in initial rehearsals Balanchine spoke openly about using Mitchell's brown skin to contrast with Adams' white skin.[28] One example of this visual contrast comes early in the ballet's central *pas de deux* when the two dancers link arms. The ballerina's white arm snakes over and through the man's darker arm, and then the two flip their arms up, an interlocked diamond of black and white skin.[29]

Sonically, jazz rhythms lurk within Stravinsky's music for *Agon* and Balanchine's choreography. Baroque and jazz music contribute to *Agon*'s complex rhythms, and, as Stephanie Jordan has written, the influence of African American jazz can be seen in *Agon*'s "jazz-style freedom," including the choreography's "slightly 'offbeat' phrasing."[30] In a 2006 video filmed by The George Balanchine Trust, Mitchell teaches the *Agon pas de deux* by isolating the ballet's syncopation. As he coaches the dancers, Mitchell breaks down the music by singing in an almost bebop style, emphasizing the "offbeat" rhythm Jordan has identified.

Race is also a social question, even a controversy, in *Agon*. The central *pas de deux* between a black man and white woman, made in 1957—the same year the National Guard forcibly intervened to integrate schools in Little Rock, Arkansas (and the year the USIA first surveyed foreign nations about their perceptions of American race relations)—was a notable gesture for the time. Perhaps Balanchine's most radical choreographic choice was creating a *pas de deux* that required black and white dancers to share energy. For instance, in one phrase from *Agon*, Mitchell grabs Kent's arm as she pulls away in arabesque. Next, they switch positions, pulling in opposite directions, again achieving a shape through a tug of war of arms and legs. In both of these positions, Mitchell and Kent need each other to remain standing. Put another way, the black man needs the white woman and the white woman needs the black man, a controversial relationship when interracial couples remained an absolute taboo. (*Loving v. Virginia*, the Supreme Court ruling that struck down anti-miscegenation laws across the United States, did not happen until 1967.) Historian Peggy Pascoe has argued that miscegenation posed a real threat to twentieth-century American society's cultural investment in the nonrecognition of race because defining miscegenation required a public recognition of race.[31] By putting an interracial couple onstage, particularly an interracial couple that embodied the iconic sexualized taboo of the black man and white woman, Balanchine opened modernism's coat of abstraction, revealing the racial presence at its core.

Fully comprehending the stakes of Mitchell and Kent dancing *Agon* on a 1962 State Department tour requires rewinding to the mid-1950s, when the ANTA Dance Panel first began selecting dance companies. Panel meeting minutes illustrate how the group connected formal innovation and racial politics when discussing values to be promoted on tours. In a March 1957 discussion about the opening of Berlin's Benjamin Franklin Theatre, the panel imagined its "ideal" program: an "American Indian dancer, American Negro dancers, American ballet dancers, and American modern dancers."[32] With this racial and formal mix, this ideal cultural diplomacy program would present a picture of the United States as racially inclusive and at the forefront of modernism.

A January 1956 panel conversation suggested that Mitchell's presence in the New York City Ballet represented a perfect coupling of race and form. Kirstein told the panel that "a Negro dancer as soloist will appear with all the classic ballets, as just one of the dancers, completely integrated with the company,"[33] an idea that "the Panel approved wholeheartedly."[34] Unnamed in the minutes, Mitchell, City Ballet's only African American dancer from 1955 to 1970, is not a person, but an abstraction. A "Negro dancer" in the company presents ballet as becoming American—democratized even—in its integration of a black dancer as "just one of the dancers."

In the Soviet Union, however, Mitchell was not just another dancer or "the black dancer." By Mitchell's partners' accounts and his own, Soviet audiences were obsessed with him. In Tbilisi the company attended a performance by former Kirov star Vakhhtag Chabukiani in his ballets *Laurencia* (1948) and *Othello* (1958). Mitchell remembers a long pause after a Chabukiani solo, and looking around the theater only to realize that most of the audience was looking at him. Once Mitchell began to clap, the audience joined him.[35] His presence as a black man in the theater was such a singular event that it disrupted theater etiquette.

Almost all the dancers I interviewed said Mitchell had an equally strong effect on audiences when he performed, although the interpretations of the interest in Mitchell ranged widely from positive to negative. As Allegra Kent talked about the tour, she switched into a fake Russian accent only once: when she repeated for me what she heard while onstage dancing with Mitchell, Soviet voices chanting "Arthur, Arthur!"[36] Remembering dancing with Mitchell conjured those Soviet voices in Kent's mind. Gloria Govrin described Soviet audiences' reaction to the programs she closed with Mitchell in *Western Symphony*: "They were very taken, especially with Arthur. . . . 'Arthur Mitchell!' they were chanting."[37] Violette Verdy remembered audiences chanting *chernyi* whenever Mitchell danced.[38] Translated literally, *chernyi* means "black," although the word is usually used in a derogatory way. Verdy, who was not fluent in Russian, interpreted the chant as positive, but what read as enthusiasm to the American dancers may have been fetishization or even taunting, as the choice of the pejorative *chernyi* suggests. Reviews of the company published in Soviet and Canadian newspapers corroborate the dancers' memories that Mitchell's reception was exceptional. Canadian writers did cover Mitchell's success, noting the Soviet "enthusiasm" for him in both his "sensuous duet" and his "freewheeling cowboy finale."[39]

Most American newspaper accounts, however, offer only brief mentions of the acclaim Mitchell received. *Times* critic Martin positioned Mitchell as just further evidence of Balanchine's innovation. He named Mitchell twice in his review of NYCB's opening Moscow performance, noting that Kent and Mitchell's central *pas de deux* in *Agon* had elicited the "first sign of genuine enthusiasm" from the audience. In the same review, he said that Mitchell and Govrin's performance in *Western Symphony*'s fourth movement "stopped [the performance] in its tracks."[40] After this initial review from Moscow, however, Martin shifted his focus almost entirely to Balanchine, attributing the unexpected success of the more abstract ballets, such as *Agon* and *Episodes*, solely to the choreographer's "genius."[41] Because Martin was the only critic to travel with the company to all of the tour's five stops, his minimal coverage of Mitchell's success leaves a substantial historical gap. Abstraction and choreographer move center stage. Dancer and Africanist presence slide to the margins (at best).

Sometimes Martin's cryptic word choice seemed to refer to race without naming it. For example, Martin described the opening night performance of *Agon* in Leningrad as a "braintwister" that "carried the house along with it gratifyingly, even beyond the customary burst of enthusiasm for its curiously inventive *pas de deux*."[42] Martin's "curiously" perhaps implies something more than formal invention. Perhaps he alludes to the *pas de deux*'s entanglement of a black man's and white woman's bodies. Again, race is relegated to subtext.

Dance reviews too frequently leave dancers unnamed or unmentioned, so some of Martin's erasure of Mitchell can be attributed to the genre in which he writes. Martin, however, wrote an unusual form of review on the Soviet tour, reporting more about Soviet audience reactions—when people did or did not applaud—than is customary in a dance review. Since there were no premieres on the tour, it seems an appropriate reportorial choice to see the Soviet perception of the ballets rather than the ballets themselves as the "news" of the government-sponsored tour. Martin's focus on the audience, then, makes his exclusion of the response to Mitchell seem a conscious omission (or, he unconsciously attributed it to Mitchell's blackness and therefore not newsworthy). Most other American newspaper reports about the tour followed narratives similar to Martin's: the tour was triumph for Balanchine. Newspapers' dismissal of the subject of race on the tour is probably not surprising given the era, but closer attention to Mitchell's performances would have flipped the script about what American modernism really said about American culture: that black people and black culture were present in anything deemed "American" but only enjoyed the partial benefits of American citizenship.

Mitchell's exuberant performance style and his self-professed consciousness of blackness as a performance not just phenotype—another physical reference he made in our interview—opposed modernism's positioning of African Americans as not important enough to be named. Mitchell's dancing, the attention he received from Soviet audiences, and the radical racial politics of *Agon*'s *pas de deux* catapulted him beyond American cultural diplomacy's usual packaging of race in modernism. Mitchell's performances constituted what performance theorist José Muñoz has called "feeling brown." Muñoz described performances of excess, especially by Latina/o performers, but also other minoritarian groups, as "specify[ing] and describ[ing] ethnic difference and resistance not in terms of simple being, but through a more nuanced route to feeling," a route that separates a performer of color from "an official, 'national affect' that is aligned with a hegemonic class."[43] By refusing to fade into a racially integrated collage—just another dancer in the company but one who happens to be black—Mitchell made his presence known and commented on the prevalence of white bodies and the performances of whiteness on the ballet stage.

Mitchell's explosive performances cracked the cool austerity of Balanchine's formal abstractions. He remembered a conversation with Govrin after a performance of *Western Symphony*. Mitchell said, "Gloria said, 'You bent over so far back, your head was—you went into a back-bend and your head was touching the floor.' And I'm telling Gloria, 'I'm in Russia; what am I going to do?' And that's the extrovert part of me that comes into play, and the pride that you have that you're onstage with Mr. Balanchine."[44]

Mitchell went on to tie his performance style to an intentional performance of race. When principal dancer Conrad Ludlow was injured on the tour Mitchell had to perform *Divertimento No. 15* (1956) in Ludlow's place with little rehearsal. Lincoln Kirstein and Mitchell talked about how Mitchell would learn the forty-five-minute ballet quickly. Mitchell remembered Kirstein asking, "'Arthur, what are you going to do?' Mitchell responded, 'Nothing. I'm going to go out and think 'white.'"[45] As Mitchell told me the last line of this story, he sucked his cheeks in, puffed his chest out, and looked down his nose, showing me what it meant to perform "white," demonstrating a body posture of rigidity and pretension. In that moment, Mitchell illustrated how he consciously deployed white and black as performative categories.

Mitchell's comments help return the burden of racial representation experienced by Mitchell on the Soviet tour to NYCB history. Difference did not just derive from Mitchell's distinction as the company's only black member on the tour. He used his performance skills to separate himself from the cast, making ballets' structures and demographics more visible. When Mitchell performed, he did so under a heavy burden of representation, but his efforts also meant that African American identity could not be overlooked—it was not just a category the State Department and the Dance Panel could include as evidence of American racial inclusivity. As was true with the photograph that drew my eye in Mitchell's office, modernist abstraction cannot entirely camouflage performances of blackness, nor can it frame blackness as only an object to be appropriated for hegemonic ends. Just one black dancer, Arthur Mitchell, had challenged a variety of frames that could have curtailed the public visibility of black power *as* black power, not *only* American power.

ALVIN AILEY AMERICAN DANCE THEATER, AFRICAN AMERICAN MODERNISM, AND SELF-DETERMINATION

The racial makeup of the Ailey State Department tours was almost the exact opposite of the 1962 NYCB tour. Since founding the Ailey company, Alvin Ailey had made sure the company was predominantly African American, and also had Latina/o and Asian American dancers. Ailey expanded the company's racial mix when a white dancer joined the group just prior to the company's first State Department tour in 1962.

Ailey's work—the choreography and the company members' dancing—always told a story of African American self-determination, even amid a modernist landscape.[46] The song lyrics and movement of Ailey's *Revelations*, which was included on every one of Ailey's State Department tours, depict African American people overcoming obstacles through individual will drawn from community strength. Seen through the lens of self-determination, *Revelations* is not just representative of modernist formalism, although that proliferates through its abstract scenic elements and dance techniques that emphasize making shapes with the body. *Revelations* is a quintessential example of African American modernism, too. Performance scholar Kimberly Benston has described African American modernism as artistic work that stresses "an autonomous black poetics" while also "seeking to situate black poetics within a larger, more continuous, and more textured field of expressive desire."[47] Ailey's aesthetic fits within this reframing of modernist autonomy as still part of a specific community, while also commenting upon the larger cultural world in which black culture moves. Modernist aesthetics, with its tendency toward including but obscuring the specificity of blackness, helped get Ailey booked on tours. Making explicit modernism's debt to African American modernism made Ailey's choreography, particularly *Revelations*, a statement about African American self-determination that disrupted the progress narratives about African American life circulated in other USIA materials.

Self-Determination in Politics across the United States and Africa

Throughout the decades that the Ailey company toured most frequently on behalf of the State Department, Ailey clarified and expanded his choreographic vision of African American self-determination. The company was quite new when it first toured with State Department support in 1962. Compared to larger, better-supported tours, the small, young Ailey company sometimes scrambled to keep itself going on tour. The early Ailey tours were very small affairs compared to those of the big ballet companies in the 1950s and 1960s, or even in comparison to some of the tours by the Graham and Limón companies. For instance, Ailey's 1967 tour of ten African countries included only Alvin Ailey, an ensemble of twelve dancers, lighting designer Nicola Cernovitch, and USIA escort officer Harry Hirsch. Dudley Williams recalled that dancers "didn't have substitutes or understudies."[48] While the absence of extra dancers was not uncommon for State Department tours, the limited staff was more exceptional—and challenging for the young company. Dancer Lynne Taylor-Corbett recalled boarding planes and watching Ailey run across the tarmac as cassette tapes of the music used for the performances spilled from his bag. Now a well-known choreographer herself, Taylor-Corbett remembered this harried vision of Ailey and thought, "Imagine being responsible for all that and not having a support system."[49]

Tour repertory was quite expansive, representing a typical, mid-century Ailey mix of works by Ailey and other, mostly African American, choreographers all generally working within modernism—many of them African American modernist works. The exact repertory of the 1960s and 1970s tours is unclear, but the 1960s Africa tours definitely included Ailey's *Blues Suite*, Talley Beatty's *The Road of the Phoebe Snow* (1959), Geoffrey Holder's *Prodigal Prince* (1967), Louis Johnson's *Lament* (1953), Beatty's *Congo Tango Palace* (1960), and Paul Sanasardo's *Metallics* (1964). In 1970 most of these pieces were repeated in the Soviet Union with the addition of Ailey's controversial *Masekela Langage* (1969), which caused a stir in the United States and abroad for its comparisons of racism in the United States and in South Africa.

The State Department, which chose tour destinations, primarily placed Ailey in countries in the throes of building new governments after throwing off European colonial rule. For instance, the Ailey company first appeared for the State Department in Southeast Asia in 1962. Thinking back to that first tour, Dudley Williams and Carmen de Lavallade (de Lavallade shared top billing with the then little-known Ailey) remembered riots in the streets of Indonesia's capital during performances.[50]

In the late 1960s, the State Department mainly sent the Ailey company to the African continent, a pairing of company and tour destination that explicitly brought together African and African American self-determination movements. The Ailey company (no longer appearing with de Lavallade) first traveled to Africa in 1966 for the First World Festival of Negro Arts in Senegal, a festival organized by Senegalese President Léopold Senghor to celebrate the global impact of black culture. The Ailey company was a last-minute addition to the American artistic roster, added when a replacement was needed for the ballet company Arthur Mitchell had begun to build. The 1966 engagement was a smashing success, in part, because Ailey's fluency in French made him an ideal American spokesperson in former French and Belgian colonies, including Senegal. The State Department sent Ailey for a longer African tour in 1967.

On the later tour, dancer George Faison and other dancers said they found their proximity to African anti-colonial movements palpable and poignant, knowing they were in the places that, as Martin Luther King Jr. famously put it, had moved with "jetlike speed toward gaining political independence."[51] The US government hoped African audiences, too, would be inspired—inspired by the Americans' presence to bend African postcolonial movements toward American democracy.

The 1967 tour included several stops in newly decolonized African countries still in postcolonial tumult and where the United States worried about increasing communist leanings. For instance, in 1967, the United States had pressing interests in Ghana since a coup had dislodged the socialist-leaning Kwame Nkrumah the year before. Later in the tour, the company was in the Congo during one of several violently crushed rebellions that attempted to overthrow leader Joseph Mobutu, who the US had controversially helped put into place based solely on his anti-communist stance.

On some tour stops, the company found themselves sharing space with African leaders best known for their work in anti-colonial movements. A photograph taken by State Department staff (figure 2.5) documents the young Ailey kneeling before Kenyan President Jomo Kenyatta, who (with Ghana's Nkrumah) was an important leader in the Pan-African movement and a key negotiator of Kenyan independence in 1962. In 1967 when the picture was taken, Kenyatta was the newly independent country's first president. The company performed for Kenyatta, as Judith Jamison (who made a huge impression on the leader) remembered, on the president's lawn in 110 degree weather.[52] The photo, taken at the president's home, where the company gave its command performance, quite literally brought together Africans and African Americans invested in self-determination and reimagining democratic systems that would not just include black people but in which black people would be leaders.

Beyond meetings with visible leaders, the dancers did not always know about the larger historical contexts in which they moved, much as the NYCB dancers were not always aware of the Cuban missile crisis (see chapter 1). They often learned about ongoing tension and violence in mundane ways: a boy who helped carry suitcases at a hotel in Kinsasha, Congo, told Lynne Taylor-Corbett that forty people had been shot by government forces in a nearby square the day before.[53] More positive experiences, however, often overwhelmed stories of violence: on the same Congo stop, dancers mainly remembered being greeted by local drummers at the Kinsasha airport.[54]

Figure 2.5
Alvin Ailey kneels before Kenyan President Jomo Kenyatta, one of the best-known lead-
ers of decolonization in Africa and the first president of Kenya. Mbiyu Koinange, Kenyan
Minister of State, sits to Kenyatta's right, and Mama Ngina Kenyatta, Kenyatta's wife,
sits to his left.
Source: Courtesy of Special Collections, University of Arkansas.

Though embassy staff planned meetings with locals like the one at the
airport, the dancers say Ailey was often frustrated to not have access to
more parts and peoples on the continent. In 1967, Ailey wanted the company to perform in South Africa, but State Department officials refused,
saying it was too dangerous. The dancers, however, recalled another Ailey
protest—to perform for local African audiences, rather than for elites and
expatriates only—that was eventually heeded by the embassy and the
USIA officers. Alhough the 1967 tour occurred as the State Department
was beginning to expand all its arts tours to reach broader, often younger
audiences,[55] Dudley Williams remembered that Ailey still had to fight for
performances with lower-cost tickets: "He didn't want to dance just for
the people with gloves on. . . . He wanted to dance for the people, and the
tickets were so expensive. . . . He demanded that we dance for the people
and lower the tickets [prices] so people could come in."[56] Taylor-Corbett
noted that Ailey's request to perform for "the people" in Africa had a racial
dimension. She was often shocked when curtains would open at the beginning of a performance in an African country and all she saw was a "sea of

white faces."[57] At Ailey's request, the embassies added several informal outdoor shows to ensure that a wider swath of the local population could attend.

Performing Self-Determination: *Revelations*

On every bill, on every tour stop, *Revelations* closed the program. Ailey's signature work may be best known for its boisterous closing dances as women in bright-yellow dresses fan their male partners with straw fans— the dancing Sharron Miller referenced in the anecdote that opens this chapter. *Revelations'* combination of emphasis on the lines of the body and celebratory reenactment of African American culture made it one of the most popular exports for the State Department. Yet the role the Ailey company played in State Department programming becomes much more complicated if *Revelations'* opening, more somber dances are examined alongside its happy ending, and in interviews dancers frequently pointed to these dances as absolutely crucial to understanding *Revelations*. (figure 2.6).

Figure 2.6
The full Ailey company in the early 1970s in the final joyous image of Alvin Ailey's *Revelations*.
Source: Photo by Johan Elbers. Courtesy of the Alvin Ailey Dance Foundation, Inc.

Revelations' expressions of violence, sorrow, and struggle undermined the progress narratives of African American history being presented elsewhere in American cultural diplomacy in the 1950s and 1960s. Most USIA materials, particularly a series of pamphlets about African American history, positioned slavery as a long-ago event, the starting point in the story of American racial progress, rather than as a horrific historical event that still shaped American attitudes and practices. In contrast to these kinds of materials, *Revelations* offers a more layered temporality of the African American experience, intertwining trauma and celebration, past and present. Performance theorist Joni Jones describes African American theater as offering "a consideration of how a slave history has left psychic wounds on descendants of masters and descendants of slaves. The talk [or in this case, dance] with history is then a way of clarifying and contextualizing the present."[58] Ailey's live performances hurled the past into the present, making them ideally suited to comment on trauma's fluid temporality and explode a high modernist formula that had no place for culturally specific trauma. *Revelations'* opening section, "Pilgrim of Sorrow," displays the ongoing effects of slavery's trauma on people and their bodies.

By putting black people at the center of African American history, not just as one group upon which history has acted, Ailey also opened space for recognizing African Americans' role in the ongoing struggles for equality. This recognition of African Americans as actors, not just victims, contrasted with the USIA materials that positioned benevolent, white federal legislators as the primary actors in the civil rights movement. USIA's "educational" pamphlets, distributed across the African continent, emphasized racial integration as a soothing balm for the wounds of slavery. These include the 1950 or 1951 *The Negro in American Life*, and the 1965 pamphlet, *For the Dignity of Man*. Historian Mary Dudziak's close readings of these pamphlets describe how each argues for American democracy as the ideal conduit for racial "reconciliation and redemption."[59] The text of *The Negro in American Life* described the horrors of American slavery, but photographs projected images of racial integration as a smooth resolution of past horrors. In one picture, a black teacher leads a class of black and white children.[60] Another shows a group of black children standing in front of a newly constructed school.[61] These pictures connect integration and education as evidence of an American promise of increasing equality. Dudziak explains how the pamphlet's text moved from a description of slavery to an optimistic picture of African American life, where expanding educational opportunities "made 'the Negro' more worthy of equal treatment, and made him more likely to insist on his rights."[62] In Dudziak's reading, the photographs and texts created a progress narrative that did not erase slavery, but used slavery as a convenient starting point for a narrative of American progress—progress made possible because the now-educated African American could appeal to American government systems for "his rights."

The 1965 pamphlet, *For the Dignity of Man*, resurrected a familiar theme: American democracy, here embodied by white male legislators rather than a racially integrated classroom, was the best system for achieving racial progress. The text described recent developments in civil rights history, including the 1964 Civil Rights Act and the 1965 Voting Rights Act, and began with a full-page photograph of President Johnson signing the 1965 legislation (figure 2.7).[63] The pamphlet's many photographs told a story of the federal government's promotion of racial integration as a pathway for African Americans to achieve success and happiness in which white leaders are equally important—perhaps even more important— than black grassroots movements and leaders. Those unable to read the pamphlet because of language or literacy barriers would draw conclusions about American life primarily from the photographs.

Pamphlet designers cropped out of the photo the civil rights leaders present at the bill signing, including Martin Luther King Jr., making Johnson, a white, elected leader, the image of social change.[64] Dudziak describes, too, how the pamphlet distanced the US nation from racial injustice by arguing that racism is a problem only for "some individuals and state and local governments."[65] Seemingly, the President and the legislation he signed could curtail the impact of this misguided, racist minority.

The emphasis on legislation credited only the white men of the federal government with leading the United States away from its racist past. Over half of the pamphlet's pictures feature white leaders, including Presidents Eisenhower and Kennedy, as well as Johnson, signing legislation. A photo of participants in the 1963 March on Washington (figure 2.8) is shot so that it seems the marchers appealed to Lincoln's statue on the National Mall, not to the strength produced through their gathering.[66] The 1963 demonstration is the only civil rights protest pictured, and the pamphlet calls upon the photograph to emphasize that African Americans have the opportunity to appeal to civil authorities. The caption of the march photograph describes the protest as an "orderly demonstration" that concluded with a meeting between the leaders of the march and President Kennedy.[67] All of these choices, visual and textual, cohere to create the impression that the white leaders, on behalf of the American federal system, are the most capable of making change in and through American democracy. Virtually no space is given to recognizing the African American community's work or courage. This is the modernist aesthetic formula reconfigured

"The central fact of American civilization, one so hard for others to understand, is that freedom and justice and the dignity of man are not just words to us. We believe in them. Under all the growth, and the tumult, and abundance, we believe. And so, as long as some among us are oppressed and we are part of that oppression it must blunt our faith and sap the strength of our high purpose."

— *Lyndon B. Johnson* on signing the Voting Rights Act on August 6, 1965.

Figure 2.7
The inside cover of the USIA/USIS pamphlet *For the Dignity of Man, America's Civil Rights Program* shows President Lyndon B. Johnson signing the 1964 Civil Rights Act. Martin Luther King Jr. and other civil rights leaders who stood around Johnson at the moment of signing were cropped from the photo.
Source: Courtesy of the Lyndon B. Johnson Library and Museum.

as a political strategy: American innovation and strength consume all nonwhite culturally specific markers, retooling the presence of black culture and black people into evidence of American democratic superiority.

When civil rights protests do appear in the pamphlets, they, like slavery, are framed as events of the past. For instance, in *The Negro in American Life*, one photograph shows African Americans eating at a lunch counter—a triumph over segregation secured, according to the photograph's caption,

Figure 2.8
Image of the 1963 March on Washington from the USIA/USIS pamphlet *For the Dignity of Man, The Civil Rights Program*. Only the looming figure of President Lincoln is recognizable, whereas the thousands of marchers are an indistinguishable, barely visible mass.
Source: Courtesy of the Lyndon B. Johnson Library and Museum.

not by sit-ins in Greensboro, North Carolina and other Southern cities, but by the 1964 Civil Rights Act.[68] The pamphlet's remaining photographs depict happy scenes of an integrated America: children of different racial backgrounds playing together in a park and African American teachers working with white students.[69] According to the pamphlet, democratic, federal structures have ensured equal access for all Americans—a far cry from the truth of African American life in 1966, 1967, and 1970, when the Ailey company represented the United States on State Department tours.

Revelations' choreographic procession from depictions of pain in "Pilgrim of Sorrow," the work's opening section, to its final joyous moments does not completely dispense with the USIA pamphlets' progress narratives. The Dance Panel (no longer known as the ANTA Dance Panel, but rather as the State Department Dance Advisory Panel after 1963) definitely thought of *Revelations* as an optimistic work. In a 1970 memorandum in which the panel members expressed concern about including Ailey's relatively violent *Masekela Langage* on State Department tours, they described *Revelations* as "warm and lovely," a suitable counterpoint to *Masekela*.[70] Dance historian Thomas DeFrantz has argued that *Revelations'* "economy of dance motion, brevity of musical selections, [and] the confident dispatch of its staging" softens its political potency for some.[71] Judith Jamison noted that *Revelations'* joy is political, too: "Some people say 'Rocka My Soul' is a whole bunch of happy people onstage. That's not exactly right. It is the faithful understanding they have joy."[72] Joy comes from surviving through struggle, but it does not erase that struggle.

In comparison to the USIA pamphlets, however, *Revelations'* choreographic politics are overtly radical. Violent images of slavery and the ongoing, painful effects of slavery and racism on African American people and their bodies are inescapable in *Revelations'* first three dances. The dancers' earth-tone costumes and the bare stage make "Pilgrim of Sorrow" *Revelations'* most abstract section. Rather than only invoking modernism's abstraction, however, the three dances in the section direct audiences to the haunting pain in the work's accompanying spirituals. The spirituals are not only anthems of African American Christian celebration in "Pilgrim," as they might be in *Revelations'* final dances, but, to borrow W. E. B. Du Bois's term, they are truly "sorrow songs." Much like Mitchell's joyous leap in the iconic *Agon* landscape, dancers' affective and physical performances exceed the framing of modernism's bareness, making the section an example of abstract formalism but also of African American affect, pain, and power.

In the movement vocabulary of *Revelations'* two opening dances, heaving torsos and jerking limbs reinsert images of slavery into American cultural diplomacy. The tempo of *Revelations'* opening piece, "I Been 'Buked," dramatically shifts from slow to fast as baritone voices sing, "There is trouble all over this land." With these words, the Ailey ensemble moves away from *Revelations'* well-known opening cluster, in which dancers stand shoulder to shoulder, palms forward, fingers flexed, chests and chins high.[73] An abrupt tempo change sends the dancers barreling out into space. Each dancer performs an individualized phrase as he or she moves away from the group. The diversity of the dancers' steps, coupled with their general spinning quality, produces an image of anxious chaos that contrasts with the sustained, heavy choreography of the opening cluster.

Throughout "I Been 'Buked," percussive, jerky dancing disrupts slow, somber postures. In the piece's final moments, the dancers return to the opening cluster. As they simultaneously stretch their arms slowly upward, it seems the piece will close with the sustained unison movement with which it began. But then, one by one, the dancers' arms go rigid at the elbows, and then open into a "V." Finally, in tiny spasms of pain, the dancers jerk their arms out and down.

The impact of slavery's cruelty on people and their bodies reappears in the movement vocabulary of much of "Didn't My Lord Deliver Daniel," the second dance in "Pilgrim of Sorrow." Angry, tired sobs wrack the dancers' entire bodies. Pain travels from the dancers' arms into their hunched, pulsing torsos. Near the beginning of "Daniel," the three dancers, one man and two women, squat in a deep second position, their bodies turned on the diagonal, giving the audience a view of their perfectly curved spines. With heads bowed, arms stretched forward, and hands clasped, the dancers' posture conjures images of fields being plowed. But as the dancers pulse their bodies to the percussive singing of the word "Daniel," labor turns to agony. The choreographic layers of physical activity and emotional response specifically refer to the physical and psychological toll working in the field took on slaves, just one instance of what DeFrantz has described as *Revelations'* "reenactments of physical bondage."[74] Another obvious, even more violent example of a reenactment of slavery comes earlier in "Daniel." Just before the series of contractions, the trio of dancers stand, feet apart, arms high, wrists crossed as though bound, referencing the position of slaves, hands tied, stealing themselves for the strike of the master's whip.

"Pilgrim" does not, however, only position black people as victims. *Revelations* also presents black people, as individuals and as a collective, fighting to overcome forces that oppress them. In "I Been 'Buked," the dancers spin away in individual phrases, but they always return to the large group in the center. Moving in slow, controlled unison, they gather strength and create some of *Revelations'* most iconic images of community power. Standing in the dance's final grouping, the dancers jerk their arms downward one at a time—but they never drop their heads or chests. They stand, looking up in defiance, as the lights dim.

"Daniel," like "'Buked," ends with an image of bodies refusing to go down. In the music's last phrase, the three dancers step forward, then spiral their bodies to the floor. On the final drumbeat, they press their hips up into a bridge and shoot their arms, fingers spread, straight to the ceiling. Throughout "Daniel" the dancers have been knocked down and their bodies have been wracked with pain, but Ailey created a final image of people refusing to give up. The moment illustrates dancer and director Judith Jamison's point that *Revelations* is, all at once, about "struggle and the triumph of hope."[75] By reenacting these images on every program on the State Department tours, Ailey and the company dancers challenged the dominant government narratives about African American life.

Offstage Ailey also confronted American racism directly, shifting agency from the white American presidents featured in the pamphlets' photographs to the black-led grassroots civil rights movement. In a 1966 interview with the National Radio of Senegal during the First World Festival of Negro Arts, Ailey spoke about African Americans' courage, explaining that his company allowed African Americans to celebrate American culture and self-determination. He said,

> When I started to have a dance company, I decided I wanted to do something to show what the Negro had done. . . . In the United States, we have a little problem, as you know. They think we're not first-class citizens. . . . They don't recognize [our music and dance] for what it is. So I made a dance company mainly to illustrate to them what the Negro had contributed to America, . . . what the Negro made out of adversity, what the Negro made out of his sorrow, what the Negro made out of being held down in America. That's what the blues are. . . . I've taken these beautiful things and put them in dance.[76]

Ailey named the discrimination black people face in the United States and made fun of the dismissal of contemporary racial grievances with his ironic quip, "we have a little problem." Building emphasis through verbal repetition—an astute rhetorical move for a radio broadcast—and making "the Negro" each sentence's active subject, Ailey described "the Negro" as the source of overcoming, the source of creativity. He gave black people credit, and he gave them the stage.

Dancer George Faison remembered that, as was the case in the 1966 radio interview, Ailey was often critical of the United States—or at least truthful about the complications of American life for African Americans. Faison said of the 1967 tour, "[When] Africans asked Alvin, 'Is this [your choreography] a clear depiction of what goes on in America?' . . . [Ailey answered,] 'No, because there is prejudice. There is segregation.'"[77] Other dancers reported that over time Ailey toned down his rhetoric in interviews, perhaps because he had been, as the next section discusses, warned about how, as a black, gay man, he should appear in public while on government tours.

Ailey's choreography and his dancers' performances of that choreography expressed the strength and depth of African American culture. The lyrics of "I Been 'Buked" were right: There was "trouble all over this land"—all over the United States and all over Africa. The wounds of slavery had not faded into a long-ago past, as the USIA pamphlets suggested. In the 1960s and 1970s, black people and other citizens of color continued to face racial discrimination and violence and to fight for equality and representation on the streets of American cities—and on the stages of newly independent African nations.

MODERNISM OFFSTAGE

While Mitchell and the Ailey dancers found ways from the stage to challenge modernism's push of racial identity to the margins of representation, artists said such challenges were harder to sustain offstage. Strategic maneuvering was harder to accomplish offstage because oppressive attitudes around identity, namely racism and homophobia, were embedded in policies about how the dancers were to behave—and those policies more often came in the form of directives rather than discussions. Too, offstage the State Department Dance Advisory Panel and government officials exercised great power over how the tours were framed—in programs, publicity materials, and so on. Taken together, onstage possibilities coupled with offstage disciplinary structures formed what musicologist Nadine Hubbs and dance theorist Susan Foster have described as mid-century modernism's paradoxical entanglement of redemptive and regulatory forces.[78] When artists were offstage on the tours, they felt more regulation than redemption. They had to submit to what the State Department considered to be "good behavior," although many, particular Alvin Ailey, still found ways to manipulate the system even as they also suffered under oppression's weight.[79] These situations arose most clearly around homophobia and around Ailey's most controversial piece performed on State Department tours, *Masekela Langage*.

Dancing Through the Lavender Scare

While supporting Ailey in public, State Department officials reprimanded Alvin Ailey in private. The State Department knew Ailey to be gay because of information in his FBI file. During a routine background check preceding Ailey's 1965 visit to the White House, State Department officials learned of his 1950 arrest in Los Angeles for what was described as "vagrancy–lewd."[80] After this discovery, State Department requests for information about Ailey always referenced the 1950 arrest, and after 1967, also mentioned his arrest in Italy for "engaging in homosexual acts," thus criminalizing his sexuality.[81] Every time Ailey worked on behalf of the government or was invited to the White House, the paper trail documenting his sexual life would again circulate. At a time when the State

Department and many other government agencies fired people who under even the slightest suspicion of being gay, it seems remarkable Ailey, who was relatively open about his sexuality with fellow dancers documented as having engaged in homosexual acts, continued to receive State Department support.

To get this government support, though, Ailey had to navigate a terrain marked with racism and homophobia. A formerly classified State Department memo from June 1967, written to Cultural Presentations officer Thomas Huff, documents the department's suspicion of Ailey because of his sexuality and the department's attempts to control his behavior. The memo outlines Ailey's and dancer Miguel Godreau's arrest records (Godreau had been arrested for forgery) and mentions lighting designer Nicola Cernovitch's possible connection to a pro-Cuba group. According to the memo, government representatives briefed Ailey about their knowledge of the arrests, specifically mentioning his, as they called it, "lewd disposition." Officials told Ailey that the company, which was then preparing to leave on its 1967 Africa tour, "was to walk the straight and narrow path and that failure to do so could result in immediate cancellation of the tour." Ailey assured the officials he would "insist on proper conduct" from the company, which would "cooperate with the Department in every way."[82] The conversation between the State Department officials or panel members (it is unclear who met with Ailey) and the gay, black choreographer must have felt like a threat, a reminder that on tour Ailey worked for an American government that considered him suspicious and held his company's future in its hands.

The private conversation with Ailey and the citation of his "lewd" arrests occurred within the larger context of the State Department's institutionalized homophobia. Of all federal agencies, the State Department fired the largest percentage of suspected homosexuals during the Cold War. As historian David K. Johnson has charted, since the late forties, congressional inquiries had led to the firing of thousands of federal employees suspected of being homosexuals because they were thought to be "security risks."[83] Senator Joseph McCarthy, among other vocal figures in the late forties and fifties, argued that homosexuals' "perversity" made them, particularly those in diplomatic roles, susceptible to blackmail by Communists.[84] (Of course, it was not their sexuality but the criminalization of their sexuality that would have made blackmail possible.) The federal government's most public sexual inquisitions had ended before Ailey began touring for the State Department in 1962, but the institutional barriers to homosexuals' participation in diplomacy remained. Through the late 1960s, the State Department's annual reports to congressional committees always included the number of homosexuals fired that year.[85] As late as 1966, all male applicants to the State Department were asked if they had ever engaged in a "homosexual act."[86]

How did a State Department saturated with homophobia in its personnel practices and written policies come to fund a number of dance tours led by only partially closeted artists, including Ailey and José Limón? One answer might be the entanglement of homosexuality and artistry in mid-twentieth-century popular culture. To support artists at that time meant not just overlooking homosexuality but consciously constructing codes to shield audiences from its assumed presence in the art world. The post-war generation inherited Hollywood codes that used the words "artist" or "poet" to connote a male character's homosexuality. (The former term was used in Alfred Hitchcock's 1948 film *Rope;* the latter, in the 1951 film version of Tennessee Williams's *Streetcar Named Desire*.) Homosexuality was not imagined as something that could be eradicated in artistic circles, but it could be obscured and/or managed.

On tour, the State Department charged the USIA escorts with the job of watching for homosexual activity, a monitoring system that allowed government officials to express their homophobia, although it also meant they endangered themselves by documenting their knowledge of homosexuality on tour. (By knowingly keeping homosexual artists in circulation with State Department funding, government officials associated themselves with gay people and thus could have been fired, too.) In one unsigned internal memo, a government official traveling on the Limón Dance Company's 1973 Soviet tour (most likely the USIA escort) dedicated several pages to a meeting with the company manager Judith Hawkins, lighting designer "Spence," and stage manager John Towland. The memo writer directed his primary ire over tour problems toward Hawkins but also noted: "It is only too relevant to this tale of company intrigue and backbiting to mention that Spence and Towland are flagrant homosexuals, whose appearance, demeanor and conversation detracted from the otherwise excellent public image the company projected."[87] Being a "flagrant homosexual" was the opposite of having an "excellent public image."

As late as 1975—the year the US Civil Service Commission removed "immoral conduct," another euphemism for homosexuality, from the list of disqualifications for federal government employment[88]—Foreign Service officers strained to keep dancers' homosexual activity under wraps while abroad. In a report for the State Department about the Joffrey Ballet's Soviet tour, the tour escort wrote, "By Vilnius, homosexual contacts of Company members with Soviets were obvious, and actions taken have been communicated to the Department."[89] The author did not specify what "actions" he took, but the phrasing suggests that it was not so much the homosexual encounters but the fact they had become "obvious" that created the problem. "Behaving well" meant keeping homosexuality private. The statement shares the negative attitude of the earlier memo about the Limón employees, but it also raises questions about transnationally institutionalized homophobia. Being arrested for an "obvious" homosexual act in 1975 in the Soviet Union would have both embarrassed the State Department and possibly led to a scary fate for the American in question. Sexual acts between men had been illegal in the Soviet Union since 1936, and the ruling Communist Party remained staunchly anti-gay well into the 1980s.[90]

By 1966, when the State Department discussed "good behavior" with Ailey, the federal government had begun to make strides in more equal hiring practices. According to Johnson, the combination of "affirmative action toward racial minorities [and] liberalization of policies concerning heterosexual conduct" and the continued "hard-line toward homosexuals created a great deal of frustration."[91] Liberalizing race politics may have been a factor in the government letting Ailey off with a warning rather than a dismissal. Being black and leading a predominantly black company may have helped Ailey continue to receive government funds given State Department concerns about American race relations' effect on foreign policy. But being told to "walk the straight and narrow path" had higher stakes for the black Ailey and his predominantly black company than for a largely white arts organization. The NYCB and Graham dancers also remember State Department officials warning them to behave well on tour, and the NYCB sent one dancer home after he caused a drunken scene in a Moscow hotel lobby.[92] But what counted as acting out—looking suspicious—for dancers of color, and particularly gay dancers of color, was different than for white dancers.

The possible consequences of being black and not walking "the straight and narrow path" in 1967 became painfully apparent when Ailey briefly returned to the United States at the end of the company's European tour, before traveling to Africa. While dining with friends near Lincoln Center, Ailey was arrested by two policemen, who had mistaken him for a bearded black man who had murdered four policemen in Cincinnati. Ailey spent a night in jail and was beaten by police officers.[93] Ailey biographer Jennifer Dunning described the arrest's effects on Ailey, noting that it illustrated the "specter of imprisonment [that is] part of the racial unconscious of black men."[94] Ailey's arrest for "homosexual acts" in Milan only a month earlier must have made that specter all the more intense. Ailey rejoined his company in Athens, carrying a conscious reminder of the possible consequences of attracting suspicion and aware that no artistic engagement could overcome the real consequences of American racism, or the domestic and international consequences of homophobia.

Situating the State Department's request for Ailey to act appropriately within the context of 1960s homophobia and racism demonstrates how the department held Ailey more responsible for his actions than other artists the State Department employed. Ailey was an excellent representative of America in many ways. Reports from Africa and the Soviet Union praise his engagement with local dancers and audiences. After the 1970 Soviet tour, tour escort Joseph Pressel described Ailey as "going out of his way" to attend local dance rehearsals and sitting on the edge of the stage to greet audience members after shows.[95] On other tours, however, Ailey's struggles with drug abuse and bipolar disorder made him a difficult (and perhaps sad) figure with whom Foreign Service officers had to contend. An unsigned, handwritten letter to the State Department, apparently written by the USIA tour escort on the company's 1974 Eastern European tour, described Ailey as "an unhappy, moody, caustic, and solitary figure" whose "offstage leadership sets either negligible or negative" examples, even as the author described the company's "outstanding success" as a "very personal tribute to Ailey."[96] Ailey contributed to his problems on tour, but he also moved within a complicated web of institutionalized, social oppression.

Even in this difficult climate, Ailey managed to get the funding he wanted for his company. In late 1969, Ailey announced that the company did not have sufficient funds to pay the dancers, in DeFrantz's words, "cunningly" leveraging the State Department's recent choice of the Ailey company for a fall Soviet Union tour to obtain more government funding.[97] In response to the announcement, the State Department found the funding for several weeks of rehearsal and a North African tour, which kept the company together until its departure for the Soviet Union. The government's paternalism could not thwart Ailey from his goal to keep his company going.

Regulating *Masekela Langage*

Behind closed doors, however, the Dance Panel, with State Department support, repeatedly tried to regulate Ailey's performance of identity and critique, in both his personal identity and in his choreography. The most blatant examples come from discussions preceding the 1970 Soviet tour. The State Department expressed concern over Ailey's *Masekela Langage* because of its violent depictions of racism and Ailey's insistence that program notes frame the piece as a comparison between racism in the United States and in South Africa. Created to the music of South African trumpeter Hugh Masekela, *Masekela Langage* unfolds in a lower class road-side bar, where the dancers flirt, drink, and cavort. Their socializing is interrupted when a bloody, beaten man rushes into the bar and performs a heartbreaking solo. The group, previously splintered, coheres around the man and seems poised to retaliate against those who have beaten him (a group never seen onstage). The ballet has an open-ended feeling at the end: the man dies and at least one dancer steps over him as though the death will be ignored, but tension lingers and proliferates. Whether outrage over the violence will be the thing that initiates a black revolution seems to be the question at the work's end.

The dance panelists eventually agreed that the piece could travel, but wanted the program notes changed. Longtime panelist and dance critic Walter Terry sought ways to reframe the piece as race-blind modernist abstraction. He told Cultural Presentations administrator Beverley Gerstein that Ailey's description could be deleted because, while the piece looks like "a sultry South African town . . . it could be anywhere in the world." Another panelist, William Bales, said the reference to the US (the program note compared South Africa and Chicago's Southside neighborhood) seemed inconsequential. Bales suggested that Clive Barnes, an English critic who was thought to "know Russia" be consulted. Ultimately, Terry and Bales, two white men, agreed to excise Ailey's remark about *Masekela's* racial politics. Language highlighting race had to disappear, and the panel comfortably chose their politics over Ailey's.[98]

Similar arguments arose over program notes for Lester Horton's *The Beloved* (1948), which categorized the central character as "an unliberated female." Terry argued to Gerstein that the character is "nothing more than a high class servant," dismissing the gendered commentary. Terry suggested that instead of using the notes submitted by Ailey, Gerstein should find "old reviews from John Martin, Clive Barnes or himself to describe the work."[99] Terry wanted the words of three white, male dance critics instead. Terry continued, making a more damning point, noting changes in the program notes need not be discussed with Ailey. The memo recounts Terry's reasoning: "Since it [the program] will be in Russian, Ailey will never know."[100]

Through a logistical accident, Ailey did find about the program note changes, and he regained some control. The State Department sent the panel-approved program notes minus Ailey's South Africa–Chicago comparison to the Soviet cultural bureau, the Gostkoncert, for printing. The company arrived in the USSR to find the printed programs riddled with obvious errors: a photo of the Paul Taylor Dance Company in Taylor's *Three Epitaphs* was on the cover, and all the program notes had disappeared.

The program notes then became an issue, and so Ailey saw the State Department's notes with their English translations. Ailey judged the revised notes "inadequate." He also disliked Gostkoncert's description of the Ailey company as an "ethnic dance" company rather than, as Ailey preferred, a company versatile in "nearly all the modern styles of dance." Ailey wrote new program notes, which were never printed but were read as a pre-performance announcement in each city. There is no documentation of Ailey's script for these announcements, though given what he said in the *New York Times*, recounted earlier, it is likely that he wrote out any references to black culture and inserted the label "American" where he could, and potentially also wrote racial and gender politics about *Masekela* and *The Beloved* into the announcement as well.[101]

The controversy surrounding *Masekela* extended beyond the program notes. While the State Department implored Ailey to submit to their model of morality while on tour, USIA officials bristled when Ailey submitted to—even briefly—another authority. Mid-tour, Gostkoncert protested that *Masekela* and Paul Sanasardo's *Metallics* be removed from the repertory. Gostkoncert criticized the former for being "unintelligible" to Soviet audiences, and the latter as "too sexual."[102] Reports sent to the State Department during and after the tour describe the standoff over the programming as difficult because of what tour escort Joseph Pressel saw as Ailey's tendency to acquiesce to Soviet demands. From Moscow, Pressel wrote, "Alvin is too easy on the Soviets and lets himself be moved too easily by their objections, only a few of which have any basis in fact."[103] Once the Soviets began protesting the programming, Pressel again complained of Ailey's tendency to submit. Pressel wrote, "Curiously, one of the problems in resisting the Soviet importunings [sic] was Alvin Ailey's own desire to please. This caused him to be far less obstinate than one might have wished. To be sure as time went on Ailey became rather more willing to stand his ground."[104]

The 1970 tour was, like all the Ailey State Department tours, a great success, although the *Masekela* controversy continued after the company's return home. Ailey seemed interested in keeping the scandal and thus his work visible. As he did in 1969 when he got more State Department funding, he used the public stage (rather than being used by the State Department as a spectacle *for* the public). In the *New York Times* article quoted earlier, Ailey told Anna Kisselgoff about the Soviet objections to *Masekela* and *Metallics*:

Masekela is the most negative piece I've ever done. . . . It was certainly not the kind of positive image Soviet dance companies present in their own works abroad. . . . It's almost as if the Russians were concerned for us. If you're in a foreign country and you see all those tacky people in *Masekela*, you think that's America. It looked like contemporary America, a piece de genre, which in America, you know it does not. You know those are very down people, right? But when Russians see it, they say that's the way America looks today. But I told them I wanted them to see every aspect of what we do. Negative works as well as positive ones, to see the variety of styles our company could dance in.[105]

Just as he had done in the initial *Masekela* program notes, Ailey described the piece as a critique of a community he thinks will be recognizable as American. Ailey commented on the State Department's inclusion of such a negative depiction of the United States as a good thing. By including a range of opinions, the United States differentiated itself from "the kind of positive image Soviet dance companies present in their own works abroad."

The State Department felt differently, according to an internal memo circulated two days after the *Times* article appeared. The memo described *Masekela* as though Ailey did not understand its roots, marking it as a piece with potentially African, but not American roots. The 1970 memo goes beyond the Dance Panel's concern about the comparison of American racism and African racism, describing *Masekela* as a critique of "poverty, frustration and despair," traits described as having "universal application" but not necessarily representing American reality.[106] The memo also clarifies that the State Department did censor *Masekela*, forcing the removal of the final scene; everything violent was cut, including the dying man's solo, his death, and the ensemble's painfully ambivalent response: "Dept [*sic*] officers and the Department's Dance Panel auditioned the dance and did not feel that it depicted any relevance to the American scene, as long as the last sequence of the dance was dropped." The last scene posed a danger—connecting a representation of the United States to apathy and violence that probably came too close to images of urban race riots erupting across the United States at the time, and thus tossing off the necessary veneer of universality. A dance work could inch toward a political stance, but must always stop short of placing its politics in too specific of a place or time.

This rejection of a piece that publicly illustrated African American retaliation against oppression was not without precedent. As Constance Valis Hill has shown, Katherine Dunham, touring abroad without government support in the early fifties, faced similar censorship from government officials. Embassy officials, first in Santiago, Chile, and later in Paris, France, pointedly asked Dunham to remove her piece *Southland* (1950) from her company's program because it depicted a lynching—not the image of African American life the government wanted to promote—and ended with a black male dancer stabbing the stage with a knife. Embassy officials found the explicit violence of the hanging "intimidating," and the implicit violence of the final scene threatening.[107]

Even though the State Department took every opportunity to soften and censor Ailey's political critique offstage, it was Ailey's words and his choreography that received the most public attention, not the State Department's internal spin. In the end, as Ailey demonstrated in his interview with Kisselgoff, artists retained an impressive ability to conceptualize how they were a complicated force within the State Department programming.

CONCLUSION

According to Judith Jamison, perhaps the Ailey company's most famous dancer on tour (Lynne Taylor-Corbett remembers African audiences responding to Jamison "like she was an absolute queen"),[108] representing the United States abroad as an African American dancer meant reminding audiences that "African American culture *is* American culture . . . everything was influenced by us [African Americans] [emphasis added]." Jamison continued: "I think it's a terrible mistake when people don't understand that as African Americans our culture originated so many things that are considered to be from this country [the United States] and that when we go abroad we take what we have as black people."[109] Jamison, like Ailey before her, always described African American culture as having wide appeal and representing the United States very broadly. But this wide reach does not erase the important presence of African Americans as people, as modernist aesthetics often sought to do through the relegation of Africanist elements to the margins or background of cultural representation. Jamison placed African American performers at the active center of American culture. She noted that African Americans "originated" much of what came to be known abroad as American and argued that sending African American artists abroad corrects a "terrible mistake"—what she perceived as a widespread misconception that African Americans had not shaped American culture. Onstage and off, Jamison and other dancers were active, powerful African American figures with the ability to reshape American narratives about race. Listening to the historical record of the tours from the perspectives of African American dancers and, in some cases, dancers with minoritarian sexual identities tells a story not of cultural appropriation, but of self-determination.

CHAPTER 3

Too Sexy for Export or Just Sexy Enough?

Martha Graham Dance Company on Tour

In 1974, Secretary of State Henry Kissinger sent a memo to President Gerald Ford naming American modern dancer and choreographer Martha Graham the "grand lady of dance."[1] Kissinger conferred the title in recognition of Graham's prolific career—her company would soon mark its fiftieth anniversary—and of Graham's "contribution to international understanding," likely a reference to the Martha Graham Dance Company's (figure 3.1) many international tours on behalf of the State Department. Kissinger's staff wrote the memo to encourage Ford to invite Graham to the White House once she returned from her company's tour of Asia, one of the most sensitive tours in the then-twenty-year history of the State Department's Cultural Presentations Program. The Asia tour included performances in Saigon, the Vietnamese capital the United States would abandon seven months later.

The State Department and its advisory panels chose the Graham company for the tours, including the high-profile tours of Asia in 1955 and 1974, for many reasons. The Graham company was foundational to American modern dance, and Graham herself was an American icon. Whereas many of the State Department engagements helped young choreographers rise in public stature, Graham already had national prominence when the department began funding the dance tours in 1954. By 1974, when the State Department sent Graham to war-torn Saigon,

Figure 3.1
The Martha Graham Dance Company in 1974, still dressed in their costumes, meet the king of Thailand, Bhumibol Adulyadej, after a performance of Graham's *Appalachian Spring*.
Source: Courtesy of Special Collections, University of Arkansas.

no American dance company rivaled her longevity in the arts nationally. Even before her first State Department tour in 1955, the American government prized Graham, the woman and the company, as a symbol of American art, especially when the company represented the United States abroad.

The decades-long relationship, however, did have its contentious moments, which might be best summed up in a *Life* magazine headline that ran in 1963: "Is Martha Too Sexy for Export?"[2] The "Martha" in question was Martha Graham and the headline referenced a congressional controversy over the company's performances of Graham's *Phaedra* (1962) on a State Department-sponsored bill in Germany a year earlier. When the cultural diplomacy programs came up for funding review in Congress in 1963, the State Department's support of *Phaedra*, with its frank depictions of female desire and sexual acts, and its barely clad male dancers, ignited a controversy inflamed by prolific coverage in the national media.

The concern over *Phaedra* demonstrated that Congress knew little about Graham's repertory, but rather only knew Graham's name. Graham's work, particularly the mid-century repertory most often included on

State Department tours, overflows with desirous women, performances of sexuality, and bare-chested men. *Night Journey* (1947), *Cave of the Heart* (1946), and *Appalachian Spring* (1944), among other works, center on a female protagonist and her battle with desire. The staging and embodiment of female desire in much of Graham's repertory allows women to gain attention, gain space, and, even if they are eventually punished, to get what they want. The women, often Graham herself, who originally danced these powerful female roles, rocket across stage spaces driven by their pelvises. They express themselves freely, even if they are not free to survive that expression. (The narratives of the Graham choreographies often punish these women—both Phaedra and Jocasta, *Night Journey*'s lead woman, die as punishment for their elicit desires.)

It is not so shocking that a 1963 Congress would protest the inclusion on the State Department tours of works that were (for the time) sexually explicit. It is shocking that both the ANTA Dance Panel and the State Department permitted *Phaedra*'s inclusion in the first place and for three decades allowed Graham's depictions of sexuality to tour. Too, the support for Graham continued after the debate about *Phaedra*. In 1963, the State Department replaced the privately-run ANTA selection panel with the State Department's Advisory Dance Panel and that group, too, supported Graham unanimously.

This chapter argues that Graham's long relationship with the State Department grew from her unrivaled stature in the modern dance world and from her work's relationship to a paradoxical conception of exporting "American freedom." Graham's staged depictions of sexual desire allowed the United States to demonstrate that it did not censor its art, as did the Soviets. Graham's choreography presented just enough scandal: it was not *too sexy* for export, as *Life* posited, but was *just sexy enough*. In this chapter, I examine what allowed Graham to dance along this fine line while challenging cultural norms at the same time. As a white woman, she could stage a dance modernism that equated whiteness, universality, and American freedom, while still playing with sexual and gender norms in a way not permitted for her black female peers. Graham used the body to blur gender boundaries, commenting on cultural restrictions surrounding gender (even as she benefited from other cultural norms), taking what I term a "diva stance," an explicitly corporeal, public challenge to normative notions of gender and sexuality.

Graham dancers' roles in challenging and reimagining conceptions of freedom surface most clearly on the company's 1974 tour. The tour began after the peace treaties that supposedly ended the war had been signed and while the American military still maintained a presence in

Vietnam—a period of violent "not war" following a war long denied and then protested. Though the United States' association of itself with freedom had always been rife with contradiction—as the dancers of color in the Ailey company, among others, experienced—by the 1970s, no one could deny that the link between the United States' ideals and its practices was in question.

The Graham company members danced amid the 1970s shift in American foreign policy—and the ongoing questioning of how the United States used its military and economic power around the world. As dancer Peter Sparling described the tour, considering it within the context of his life and of US history, he said, "Well, I had just cut my ponytail off."[3] Sparling was still a young American dancer, but he no longer physically embodied the image of American 1960s counterculture—the man with the ponytail at political protests. There was sense of slight deflation in Sparling's comment—a sense of having lost faith that the American government listened to its critical citizens. This sense of flagging faith echoed through the young Graham dancers and catalyzed a different attitude about what it meant to represent the American government for the dancers on the 1974 tour in comparision to what dancers from earlier tours expressed as their feelings about representing the United States. These interviews with the Graham dancers are foundational to this chapter's second half.

Dancing as the Vietnam War still simmered, and dancing *in* Vietnam, the Graham dancers reckoned with themselves as extensions of the US nation-state. They had to acknowledge the reality that the nation they represented exported not only democracy but also war, and they knew that ideals like "freedom" were often more theory than practice. In all my interviews with Graham dancers, they told stories of how they managed these visible, often palpable contradictions, charting how an American ideal—freedom—shifts over time and how artists manipulated and managed these shifting notions.

AMERICAN FREEDOM?

In his 1953 inaugural address, President Dwight Eisenhower championed "freedom" as the United States' great Cold War weapon.[4] Ideas about which political system, democracy or communism, fostered freedom structured much of the discourse around the State Department cultural programs. When members of Congress began attacking Graham in the 1963 committee hearing, the first witness to defend her, Hyman Faine, a longtime

Dance Panel member, immediately noted that censorship was something "the Russians did."[5] For the rest of the hearing, which was ostensibly about funding levels for cultural diplomacy but that became a debate over portrayals of sexuality in Graham's work, everyone involved furiously backpedaled to avoid even hinting that they advocated censorship, a practice imagined as incompatible with American freedom.

Presenting a national attitude that embraced free artistic expression had been central to policy since the 1950s, a position that often pitted congressional conservatives against other policymakers. As discussed in chapter 2, when members of Congress had attempted to have paintings by artists with leftist affiliations removed from the USIA-sponsored 1959 Moscow Exhibition, President Eisenhower had to step in to save the paintings, since the removal of the paintings would have revealed censorship to be supported by the United States—a revelation more damaging internationally than the domestic controversy over the artists' political leanings would have been.[6] Even though the USIA only considered censoring the exhibit, the Soviet press still seized on the controversy as evidence that "once again the true worth of the fable about 'freedom' of artistic endeavor in the US" had been unveiled as empty rhetoric.[7]

Martha Graham's best-known mid-century works, *American Document* (1938) and *Appalachian Spring* among them, celebrated American freedom (or at least were perceived as unabashedly celebrating freedom), which helped place Graham on the federal government's radar. *American Document* coupled dance with excerpts from great texts in American history, including the Gettysburg Address and the Emancipation Proclamation. Graham initially paired the texts with dance in a critique of the United States. By the early 1940s, Graham had transformed *American Document* into a superficial celebration of American freedom, aligning freedom with patriotism—a strategic move as the United States entered WWII and American modern dance moved away from its earlier leftist politics.[8] Themes of frontier and freedom animated Graham's *Appalachian Spring*, too, a work that had attracted the government's attention long before the State Department programs were initiated. The Library of Congress commissioned *Appalachian Spring*, both the ballet and the Aaron Copland score, and the Office of War Information made copious notes about the work, though no record exists of a plan to act on the information that was gathered.[9]

The phenomenal success and reach of Graham's work in the thirties and forties meant that when the ANTA Dance Panel first met in 1954, the members assumed the Graham company's artistic value. The panel nominated Graham as its first choice for a State Department tour. (State Department officials, not the Dance Panel, had selected the José Limón company for the 1954 tour before the panel began meeting.) In making the decision to recommend Graham (the panel recommended the artists, while the State Department chose the tour destinations), the panel so enthusiastically supported Graham that there was little discussion of *why* the Graham company should be chosen. The panel's primary point in discussions of Graham can be summarized in one sentence from May 1955 meeting minutes: "Martha Graham is a symbol, even to people who have never seen her."[10] The panel assumed Graham's international value.

Graham ascended in the government's evaluation, too, because unlike Limón, her most frequent competitor for early State Department support, she could claim the United States as her familial home. Memos from American embassy staff express concern that Limón's immigrant background—he had immigrated to the United States from Mexico at the age of eight—made him less billable as purely American.[11] Graham, on the other hand, made much of her American roots, even claiming to be a descendant of Myles Standish, and thus tying herself to two centuries of American history.[12]

With Graham's work framed as the ultimate American symbol of freedom and her personal biography soundly rooted in American soil, the next question is how Graham became so intimately tied to cultural diplomacy for so many decades. Graham became synonymous with both "American" and "universal," categories assumed to be one and the same in Cold War foreign policy.[13] American modern dance, largely because of the writing of John Martin, had become an art form on its own merits (rather than as only complement to music or theater) through the assertion it was uniquely universal in its communicative abilities[14] According to Martin, modern dance had American roots but could be universally understood. Dance's reliance on physicality, rather than written or spoken language, Martin argued, tapped a "single underlying reality."[15] In watching and experiencing live dance, Martin imagined that all could access the same emotional well, regardless of personal background. Martin anointed Graham as an exemplar of dance's universalizing communication, and Graham shared his belief in dance's potential. Reflecting on her 1955 Asia tour, Graham said, "I am not interested whether they [the foreign audiences] understand or not. I am only interested if they feel it. And it's on that basis that I've tried to reveal—through women, through whatever means I had available—the quickening of people's sensitivity."[16] Graham imagined she could reach any audience, and so did those who selected her for international tours.

Imagining that audiences of all kinds would understand Graham's choreography, however, required ignoring the cultural specificity of spectatorship. The modernist formula of considering all (or most) elements of a dance work as abstract also denied cultural specificity in artistic choices. Universalist rhetoric about dance and modernism, as discussed in chapter 2, bolstered the prominence of whiteness. Writing about race and cultural diplomacy, dance historian Susan Manning has described the companies chosen for the tours as exhibiting "mythic abstraction . . . stag[ing] universal subjects without the mediation of bodies marked as cultural other."[17] Mythic abstraction gave Graham wide-ranging power as a white female choreographer in the context of State Department tours. Examining how the repertory of the Graham company fits the category of "mythic abstraction" opens a path to consider how race and gender intersected on the tours, why race rather than gender has been foregrounded in American cultural diplomacy history, and finally, how Graham's status as a white woman facilitated her role on the tours. Indeed, for three decades, Graham was the only female choreographer to frequently receive State Department support. The US publicly marketed artistic freedom as its key export, but selectively chose who could represent that freedom.

As a white woman, Graham had particular access to staging "freedom." Both Manning and historian Ellen Graff have discussed Graham's strategy for creating a universal American subject: placing a white female body against a literal or figurative backdrop of multi-racial performers. In *American Document*, one white female body, or a group of white female bodies, signified American identity as a composite of all racial, ethnic, and gender identities. An abstract mise en scène offered little suggestion of a specific location or time, a choreographic dislocation that made the work's textual references to specific events in American history mere frames.[18] For instance, in "Emancipation Episode," text read during performances of the piece from 1938 to 1940 referenced violence toward African Americans, including the wrongfully convicted Alabama teens known as the Scottsboro Boys. As audiences heard the text, they saw a group of white women leaning with their torsos and flying through the air with abandon. The text pointed to specific atrocities in African American history, but the choreography translated those events into physical emancipation for white female bodies.[19] When Graham cut the text from versions of the piece performed after 1940, "mythic abstraction" was complete: the racial violence disappeared leaving only white women dancing. Graff describes this process as not just about white, female bodies erasing the presence of African Americans, but as choreographing the white female body as the "universal American body, traversing the limits of time, space, and race . . . [capable] of subsuming every other identity."[20] Whiteness facilitated Graham's entrance onto the national stage and her ability to stage the nation.

Graff's and Manning's arguments raise questions about how the tour selection panels considered gender and race. Why was the Graham company the only female-led group to be consistently funded? Of the fourteen single-choreographer companies on the Dance Panel's "approved" roster in 1963, the year Graham faced congressional scrutiny, only four had female leaders, and one of those four, the African American choreographer Katherine Dunham, has been approved "with reservations."[21]

Historians have paid less attention to how gender, as opposed to race, affected the State Department tours because racial politics had a much more explicit impact on the tours—shaping who went on them, where the tours went, and what the government hoped the tours would accomplish. Many music tours featured African American performers, especially jazz and gospel musicians, as historian Penny Von Eschen has shown. Dance tours, too, frequently included predominantly African American companies. Von Eschen has argued that black jazz performers offered the State Department a chance to publicly embrace African American culture and to claim modernist jazz as an example of American innovation and individualism.[22] A similar project unfolded on the dance tours, as discussed in chapter 2, as black artists maintained a careful calibration between modernist aesthetics and African American culture.

The Graham company's commitment to racial integration benefited it in the artist selection process. Although led by a white woman, the company presented an image of racial inclusion. On every major Graham company State Department tour, Asian American, African American, and Latina/o dancers, performed in the ensemble and in soloist roles. On the 1974 tour, when the eighty-three-year-old Graham was no longer dancing, the Japanese-born dancers Takako Asakawa and Yuriko Kimura danced most of her major roles. On the 1974 tour, too, the company also featured African American dancers, including Shelley Washington, Carl Paris, and Daniel Maloney. Graham became so well known for having a racially integrated company that the New York Times highlighted the fact in her obituary.[23]

The Dance Panel frequently discussed the value of selecting racially integrated troupes, though no record exists of panelists making this argument about Graham. There are, however, conversations about Graham's interest in borrowing Asian aesthetics (which from a contemporary vantage point might be labeled as "appropriation"), as reason to send her company abroad. When the panel first voiced its support for Graham in 1955, they unanimously suggested her for "the Orient."[24] Graham displayed her interest in Asian cultural forms through her heightened choreographic theatricality and use of formalism as a means to express emotion, but also in what bordered on a fetishization of Asia: on the 1974 tour she traveled with an ornate Chinese chair, which the company hauled to every tour destination and which Graham sat in when she introduced performances. The white female body again appeared surrounded by markers of racialized "others," and then that consumption was taken as evidence of American openness.

Though race—in all kinds of ways—was discussed around tour selection and logistics, gender did impact the tours. As Von Eschen notes, when the mostly male musicians traveling on the jazz tours behaved in a manner the State Department found unseemly, officials excused them as "eccentric" artists; when female musicians engaged in similar behavior, they were deemed "unstable."[25] Less can be said, however, about the different treatment of men and women on the jazz tours because men so dominated the mid-century jazz world.

The dance tours developed differently: almost every company that toured had either equal gender representation or more women than men. ANTA panel meeting minutes from the first twelve years of State Department support for dance—the period when Graham emerged as the primary modern dance artist recommended for tours—reveal two trends related to gender. The first emerges in how the panel discussed female choreographers, and the second tells a complicated story about the intersection of race, gender, and national identity.

The panel discussed female-led companies and female solo artists as often as they discussed male choreographers. Panel minutes describe many women as good performers but incapable of maintaining larger, evening-length performances. The panel expressed this fear about the African American ballerina Janet Collins and, occasionally, about the former Graham dancer Pearl Lang. Many female choreographers also failed the universal accessibility test. The panel eventually rejected Lang because it felt that her repertory did not focus on "traditional American themes."[26] The ANTA panel worried that several choreographers whose work it saw as satirical—Myra Kinch, Mata and Hari, and Valerie Ladd—would confuse foreign audiences.[27] Similarly, the panel rejected Anna Sokolow because her work was "good" but "would escape foreign audiences."[28]

Other issues that arose around female choreographers were structural: discussions framed women as teachers, not leaders, and noted that female-led companies lacked sufficient financial support. The panel often recommended these women for the Leaders and Specialists program, a State Department program that sent individual artists abroad to teach rather than perform.[29] In twelve years of panel minutes, the panel never recommended that a man be referred to Leaders and Specialists.

After Graham, the panel's next-most-discussed female choreographer was Agnes de Mille, who did not have a company sustainable enough to tour (and, in some moments, had no company at all). The panel thought de Mille should create a dance company based in American folk-dance techniques, such as square dancing, which the United States could then send to the Soviet Union as an answer to the popular Moiseyev Dance Company, with its virtuosic versions of "folk" dances.[30] Despite the panel's feeling that de Mille was perfect for such a troupe, de Mille, like many of the women considered, never had enough financial support to keep a company together. Graham, unlike de Mille, had intense support from friends and patrons, including from panelists, such as the arts education leader Martha Hill, dance critic Walter Terry, and patron Bethsabée Rothschild. Private support translated into public support.

While many factors contributed to the panel's overwhelming support for Graham, race mattered in a way that had everything to do with gender and sexuality. As a white woman working within a modernist, universalist aesthetic, Graham had greater latitude to present female sexuality. Graham's mid-century works, the pieces derived from Greek myths that formed the company's State Department tour repertory, centered on female protagonists who expressed their power and desire through pelvic contractions and onstage depictions of sexual encounters. As dance theorist Ramsay Burt has written, Graham had "unprecedented autonomy as a cultural producer and was thus able to articulate a feminine point of view that was unconceivable . . . in other fields" at the time.[31] The panelists expressed concern about other choreographers' sexual content, particularly Katherine Dunham's, but such concern never surfaced about Graham. Even after the congressional controversy surrounding *Phaedra*, the panel strongly supported Graham. In a September 1963 panel meeting, when the panelists worried about how to assess dance works containing sexuality explicit material, Walter Terry described Graham's *Phaedra* as exemplary because "the so-called 'eroticism' had a point."[32] To tell a story—a story the panel imagined would be accessible to all because of its "universal" themes and safe framing within classical Greek myths—with and through "eroticism" was acceptable when Graham did it.

The government gave less latitude to African American Katherine Dunham's performance of female sexuality because it emerged from a black modernity borne of cultural fusion rather than race-blind universalism.

In Dunham's estimation,[33] the State Department did not offer Dunham funding because of her earlier refusal to bend to State Department admonishments to stop performing her piece *Southland* abroad—a work that explored interracial tension and violence, as discussed in chapter 2.[34] Panel minutes, however, make no mention of *Southland*. Instead, when the panel denied Dunham approval in 1958, minutes described Dunham's work at the time as "too theatrical," seemingly referencing work done outside the "highbrow" dance world and less worthy of support than earlier work that the panel considered more serious.[35] Foregrounding sexuality proved to be a particular liability for Dunham in the late 1950s, especially after the publicity materials for a privately funded international tour featured a coy, provocative Dunham.[36] Letters between ANTA president Robert Schnitzer and Dunham describe an overt, cruel dismissal of her as too interested in what was seen as too sexy—mere entertainment—and thus unworthy of support.[37]

The ANTA Dance Panel did take Dunham seriously (more so than Schnitzer did) but even when these cultural gatekeepers found Dunham's work acceptable, they considered it suitable only for certain audiences. Graham had the panel's unconditional support and, they said, could tour anywhere. Panel minutes in 1958 report, "The Panel is favorable to anything that Martha Graham can do and hopes she can be helped in some way."[38] In 1960, the panel augmented a vote to select a group for the USSR (they chose Graham) noting that if the Graham company could not go to "Russia," then she would be well suited to tour anywhere else in the world.[39] Panel minutes from the same period document positive commentary about Dunham and her fellow African American choreographer and anthropologist Pearl Primus,[40] but the panel only seriously considered the two women for African tours. Even when the panel approved Dunham in 1961, it stipulated that the approval was only for Africa. Since the State Department had already slated a company for an African tour that year, the panel decided to exclude Dunham and Primus from their recommendations.[41] The one "black artist" slot was taken.

The panel imagined greater possibility for Graham's body and what she could do with it than they could for African American artists. When State Department representative Glenn Wolfe visited the panel in 1963 to cite concerns that the still-dancing, seventy-two-year-old Graham gave mediocre "personal performances" on the 1962 tour, the panel rebuffed him. They responded that Graham's recent "emphasis . . . of her role has been toward acting, rather than dancing."[42] In the same meeting, the panel again recommended Graham for a Soviet tour. Primus was not treated with the same equanimity. The panel twice blocked her from touring for physical reasons. In 1955 and 1961, the panel minutes described Primus as "about thirty pounds overweight" and as having a "weight problem," though on the latter occasion the minutes note that Primus remained "capable of doing her dancing."[43] In 1955, the assessment of Primus's body contributed to her company's rejection; and in 1961, to her company being approved "with reservations." While the minutes mention no explicit tie between the assessments and race, it is impossible to ignore that, while dancers and the dance community do discuss people's bodies in ways not often done in other fields, no other mention of any person's weight is made in more than twenty years of declassified panel minutes. Primus never toured with her company with State Department support.

The comments about Primus and Dunham suggest that being a woman of color made winning State Department support difficult. A series of 1964 memos record that State Department officials polled the Dance Panel members about Dunham for the Leaders and Specialists program. These memos contain coded racialized language, describing Dunham as "hard to handle" and having a "difficult personality."[44] Walter Terry, Graham's biggest supporter, was at first supportive of Dunham then changed his mind because he found Dunham's work depicted "the Negro" as "different" from other Americans, and that was not in keeping with the program's goals.[45] Again Dunham paid a price for working outside modernist universalism. Dunham eventually received State Department support, but only after Senegalese president Léopold Senghor invited her to Senegal to open a dance school prior to the First World Festival of Negro Arts in 1966. Eventually, Dunham and the 1966 festival received State Department support, possibly because the philosophy of Negritude that guided the festival organizers recognized African diasporic experience as "different" from other American experiences, and thus Dunham's black modernity fit within the festival better than it did broader American cultural diplomacy. Claiming one's difference, though, was not an option equally available to all.

REPRESENTING GENDER IN POLICY AND PERFORMANCE

The ANTA Dance Panel's sustained recognition of Graham as an extraordinary national symbol put all things Graham—the woman, the company, the technique, and the choreography—into national and international circulation in performance and political realms. As such an exceptional female figure, a status derived in part from the State Department's support of her work, Graham moved within a discursive landscape of Cold

War–era female stereotypes. While many American gender stereotypes circulated in the 1950s and 1960s, three types overlapped the fields of foreign policy and cultural performance—in live venues and increasingly on television and film screens. These were woman as domestic safekeeper, woman as benevolent pedagogue, and man as virile masculine warrior. These frames, as well as how Graham remixed and provocatively exceeded them through embodiment, are important precursors to the 1963 congressional controversy about Graham's work.

The first of the Cold War female stereotypes common to both performance and politics positioned women as guardians of domestic spaces and nuclear families. Many women returned to the home after holding jobs during WWII. As historian Elaine May has argued, these women became guardians of the homefront, bringing containment from the public sphere into the private.[46] Versions of this woman proliferated on television: think of Barbara Billingsley's portrayal of June Cleaver in the CBS (then ABC) show Leave It to Beaver, which ran from 1957 to 1963. The show confined June, always the mother and wife, to domestic spaces, but also positioned her as the person who made the home welcoming for all. This is the female figure government brochures instructed on how to keep the home safe for families during the Cold War, helping build the rhetorical juncture that conflated healthy families and a safe nation.[47]

The second Cold War female role that crossed performance and politics positioned women as pedagogues who instructed racialized "others." Writing about American interventions in Japan post–World War II, feminist scholar Mire Koikari argues that the United States enacted what she calls a "pedagogy of democracy," placing American women abroad and imagining they would teach foreign publics, often foreign women, to fight for freedom and equality. Yet these women were to teach others, not be students of other cultures themselves.[48] Embodied in the caring female teacher, US imperialism looked benevolent—the more evolved foil to European colonialism. The figure of woman as guide to democracy was a fixture in mid-century American musicals, books, and films.[49] For instance, in the 1951 Rodgers and Hammerstein musical The King and I and the 1956 film of the same name, the white teacher Anna teaches the Thai royal court Western ways, including how to speak, how to dance, and how to love—all actions configured, as Christine Klein has noted, as sentimentalized routes to Western-style democracy.[50] The conception of women as teachers to foreign publics shaped State Department programming, explicitly and implicitly, as is especially evident in the large numbers of women recommended for the Leaders and Specialists program.

Of these first two types, domestic guardian and international peda-gogue, Graham does not resemble the former, but she does fit the latter to some degree. Her works that most explicitly address marriage, such as *Appalachian Spring*, suggest a woman's ambivalence about marriage and domesticity.[51] Although *Appalachian Spring* has often been interpreted as joyous by critics overly focused on the energetic Copland score, cho-reographically, the piece centers on the bride's anxiety, even fear. Other Graham women, such as Phaedra and Jocasta, so tortured by their famil-ial roles, make the domestic space a monstrous one. These are choreog-raphies of marriage and motherhood as unsafe for women's well-being and desires. Graham does, however, overlap with the female teacher type, particularly given the global spread of her dance technique through Asia, Mexico, and the Middle East. On the 1974 Asia tour, the Graham company members frequently met local dancers who had trained at the Graham school and then returned home to teach Graham technique.

The third gendered type familiar in Cold War foreign policy and cul-tural performance—and the type with the greatest overlap with Graham's female protagonists—is not associated with women, but with men: the strong, white, heterosexual man who conquers the world through his sexual virility.[52] Foreign policy's most explicit and often-cited example of the entanglement of male sexual virility, fear of homosexuality, and American global power is George Kennan's 1946 "Long Telegram," the document that outlined post-World War II American policy toward the Soviet Union. Kennan named groups in the United States, labor unions and student groups among others, as weak because they were vulnera-ble to Communist "penetration."[53] To be strong in a Cold War standoff, a nation must resist being penetrated, a position deemed weak and passive, and be instead the active (male) protagonist. In terms of cultural produc-tion, this masculine figure proliferated in movies and on television shows centered on espionage. The British spy—and American craze—James Bond, was the iconic Cold War man: able to travel, battle Communism, and bag babes.[54]

Graham created female protagonists with a sexual virility primarily seen in both foreign policy and performance arenas only on male bodies. These women were sexual agents and sexual partners. They simulated sex-ual acts onstage, sometimes controlling the encounter and taking pleasure in it. For instance, Graham's *Night Journey* features Jocasta actively seduc-ing her son, Oedipus; *Phaedra* follows a similar narrative of a woman who is mobile and sexually desirous. Dance theorist Mark Franko has argued that myth, Graham's primary dramaturgical frame mid-century, offered a "means to navigate between issues of feminine identity and male-identified power."[55] By taking on powerful, sexually desirous roles and focusing on the female characters in myths, as in *Night Journey* and *Phaedra*, Graham and her dancers brought previously exclusively masculine power and feminine power together in a single body—a single female body.

In addition to choreographing sexual desire to merge masculine norms and the female body onstage, Graham often enacted similar strategies in her offstage persona, speaking about sex in public as a physical, visceral act. For instance, after the 1963 *Phaedra* controversy, Graham chastised Congressman Peter Frelinghuysen, one of her key detractors, teasing him for imagining so many dancers on the set's bed: "There is only one couch in *Phaedra*. It is very small; it is tilted. I have to hang on to it to stay there and if Mr. Frelinghuysen thinks it's possible to have a lot of assignations on it, he's a better person than I am." Walter Terry, who reported the story, later described Graham's comment in even more lascivious tones, saying that Graham had also said that "if the Congressman thought that anything of an amorous nature could be accomplished on it [the bench/bed], he was welcome to try it out."[56] Graham publicly joked about her own sexual knowledge, as well as a congressman's, and she did so with an explicit reference to the body—having to "hang on"—inviting readers to imagine herself, the Congressman, and perhaps even themselves on the bench.

NAVIGATING AND RESISTING COLD WAR GENDER NORMS THROUGH THE BODY

Graham transgressed gender boundaries with dancing bodies and public commentary focused on the body, putting masculine power onstage under the control of women's bodies. I call this corporeal remixing of gender codes a "diva stance," to describe how Graham deployed physical action to "disorder" gender, critiquing and re-imagining gender norms through the body.[57] Through the diva stance, Graham assembled a hybrid gender identity to perform an assertive female sexuality that borrowed from dominant modes of masculinity and denaturalized the typical feminine roles of the Cold War Woman.

Graham's strategic position is a diva "stance" because it is a gender transgression enacted verbally through appeals to the body and corporeally through dancing. Graham's choreography and the dancers' interpretation of that choreography highlight the body, not as an essentialized source of "true" knowledge, but as a mode through which people make meaning and challenge cultural norms. The body, then, is revealed as having "sedimented layers of signification," and the dancers use the body to call attention to and reorder those layers.[58]

Much performance work that is focused on the body and identity has (or tries to have) this effect, but Graham had a uniquely public stage to enact her diva stance because of the State Department's support. Feminist cultural theorist Lauren Berlant has described such national disruptions as "diva citizenship."[59] But unlike the African American women Berlant discusses, who faced great risk because of their double minoritarian status, whiteness made national and international stages available to Graham. Privilege, in part, brought Graham to national attention, but the corporeal skill that brought her to national attention also allowed her to critique gender norms.

Phaedra exemplifies Graham's choreography as diva stance. The work emphasizes the female body as a source of power, flipping the usual script of women as passive objects in the face of male control and desire. Phaedra uses her body to lead in a world in which women have desires and men are objects of desire. In *Phaedra*'s beginning sequence, the lead female dancer (in 1962, Graham) immediately uses her body to focus the audience on female desire. Phaedra lies on a bench-like structure at center stage. She writhes as tight contractions of her abdomen and pelvis fold her in half over and over again, a signature of Graham's movement vocabulary, and an action that transforms the stark modernist bench into a bed (figure 3.2).

Phaedra's body swallows her in ecstasy or perhaps grief. Her dancing brings the audience into her private chamber, and that chamber, her room, and her body overflow with tension and desire. As the next character, the goddess Aphrodite, emerges, the choreography's spatial dynamics further mark Phaedra's world as feminine. A Noguchi sculpture that appears to be a cocoon opens, revealing a pink interior with Aphrodite inside. The sculpture stretches out behind the dancer like a Georgia O'Keefe flower. With the body inside, the image also conjures a womb. It is only a few minutes into the piece, and the audience knows that *Phaedra* occurs in a woman's world where bodies, usually feminine forms in motion, offer the keys to interpretation.

The next character's introduction, the partial reveal of Phaedra's stepson Hippolytus's male body, helped make *Phaedra* the object of public debate in 1963. The audience meets Hippolytus as a male body, not a full man. Aphrodite opens one panel of a rectangular box, revealing only Hippolytus's pelvis, clad in the tiniest of briefs. From the audience's perspective, Hippolytus is introduced as an object of lust. As Phaedra draws closer, Hippolytus steps out of the box and begins to dance. But, whereas Phaedra extended her arms and legs to travel across the stage with great

Figure 3.2
Martha Graham in *Phaedra*, featuring set pieces designed by Isamu Noguchi.
Source: Photograph © 2014 Jack Mitchell.

mobility, Hippolytus moves little, passing through a series of statuesque poses. In this sequence, the usual scenario of objectification is reversed. The scene unfolds from the woman's perspective, publicizes her desire, and relies on her mobility. The man is fixed as the object of her gaze. From the vantage point of *Phaedra*'s script-flipping gender discourse, I turn to the 1963 congressional debate about Graham, offering Graham's successful navigation of governmental scrutiny as proof of the diva stance's powerful operations.

PHAEDRA: CONGRESSIONAL DEBATE, CENSORSHIP, SEXUALITY, AND FEMINISM

Graham's choreography and the controversy it caused makes explicit the gendered impulses behind Cold War policy debates. Who enacts gender norms and who is allowed the freedom to challenge those norms? Under what circumstances? The controversy around *Phaedra* demonstrated how much the United States needed publicly visible, challenging artworks to prove itself the home of "freedom," while also raising questions about freedom for whom. The congressional hearing at which *Phaedra* first drew criticism provides insight into what falls beyond the limits of acceptability—namely, male homosexuality—and in what scenario a strong, outspoken woman can (and cannot) be tolerated.

In September 1963, *Life* magazine, as mentioned earlier, ran a two-page spread with the provocative headline "Is Martha Too Sexy for Export?"[60] The article's photographs showed Graham in *Phaedra*'s title role and potentially offered Graham's critics ample reason to decry her work as being, indeed, too sexy for export. In one photograph, Graham as Phaedra grasps for Bertram Ross's (as Hippolytus) barely covered crotch. In the other (figure 3.3), she wrestles seductively with Ross. In both photographs, the dancers' bodies entangle in erotically charged choreography—made even more charged because neither photograph makes clear who wants whom. Is Ross moving Graham's hands away from his briefs or about to place them there? Are Graham's legs pushing Ross away, or does the press of her legs send him arching in ecstasy? Desire is all consuming in these photographs, and is equally available to the female dancer as it is to the male. Phaedra's desire is not entirely her own (the gods have cursed her), and not without cost (she ultimately kills herself), but desire is not danced as unwanted or illicit in *Phaedra*—a possibility made all more important since the choreography's plot is extremely hard to follow. Graham's choreography and dancing put female desire center stage and made it the primary door through which spectators enter the piece.

It was this performance of bold sexual desire that threw *Phaedra* into the national spotlight. By 1963, the Graham company could have easily assumed that it would enjoy government support for decades to come. A House of Representatives subcommittee hearing in September of that year cast doubt on that assumption.[61]

The congressional hearing covered many topics, with everyone—witnesses and government officials alike—insisting that the United States send its "best" artists on tour, implicitly equating "best" with an idealized, sanitized version of American culture. One of the most outspoken voices championing "the best" was Congresswoman Edna Kelly, a Democrat from Brooklyn known for her work on the recent Equal Pay Act. In the hearing, Kelly posed the question "What is the image of America abroad?" and then answered it herself by saying that the American image abroad should not just be "what we want, but the best."[62] Kelly raised the idea of "the best" to note where she saw standards lacking—namely, a 1962 Graham performance in Germany she "almost had to walk out on."[63]

Kelly explained that the Graham piece offended her because it presented the "seamier side of life." Peter Frelinghuysen, a Republican congressman from New Jersey, among others, agreed. He offered a performance

Figure 3.3
One of two photographs from Graham's *Phaedra* that appeared in *Life* magazine in 1963 under the headline "Is Martha Too Sexy for Export?," featuring Bertram Ross (*left*) as Hippolytus and Martha Graham (*right*) as Phaedra.
Source: Photograph © 2014 Jack Mitchell.

description as evidence of why he found *Phaedra* objectionable: "There was one act where there were a number of young men in loin cloths. Then they had some couches, which they reclined on with companions. Whether it was for recreation or relaxation—the import was quite clear."[64]

Frelinghuysen's comment carried a subtext of a perceived threat to Cold War gender norms: male homosexuality. *Phaedra*'s nearly nude all-male ensemble lounging together on a couch embodied the image of lascivious, passive masculinity denounced by Kennan in the "Long Telegram." Frelinghuysen's words, however, were more a revelation of anxiety over what *could* happen among such men than what *did* happen, since what he described does not actually happen in *Phaedra*. The cast's men never join one another on the bench (and Graham technique never asks dancers to appear weak onstage).[65] The only people ever together on the bench are Phaedra and Hippolytus, the male and female dancers (Graham and Ross) in the *Life* photographs. Frelinghuysen's description omitted all the women from the scene, brought the male cast members into the same frame, and draped them dangerously on the couch, and on one another. The inaccuracy stemmed, in part, from the passage of time and eyes untrained in performance analysis. It was also, however, indicative of the fear and anxiety that drove the Lavender Scare in the 1950s and 1960s (see chapter 2) when even a rumor of homosexuality could mark a government employee as gay and thus supposedly susceptible to blackmail by Communists.

Frelinghuysen's focus only on potential homosexual encounters was even more remarkable since the *Phaedra* set and choreography revolve around heterosexual sex. Hippolytus and Phaedra luxuriate in their desire to consummate their relationship, writhing and groping one another. Noguchi designed set pieces that somewhat realistically represent female and male genitalia: the soft, pink, vaginaesque structure that opens and closes around Aphrodite, and the slim, tall, phallic box from which Hippolytus emerges.

The intensity of the all-male community represented by the male ensemble (which is what Graham initially meant Phaedra to be about[66]) and men touching one another, however, overwhelmed *Phaedra*'s heterosexual representations. As American studies scholar Andrea Friedman has argued, "masculine autonomy" was a requirement for "loyalty to the nation" during the Cold War.[67] Men touching was suspect behavior; so worrisome that the Los Angeles City Council had years earlier briefly considered outlawing all public physical contact between men.[68] These fears circulated constantly in Washington: a 1954 photograph of Senator Joseph McCarthy and aide Roy Cohn talking so closely their cheeks touched provided ample fodder for gossip about McCarthy's sexuality.

Homophobia was institutionalized, too, particularly among diplomats and in the State Department. Since the late 1940s, thousands of federal employees suspected of being gay had been fired, with the largest number of dismissals happening in the State Department.[69] The federal government's most public sexual inquisitions ended before the 1963 hearing, but institutional barriers to homosexuals' participation in diplomacy remained. The homophobia so present at the State Department had intense ramifications for some of the gay men involved in State Department's dance program, as detailed in chapter 2.[70]

In pointing out *Phaedra*'s challenge to a hegemonic version of American masculinity, Frelinghuysen placed himself in a double bind. A man could not ignore the latent homoeroticism being exported by the state once it had been aired so publicly, but naming homosexuality was also risky. Social fears of homosexuality, explicitly linked to male-male touching, required Frelinghuysen to subsequently distance himself from the all-male moment. In letters to New York and New Jersey newspapers days after the hearing, Frelinghuysen clarified that his comment about young men in loincloths was about the men "leaping frequently onto couches with young women," writing women and heterosexuality back into the earlier statement.[71] Once Frelinghuysen needed a woman to confirm the existence of heterosexuality, he put female characters back into the scene. In this case, sexually desirous women were convenient for the nation, or at least for its representative Freylinghusen.

Some scenes depicting sexual desire—when they were the "right" presentations—served cultural diplomacy by offering evidence of Americans' freedom. Within a Cold War context, censorship was characteristic of Soviet Communism, not American values. In response to Kelly and Frelinghuysen calling Graham's choreography too "erotic," hearing witness Hyman Faine, a union official and a member of the Dance Panels over many years, noted that "the Russians," not the United States, would censor eroticism. An editorial in the *Washington Star* responding to the hearing summarized the ideal American position on censorship: "As for censorship, it is enough to recall that part of the point of our cultural exchange program is to show American artistic freedom as against the artistic restraint of Communism."[72] For the United States to use cultural diplomacy as evidence of American superiority over the Soviets, the programs had to be seen as free of censorship. Frelinghuysen knew that the United States could not be associated with censorship and also be the bastion of freedom to the world. Days after the hearing he attempted another semantic sidestep, saying that he had not been advocating for "government censorship, but . . . [was] suggest[ing] reasonable guidelines in a sensitive area."[73]

Whether Frelinghuysen described his position as "censorship" or "reasonable guidelines," his and Kelly's comments wielded censorship's discursive effect. As art historian Richard Meyer has noted, a call for censorship always operates within a central contradiction: "reproduc[ing] and distribut[ing] the allegedly 'indecent' images it seeks to suppress."[74] Coverage of Frelinghuysen and Kelly's comments, Graham's responses, and scores of published editorials in newspapers and magazines kept the hearing and Graham's work on the national radar for months post-hearing.

Frelinghuysen could not stop talking about *Phaedra*'s men, but the press fixated on the women. This was a Cold War catfight. A *Washington Star* editorial dramatically began: "There were three women: Phaedra, Graham, and Edna Kelly."[75] The editorial went on to say that Phaedra can no longer get an apology, Graham "needs no defense," and Kelly "needs to be schooled."[76] A *Chicago Tribune* article similarly wrote Frelinghuysen out of the controversy in its description of the scene as "the silliest bit of nonsense to come out of Washington in this . . . Congress."[77] Each woman played a particular role in press descriptions of the "silliness." First, Phaedra, like many of Graham's central female roles, was a seductress, a woman acting out her sexual desires. Some articles injected this description with negative connotations, but then deemed Phaedra's lasciviousness acceptable, since Graham's narrative sufficiently punished her for her desires (Phaedra commits suicide).[78] Many articles reiterated the need to punish overly sexual women, notably, John Chamberlain's syndicated column celebrating Graham but damning the fictional Phaedra, which ran in at least thirty-six newspapers nationwide.[79] In this line of argument, audiences could excuse Graham's diva stance because, in the end, the overly sexual women die in her works. A woman can take a diva stance to challenge hegemony, but ultimately, knowing the challenge failed made it palatable.

Graham's choice to kill Phaedra at the end of the work coupled with her celebrity separated her, even though she danced the title role, from the character. Graham largely escaped public ire in the newspaper coverage. She was, as the *Chicago Tribune* said, an "institution."[80]

Kelly does not fit easily into this public drama, or into Cold War femininity, and she, like Phaedra, provoked a public desire to see a woman punished. Unlike Frelinghuysen, Kelly made no public statements after the hearing. Her only recorded response was a short telegram sent to Graham, in which she apologized for misstating the location of the German performance and said that she—Kelly—had the "right to object to any part of a performance sent abroad at taxpayers' expense which in my estimation does not represent the culture of these United States."[81] Kelly positioned herself as the nation's moral arbiter, something like the domestic guardian June Cleaver type. The main difference—and an important difference— between Kelly and the stereotypical domestic guardian is that, as a member of Congress, Kelly spoke far beyond the domestic, private sphere. The press coverage argued that in this public arena Kelly did not have the tools to judge how to protect the United States. Newspapers charged her with incompetence, saying she should be "schooled" and that *Phaedra* offended her only "as a lady." The *Life* article described Kelly as a "widowed grandmother" and questioned her education and judgment. When writers mentioned Frelinghuysen, they only attacked his logic. When writing about Kelly, which they did much more often, they attacked her personally.

Kelly's relative silence post-hearing may also have stemmed from the poor fit between Graham's diva stance and Kelly's political agenda, which operated from a liberal feminist vision predicated on equality and universal human rights, whereas the diva stance forcefully marked women as different from men and formulated that difference as a source of power. Even though Kelly did not describe herself as a feminist at the time, feminism circulated in the nation and in Washington in 1963. Betty Friedan had published *The Feminine Mystique* in February, and in June, Congress passed the Equal Pay Act (EPA), which Kelly had championed for over a decade. The EPA proceeded from a liberal feminist position central to early second-wave feminist legislative appeals: women and men were not just equals; men and women were not different at all. The EPA made this premise policy by legislating that men and women should receive equal pay for equal work. A woman could prove job discrimination only by providing evidence that she received less pay for a job identical to that of a male peer. This did little to help the majority of working women who worked in jobs where there were no men among their ranks. If men and women were different, which they were because of social norms, then women had no claim to recourse for low-paying jobs, a reality for which neither the EPA legislation nor liberal feminism could account.

Graham's diva stance projected a feminist politics through her choreography and self-presentation that foregrounded and re-imagined gender binaries. She revised what it might mean to be female in public—all potential claims of the diva stance that were antithetical to Kelly's liberal legislative position. The diva stance advocated overturning, not working within, an existing cultural system. While liberal feminists fought for, and won, many important advances for American women, particularly in policy arenas, liberal feminism offered less language and few analytic framings for discussions of gender difference or sexual revolution. The diva stance created full-fledged gender disorder. In a 1960s context, Graham could be considered a proto-cultural feminist in her emphasis on conveying gender difference through the body.[82] Although Graham, like Kelly, never identified as a feminist, she enacted a complex gender politics that overturned gender norms, and she did so through and with her body.[83]

BEYOND GRAHAM: DANCERS TAKE THE DIVA STANCE INTO THE 1970S

By the end of the 1963 controversy, Graham and her provocative depictions of female desire and sexuality reigned victorious over her congressional detractors. There was no doubt that Graham had unprecedented power among American dance elites and government funders. The coming years, however, would be difficult ones for Graham. Publicly, the government and cultural elite supported her; privately various officials expressed concern that the Graham company no longer represented the most innovative in American dance, especially with its septuagenarian leader onstage dancing lead roles. In a 1965 letter to the head of Cultural Presentations, Charles Ellison, an unnamed employee in the London USIS office assured Ellison that the British arts presenter Robin Howard had talked with the company about the necessity of Graham's retirement from the stage.[84] A year later, at least one American embassy in Europe, in Bonn, Germany, turned down a State Department offer of a Graham company tour. In a telegram to Washington, the embassy said it feared the Graham company would be seen as "old hat" by German audiences.[85] Graham did retire from the stage in 1969, five years later than the State Department had hoped she would.

Graham's retirement and the subsequent conflicts this produced within the company (as well as Graham's well-known bouts with alcoholism) kept the Graham company off many stages, national and international, for a time. In 1972, however, the company began to rebuild, hiring several recent Juilliard graduates. With the new dancers and veterans such as Takako Asakawa and Diane Gray, the company went to Lake Placid, New York, for the summer, beginning the Graham company's next life.

These were the dancers who brought Graham's diva stance into the 1970s. The diva stance was a physical technique that allowed not only Graham, but also Graham dancers, to examine and challenge cultural norms. Yet as the 1970s began, these norms had shifted, particularly in terms of what it meant to represent the United States. As many historians have noted, the 1970s were a "curious anomaly" in postwar American history, a dip in US global power between the heights of the immediate post–WWII period and the United States' resurgent power in the waning years of the Cold War. The diva stance of Graham's choreography in the early sixties helped Graham navigate a battle between conservatives and liberals over who would define "freedom."[86] As the Graham dancers—many of whom felt that political protests had had limited success—traveled to Asia in 1974, dancing gave them a path through which to navigate their complicated feelings in the waning months of US involvement in Vietnam.

One story from Graham's 1974 tour, an anecdote from *Night Journey* rehearsals in Singapore, exemplifies the diva stance as an embodied technique that dancers learned and then made their own while working with Graham. The Singapore stop fell halfway through the tour, when many of the dancers had dengue fever. Most of *Night Journey's* female chorus could not dance. Company newcomer Shelley Washington had to learn the ensemble's choreography, and learn it fast. The still-healthy cast members tried to teach Washington the extensive choreography while Graham watched. Eventually, Graham came on stage and said to Washington, "You'll be fine. You'll be fine. And just remember, if you forget something just stand there."[87] Almost all of the Graham dancers who told me this story felt the need to enact what Graham did as she said "just stand there." From chairs in their living rooms and kitchens, each stood, hoisted a fiercely cupped hand into the air, and let energy stream from the pelvis, up the spine, and out the chin and hand. Absorbing the whole of the stance the dancers performed was almost impossible. There was suddenly more energy than body. Graham may have commanded this kind of being into existence on that 1974 stage by saying "just stand there," but watching these dancers assume the powerful stance made "just" seem the wrong word. For those acquainted with Graham's mid-century choreography, the posture the dancers demonstrated would be a familiar one: strong, erect, driven, and anchored by the pelvis. These qualities are often associated with Graham's movement vocabulary, but they are also the elements of her choreography that transform the body into an instrument of desire and power, particularly for female dancers. When dancer Diana Hart Johnson told the Singapore story, she added, "Well, the truth is, that would be a pretty good stance for any moment a woman forgot her choreography in a Graham work."[88]

The dancers enacted a stance of power that evoked iconic political photographs of activists with one fist in the air as a stance of power and resistance: of Black Power at the 1968 Olympics and 1930s leftist-worker posters. In this instance, however, the single hand raised in defiance invoked not race- or class-based desire and strength, but gendered desire and strength. Standing in their kitchens and living rooms, the dancers showed the de facto way to be a powerful Graham dancer: stand with shoulders back, feet grounded, and hand raised, shooting power out into the world. That stance, even when taken on by the male dancers, seemed always intimately tied with a Graham-based performance of femininity. Dancer Peggy Lyman Hayes explicitly tied the stance to the wide-ranging, active possibilities of being a woman in Graham's work: "As women we got to explore a huge range of vivid emotions by acting out our characters' angers and fears and ecstasies. Where else could one do that except with Martha Graham? Not just experiencing the turmoil of life, but creating a solution out of it."[89] Through choreography and through their bodies, Graham's female dancers became protagonists in their own narratives, not just taking up a performance of masculinity with female bodies but expanding the possibilities of femininity.

These narratives extended beyond the stage for many of the dancers on the 1974 tour as they grappled with what it meant to represent the

United States in the final stages (for Americans) of the Vietnam War. The tour included the Philippines, Indonesia, Malaysia, Burma, Taiwan, Singapore, Vietnam, Korea, Hong Kong, and Japan (a private arts presenter, not the State Department, sponsored the performances in Japan). Most of the dancers thought their three days in the Vietnamese capital of Saigon would be the standout stop. The United States had officially ended its military involvement in Vietnam in January 1973, after signing the Paris Peace Accords, which temporarily stopped the fighting between North and South Vietnam. The fighting had since resumed, however, as the North kept the war going. The American military remained in the capital until 1975.

A middle-of-the-night phone call from the company manager to each of the dancers, however, underscored that the region's instability extended beyond Vietnam. The call informed the dancers that they would be leaving the United States five days late. The State Department had canceled their stop in Korea because of a failed assassination attempt on President Park Chung-hee in the theater where the company had been set to perform. (The president's wife, Yuk Young-soo, was killed in the incident.)

Once they were on the tour, the dancers also experienced how much Cold War tensions more generally, not just the war in Vietnam, contributed to Asia's instability. Many of them found Burma the most startling stop on the tour. Being in Burma taught dancers about the continuing, if somewhat dilapidated, Soviet presence in Asia. The dancers stayed in a rundown Soviet-style hotel and had less freedom to move about than they had elsewhere during the tour. As Peggy Lyman Hayes remembered, "Everything we did was very structured. We all stayed together, including Martha, and I guess the one hotel that they felt was acceptable for us was still horrible. It was awful. Like a concrete structure that was falling apart from mold and mildew—the totally wrong building components for that climate."[90] The company was told they were the first Americans to visit Burma since Count Basie toured there decades earlier.[91]

Political conflicts and resistance marked the company's work elsewhere. In Malaysia, the State Department canceled a performance when students rioted on the campus where the company was supposed to perform. It was an obvious instance of politics impacting performance, but Diane Gray said the event affected the dancers in mundane ways: many were happy to have an evening off to rest, and others used the night for a rather Orientalist tourist diversion—getting a glimpse of teenage prostitutes in the city square.[92] The dancers found themselves on the other side of power in the Philippines, when President Marcos and his now infamous wife, Imelda, hosted the company in Manila. The post-performance party lasted well past the city's official curfew. A siren-blaring motorcade escorted the dancers back to their hotels.

The trip to Vietnam happened late in the tour. When the Graham company arrived in Asia, the US military had been in Vietnam just shy of two decades—an involvement that had begun with a US victory seemingly likely and that ended with intense ambivalence about the United States' place and might in the world. The fall of 1974 brought three events in a close series that fed further doubt about the United States' stature and its choice to ally with South Vietnam, especially with then-president Nguyen Van Thieu's administration. On August 9, President Nixon resigned. On September 8, the new president, Gerald Ford, announced his extremely unpopular decision to pardon Nixon. In public spaces throughout South Vietnam, thousands protested corruption in Thieu's government.[93]

For many of the young Graham dancers, the political events of fall 1974 were just the latest in a string of political disappointments. Lyman Hayes recalled being "thrilled" to represent the United States in Vietnam at that time because she felt the tour carried American "creativity," rather than the American "war machine" to the Vietnamese people. Dancing was not protest—in some ways protest and the counterculture movement seemed politically deflated to many of the dancers. As mentioned earlier in this chapter, dancer Peter Sparling quipped, thinking back on the tour, "I had just cut my ponytail off."[94] Like Sparling, many of the dancers had protested American involvement in Vietnam in college, and one, Carl Paris, had been to Vietnam as a Marine. Dancer David Chase had been enough of an outspoken critic that Graham approached him mid-tour and asked, "Well, you won't do anything, will you?"[95] He assured her that he would not speak out while on tour.

For most, performing presented an alternative way for young Americans to engage with their national identity on the international stage. Lyman Hayes's comment about wanting to represent American creativity rather than the American war machine is indicative of a tremendous shift from how dancers sponsored by the State Department discussed their role as cultural ambassadors on earlier tours. The dancers I interviewed who had traveled on tours in the 1960s generally resisted describing their work as "political," a term most indicated they dismissed because of its connotation of a partisan political stance. In contrast, every Graham dancer I interviewed discussed the 1974 tour in relation to politics, primarily the Vietnam War, and, notably, said that exporting culture was something the government should do instead of engaging in military action. Carl Paris described the tour as a step the government could make that might be "generative."[96] Lucinda Mitchell remarked, "The government had sent so much bad, maybe it was time to send something good."[97] David Chase described the tour as a "nice" thing for the government to do but also, because of the ongoing war, "bittersweet."[98] In all these comments and others, the political, exploding on and around the tour because of the Vietnam War, among other political issues, was not something to side-step, but a concept the dancers debated, expounded on, and related to the company's artistic work. Dance was a mode of making an international political statement in a way American dancers had not imagined it to be since before WWII, when modern dancers often performed more explicit leftist politics.

Regardless of their political beliefs, most of the dancers said they would never have used the tour for overt political action. Dancer Lucinda Mitchell said,

> [W]e were all biting our tongues as we were given a lecture [at the American Embassy in Saigon] as to why the US was there and why it was important and if we weren't there Communists were going to take over the world. . . . [But] we just kept our mouths shut, [and thought], "Let them tell us what they have to tell us and shut up." . . . [I]f somebody from the State Department had marched into the Martha Graham studio in New York and given that lecture, we would have probably all walked out, but they were our hosts. At that point there's no point in getting up and ranting.[99]

Any political desires tangled with the very formal and slightly overwhelming status of being a cultural ambassador. Carl Paris said being on a State Department tour, in comparison to his usual life as a dancer in the United States, felt like being royalty.[100] On State Department tours, the company paid dancers on the usual union salary scale but with much better per diems,[101] adding a financial benefit to a tour already filled with receptions and motorcades.

At the heart of the tour was Graham's choreography. The company had initially imagined the tour as the international debut of Graham's *Clytemnestra* (1958), the last of Graham's great myth-inspired mid-century works. A pre-tour scouting report by company technical director William Batchelder aborted that plan when Batchelder (known in the company as "Batch") reported that few, if any of the stages, could support the *Clytemnestra* set.[102] In the end, the company saved *Clytemnestra* for the Japanese performances and brought mixed bills of Graham's mid-century classics to the State Department-sponsored portions of the tour. The tour repertory featured *Appalachian Spring, Cave of the Heart, Diversion of Angels* (1948), *El Penitente* (1940), *Embattled Garden* (1958), *Errand into the Maze*

(1947), and *Night Journey*. Although many, both before and after the 1974 tour, assumed that Graham's Greek-myth-driven work, with its formalism and heightened theatricality, would best resonate with Asian audiences, Asian audiences responded less to the myth-based work.[103] The State Department reports indicate that *Diversion of Angels* was the main hit of the tour.

DIVERSIONS, WAR, AND LOVE

In *Diversion of Angels*, the cast of dancers fling their arms through space, wrenching their shoulder sockets open with a sense of abandon. The men and women look as though they are coming undone at their very hinges. Every step pushes farther into space than the last: there are barreling leaps and cartwheels done in an impossibly wide X body position (figure 3.4).

The choreography demands that the dancers look on the edge of control kinesthetically and visually; both their technique and, quite literally, their

Figure 3.4
The male ensemble of Martha Graham's *Diversion of Angels* in one of many choreographic moments that asks the dancers to extend their bodies almost beyond their physical reach. The dancers are (*left to right*) Ross Parkes, Eric Newton, Tim Wengerd, Daniel Maloney.
Source: Courtesy of the Library of Congress.

skin look stretched to their limits. These images offer a different version of freedom than some of the Graham works more often associated with freedom. This is not the freedom of movement expressed, for instance, in Graham's early, more obviously political work, such as *Steps in the Street* (1936) or *American Document*, in which the ensembles hurl through space as a mass of bodies. Nor is *Diversion's* choreography one of bodies coming undone because inner emotional landscapes threaten to explode from within, as is the case with the Greek myths. *Diversion* is a group both exploding and coming together—in joy or even ecstasy. The joyful, open reaching of the group became an explicit and complicated offering of hope in performances on stages in Vietnam, which had been a battlefield—not a space of connection and certainly not a space of love—for Americans and Vietnamese for more than a decade

Graham always described *Diversion of Angels*, a work she choreographed in 1948 to the music of Norman Dello Joio, as a work about love, particularly young love or first love.[104] Generally, this description has led critics and scholars to focus on the dance's three main couples. Colored costumes delineate each pair: white for the serene lead couple; red for the fiery, fast couple; and yellow for the most playful couple. The choreography for these couples is some of Graham's most ethereal (for the Woman in White), flashy yet grounded (for the Woman in Red), and exuberant (for the Woman in Yellow). It is, however, the physicality that stretches across the choreography for the entire cast, both the ensemble and the couples that I focus on here. Rather than see love as something embodied only in *Diversion of Angels'* heterosexual pairings, how might we see love as presented in the dancing done by *Diversion's* entire cast—a way of being part of a group while being both in one's body and beyond it, out of control, yet of the fleshy moment?

Diversion of Angels closed almost every program on the Graham Company's 1974 tour of Asia. The piece's physical intensity, particularly its expression of love through dance and love among the members of a group (rather than only between couples) serves as a productive metaphor for the role the Graham dancers found themselves inhabiting both onstage and offstage on the tour. *Diversion of Angels'* performance of love became a site where young American artists negotiated a changing sense of American identity, investing in a danced embodiment of love as a way to engage in global politics. The dancers, too, negotiated their complex feelings about American politics in Asia through dance. They performed in a moment when, as dancer Peggy Lyman Hayes said, it felt as though all they could do as Americans was to make an offering of dance.

Janet Eilber, a rising star in the company in 1974 and later the company's artistic director, told me one story that she said stood out among her memories of the tour (figure 3.5).

Eilber remembers a performance of *Diversion* where she felt simultaneously spectator and performer. She watched and helped form multiple groups as she moved among her fellow dancers, the official audience, and an unofficial audience gathered to watch the performance from unexpected places:

> [W]hen we danced in Saigon . . . it was largely a military audience [in the theater], a VIP audience [of] Americans and the [South Vietnamese] VIPs who were working with them. . . . If you r[u]n off stage, usually you run into a wall eventually. But there were no walls there [that night]. The theater was open to the alleys that were beside the theater, and there were just storefront gates across them. So as we performed, and I remember specifically *Diversion of Angels* . . . these gates filled with faces from the top to the bottom of the people who lived in the alleys [who were] watching us. [They were in] awe and

Figure 3.5
Martha Graham's *Diversion of Angels* circa 1974. Downstage: Takako Asakawa. Upstage: Peter Sparling (*left*) and Janet Eilber (*right*).
Source: Photograph by Martha Swope. Courtesy of the New York Public Library for the Performing Arts.

amazement and very vocal. There'd be a lift or a fall or an "ooh, aah." And pretty soon you didn't know whether you should be playing for this very polite audience [in the theater seats]: they were there because they had to be there. Or [play for] the people [in the alley] that were just drawn to this amazing display that was happening.[105]

As Eilber finished her story, she opened her arms wide and pressed her chest beyond her shoulders, as she did at the end of the Woman in White's solo when she ran toward all those Vietnamese faces. She was another *Diversion of Angels* dancer coming undone as she ran toward the watching crowd. The choreography directed her to turn and run into the wings, but she seemed to do far more than execute the choreography in that open-hearted gesture.

The scene Eilber described is, on one hand, deeply colonial. The Vietnamese masses stand pressed to the gates and the Americans are onstage. Americans move freely, and the Vietnamese literally cannot move at all. A vision of periphery and center, invisibility and visibility unfolded, clearly shaped by neocolonial dynamics of power that influenced every American-Vietnamese interaction during (and likely after) the years of war. It requires too much squinting past the moment's historical specificity to imagine the scene of the female figure's outstretched arms and lifted chest facing the huddled group in the alley as one of transcendent connection overcoming war's strife. To read this scene that way would fall prey to the familiar narrative: the United States as the heroic white woman rushing to aid poor, anonymous, brown foreign faces in need.[106]

Eilber did not narrate the story as one of heroism, however, but of recognizing her position in the scene. She described the shift in her gaze, the moment she turned from dancing for the official audience and chose the Vietnamese audience in the alley instead. In the moment of performance, Eilber ceased to align herself only with the official, largely military audience, and instead tried to connect with the Vietnamese audience. From the stage, Eilber engaged in a transnational version of what Susan Manning calls "cross-viewing," a moment of spectatorship in which people recognize that there are multiple gazes directed at one performance. It is this moment of cross-viewing, when Eilber is seen by and also sees both the American military audience and the local Vietnamese audience, that could be provocatively imagined as what political theorist Michael Hardt has called a "properly political" form of love.

For Hardt, thinking about love as a politics requires understanding love beyond the personal, intimate sphere. The turn to *Diversion*'s ensemble as a dance of love then offers a compelling parallel. Hardt tries to imagine love as a form of global intimacy. His vision is an optimistic, even dangerously utopic, view of love's possibility in global politics, veering too close to the paternalism of neocolonial politics, where narratives of familial attachment across national divides bolster asymmetrical power relationships. In this neo-imperial formulation, love drives the more powerful entity to care for the less powerful entity; the less powerful partner loves the more powerful in return, grateful for the love and assistance. So-called First World–Third World relationships grow, fed by gratitude, as though the partners are reenacting the parent-child relationship, a demeaning metaphor for the "Third World" partner. Hardt's vision of love as global politics attempts though, too, to differ from this problematic relationship. Rather than a love driven only by a desire to mold the less powerful in the image of the more powerful, Hardt imagines a global politics of love that does not move toward sameness and unity. Another way to think through this idea in a context closer to dance might be dance theorist Judith Hamera's use of psychoanalytic theorist Luce Irigaray's concept of "I love to you" rather than "I love you" as a way to describe the affective relationship between dance teachers and students.[107] Love, demonstrated through physical relationships, allows one entity to be drawn to another without obliterating the object of desire, thus allowing space for two subjects to love one another and for both parties to change.

In this instance of cross-viewing, as Eilber was seen by and also saw both the American military and the local Vietnamese, cultural ambassadors practiced a properly political form of love. The action here does not only fulfill Hardt's call for global love across difference but also the layer cultural theorist Lauren Berlant has added to Hardt's formulation. For Berlant, love as a social rather than purely personal concept absolutely requires the recognition of contradiction. The Graham dancers performed a contradiction when they danced *Diversion* in Saigon: they were at once an extension of the military presence, the embodiment of the paternalistic love structuring neocolonialism, and an embodiment of love in which the Americans, the more powerful, come undone, at least temporarily, as part of an exchange with a nonmilitary Vietnamese audience. Eilber opened her body and rushed toward the Vietnamese, seeing them not just as victims of war, but as people with whom she could engage.

My many interviews suggest that thinking about international relationships often pitted individual or community desires against national or official desires. These layers seem particularly poignant post-Vietnam as the United States' place in the global order, and thus American identity, shifted. A quotation from my interview with dancer Peter Sparling captures this "both/and" of cultural diplomacy. Speaking about the contradictions of dancing in Asia in 1974 on behalf of the American government, Sparling said,

> Were we being sent out to colonize or show that we were the best or that our vision—American artists' [vision]—could rival any artists in the world? Yeah, definitely there was that sense. [Our performances were meant to say,] "We're not only greedy capitalists with huge militaries and a history of slavery and of holding territorial possession throughout the world . . . we also have developed our own arts and culture that promote values of democracy, of individual freedom, of freedom of expression." I think we were all those things.[108]

The dancers demonstrated through their memories of the tour that Eilber opened her arms in a genuine act of caring, using her onstage cross-viewing vantage point to see both the military intervention in Vietnam and the local people in a more complicated narrative than the one available stateside.

Although the trappings of war surrounded the company from the moment they arrived in Saigon and were picked up in military transport—big buses covered in mesh wire—many found Vietnam to be much more than a site where the United States was at war, and the Vietnamese people to be much more than war's victims, though they were that, too. The dancers worked alongside the locals to get the shows onto the stages. Diane Gray cited working with the local stage crews in Saigon and elsewhere as one of the best aspects of the cultural diplomacy tours, because it brought people together with the same goal: to make sure the curtain rose each evening.[109] Elisa Monte thrilled at the beauty of the Saigon's architecture and arts, remembering the ornate balconies and the beauty of the pottery and ceramics.[110] There was also the mundane beauty and intricacy of Vietnam. Gray says that the conversation that most struck her in Saigon was one she had with a local man who explained to her why and how the Vietnamese grew eighty-two different kinds of rice.[111]

The other theme that arose from the dancers' memories of Saigon was total shock at the poverty they saw—a theme that many said was part of the tour throughout the continent. Bonnie Oda Homsey remembered standing outside the hotel, watching large numbers of children, many of them decapitated in some way, as they begged for food.[112] David Chase found himself staring at streetscapes (albeit with a more Orientalist gaze, it seems, since he said his primary thought was looking at "all the beautiful women"), and thinking, "we were just blowing their country up."[113] Poverty was not just a symptom of war but also of postcolonialism and the ravages of the Cold War on various Asian countries. Burma was one of the sparsest countries the company visited, and the difficulties the country faced seemed clearly tied to the long Soviet grip on the region. Many dancers were horrified in Burma when someone threw an unwanted part of a sandwich to a group of stray dogs, only to see children rush the dogs and fight them for the sandwich.[114] Eric Newton noted that cultural diplomacy gave the dancers an opportunity to realize the absolute depth of poverty all over Asia—and also to realize the elite circles in which they moved as cultural ambassadors: "We were dancing for the top. And when you traveled around Manila you saw there were the very poor. So there was a big contrast between the theater and the population. We were hobnobbing with the elite; that was part of the deal of being a representative of the government."[115] While American cultural diplomacy objectives had generally shifted toward a desire to reach larger, less elite populations,[116] the dancers felt their tours remained largely focused on the elite. Eilber could open her arms wide, but she could not make the gates come down.

While the dancers desired to make real connections with local populations, and possibly did during their performances, such affective relationships would have required infrastructure to last. As Newton said, no matter how much he felt for the very poor he encountered in Manila and elsewhere, the government structured the time and the nature of the relationships. The third aspect of Hardt's "properly political concept of love," that such an intimate relationship of love at the global social level must "prompt change," cannot be fully enacted by individuals, even a group of individuals. The government structured the tour to win hearts and minds, but did little to build long-term relationships, something that might have given the tour greater chance to create a truly alternative vision of US-Vietnamese relationships. Lasting freedom could not be built only at the individual affective and physical level, even though American freedom was most often celebrated through individualism. True freedom required structural, institutional-level change.

MISSED OPPORTUNITIES

One story from the Graham company's three days in Saigon spoke to the incredible possibilities of the tours, but also to their profound limits in terms of offering extended support after initial flashes of connection. The State Department tours had catalyzed the creation of the now well-known format of the company's lecture-demonstrations, or "lec-dems," informal showings of the Graham technique for all kinds of audiences. Graham first devised a series of demonstrations of class exercises for the company's

1955 Asia tour. Dancer Peggy Lyman Hayes recalled learning that the 1955 tour was the genesis of the lec-dems when the older dancers taught her to do all the floorwork on the diagonal, rather than directly face the audience. Graham had shifted the spatial orientation to avoid offending the Asian audiences who, she had been told, would find seeing the sole of the foot rude, even offensive. Graham liked the new orientation better and it stuck, likely one of many relatively mundane choices made on the tours that had long-term impact on how the company performed.

For the Graham company's return to Asia in 1974, USIA had scheduled many lecture-demonstrations. These had even greater significance on the later tour because they featured the eighty-three-year-old Graham sitting in her large Chinese chair carried on tour. Graham would speak as the dancers went through their exercises and then performed excerpts from various pieces in the company repertory.

The company's short time in Saigon included one lecture-demonstration. Graham herself did not make the journey to Saigon. There are conflicting reports as to why Graham did not travel to Saigon—ranging from dancers who thought her absence was a form of political protest to government reports that she was too ill to travel. It seems possible that Graham may have feigned illness as a way to avoid being an American pro-war symbol in Vietnam, but, too, dancers said the eighty-three-year-old was visibly worn down by the tour and might have truly been ill. Without Graham, the dancers were left to do the lecture-demonstrations on their own with much less narration. The *New York Times* reported that the young Vietnamese dancers present at the demonstration were shockingly silent, "not a word was spoken," as the Graham dancers went through their class sequences.[117]

After the company performed, Diane Gray stepped forward to lead the young Vietnamese dancers through some Graham exercises. Afterward, one young man asked Gray if she would return to his dance studio and teach more later that day. Later, the boy and his teacher picked her up at the hotel. Gray recalled the drive and then the walk to the studio:

> They came, and they picked me up and took me faaaaaaaaaaar away [laughing]. And then, finally, we ended up in this little place—it was like a labyrinth. . . . It was just me. And so I went there and we had to go through these, like, food carts and everything, down this little tiny alley. And I didn't get there until about nine o'clock at night.

Despite the hour, a large number of people had gathered by the time Gray arrived at the dance studio.

There were all these children, and all these parents, and all these flowers. And they just clapped and clapped. I couldn't really believe it, because, I mean, who was I? I wasn't anybody. I was coming to teach. So finally, we got on with the lesson.

By then the hour was quite late, but Gray's hosts wanted more time with her: "They took me to see their temple, which was just around the bend there. And they had to wake up the people inside the temple to let us in. But they just wanted to share their lives with me. And so, then they took me back to the hotel." The new Graham aficionados came by again to give the company a proper send off. "The next day we were leaving Saigon, and they came in a busload and they brought me all kinds of pictures. . . . It was really quite wonderful." Gray said she thought about the group often thereafter, particularly the boy who initiated the entire exchange. She followed the events in Vietnam for the next several years and wondered whether, as a teenage South Vietnamese boy he had been swept into the fighting as war continued. At least a year after the tour, Gray received a Christmas card from the boy, with just a short greeting. Years later, Gray found the card again, and realized the young man had tucked a long letter into it that Gray had not noticed when she opened the card: "I felt so bad. I thought 'Well, if I had been able to stay in touch with him, maybe his life could have been different.'"[118]

In the wake of the US military involvement in Vietnam, it would be wise to be suspicious of what exactly Gray or any other Graham dancer could have offered the boy. Given, however, that one star of the tour, Takako Asakawa, left Japan for America not long after her home country had been on the opposite side of war with the United States, and went on to become one of the company's most celebrated dancers, it is not unreasonable to imagine that the same thing could have happened for another young dancer. That said, such an imagined narrative presumes not just a better life in the United States but a better life as available through American, not Vietnamese, dance. While the possibility of Graham technique as the Vietnamese savior might not be a useful moral of Gray's story (or the tour more generally), what seems more important is that while the Cold War dance tours had measurable effect on the American dancers—affecting choreography, performance choices, and political consciousness thereafter—their effect, indeed benefit, for international audiences and artists is questionable. On one level, that was not that point: the tours and the performances they highlighted were meant to make the case for "America," to demonstrate America as the home of freedom. While the dancers described performances and moments like the ones Gray experienced as profound, the dancers came and left quickly, and often there were not even Christmas cards to exchange afterward.

So is this cultural exchange? Touring and performing all over the world under the flag of the United States? This question begs an answer, but it was not to be asked again for decades. Graham's 1974 tour took place in the last years of the massive Cold War dance-in-diplomacy programs. Funding for all cultural diplomacy fell into steady decline from the mid-1960s to 1978, when the programs, much smaller than before, moved out of the State Department and into the USIA. With that bureaucratic shift, the dance tours officially became American propaganda, since propaganda was the USIA's primary mission. With the end of the Cold War in the 1980s, as policy historian Juliet Sablosky has argued, cultural diplomacy, including the dance tours, fell victim to its own premise. If cultural diplomacy was a tool of the Cold War, and the Cold War had ended, why fund cultural diplomacy? A foreign-policy apparatus forged entirely within a Cold War frame had no answer for that question.

After Vietnam, Watergate, and, later, the Iran-Contra affair, the emphasis on individual freedom seemed a dangerous aspect of American mentality, and it seemed perhaps the transparency of American democracy, too, was a myth. Without the clear foil presented by Soviet Communism—always figured as preventing freedom—the myth of American freedom fractured. It was not until the events of September 2001 jolted the United States out of its post–Cold War isolationist tendencies that the question of what it might mean to have an international relationship built through the arts began to again be asked. Toward the end of President George Walker Bush's administration, the State Department conceptualized DanceMotion USA, the international dance touring program at the heart of the next two chapters. In 2010, after decades of little support for full-dance company tours, the American government again began supporting American dance to connect to international publics around the globe.

CHAPTER 4

Negotiating Community and Diaspora

Twenty-First-Century Dance Diplomacy

A woman dances alone, her short white skirt flipping as she shoots her bare leg upward in an *arabesque* before she swirls through a series of pirouettes. The choreography mixes balletic shapes with the weighted-ness of modern dance. She glides across the floor, driving forward with her pelvis. The blending of movement vocabularies, her precision of form and technique, and her ability to ride energetic impulses creating layered rhythms marks the solo as likely a contemporary incarnation of African American modern dance. (And, indeed, the piece in which she dances, Ronald K. Brown's *Ife/My Heart,* was made in 2005 for the Alvin Ailey American Dance Theater.) As the woman exits, an ensemble of men and women enter, wearing costumes that have three times the material of the soloist's. Their white tunics, cut wide to stream behind them, and the male dancers' small round hats immediately signal their presence as of the African diaspora. The costumes, designed by Nigerian costume designer Omotayo Wunmi Olaiya, resemble the dress of those practicing the Yoruban faith, a religion rooted in West Africa. All white, the traditional dress also invokes the Afro-Caribbean religious practices of the largely Cuba-based Santería. The dancers' movement as they fly onto the stage clearly draws on the sabar dance, a high-energy dance form of ethnic groups in Senegal and Guinea. The dancers' arms swing behind them, propelling them forward as their almost-too-quick-to-track-with-the-eye running pattern sends energy into the floor with each footfall. In less than a minute of choreography, the end of the solo and the beginning of the group section, the cultures and aesthetics of the United States, Africa, and Cuba all appear. *Ife* is a dance of the African diaspora, a work by an American choreographer for American dancers that moves across multiple geographic sites connected through the history of the forced exile and enslavement of black people, and, just as importantly, through the practices of resistance and power enacted by those same people across many generations. These dancers perform a profound statement about history and bodies in motion and the degree to which American artists, particularly African American dancers, reside in one nation, but often feel connected to many.

When Joseph Melillo, the executive director of the Brooklyn Academy of Music (BAM), the State Department's private-arts-presenter partner for the touring program DanceMotion USA, called Brown to invite Evidence to perform in Africa in 2010, Brown remembered thinking, "It was amazing that I was going to Nigeria. This prayer [in *Ife*] is in Yoruban [a West African language, in addition to being a religious practice], and we're going to do it in Nigeria? The opportunity was mind-blowing."[1] The moments from *Ife* just described and Brown's comment exemplify two key characteristics of twenty-first-century American dance-in-diplomacy programs: physical connection across diverse, often international communities and public celebration by the State Department, BAM, and artists of transnational aesthetics.

This chapter explores the implications of contemporary American dance-in-diplomacy's focus on building and recognizing international relationships, particularly the ways in which this programmatic mission reimagines the concept of nation and the United States' place within global networks. In the early twenty-first century, the State Department justifies cultural diplomacy not only as a tool for persuading the world of American superiority, but as a way to, as the State Department's documentary about DanceMotion states, "increase mutual understanding and build relationships with other countries through cultural exchange."[2] The term "mutual understanding" is not new, but the mobilization of the term has changed. DanceMotion, as it has been crafted by the State Department in concert with BAM, foregrounds how American dance connects with cultural practices around the globe.

DanceMotion program materials emphasize the tours as collaborative, international spaces, rather than as presentations. The website notes that in the first three years of funding (four years have been announced as of the writing of this book), the American dance companies chosen to tour abroad led 328 workshops, but only performed in theaters seventy-seven times. This is an unprecedented investment in American and non-American companies dancing *together*. As DanceMotion's mission statement says, the State Department hopes to create space to "examine, share, and explore the American dance experience with international audiences."[3]

This exploration of connection might seem a reversal of Cold War policies based on exporting American values as though a set of values could be tied to one nation above others, but this second era of dance-in-diplomacy programs is reflective of twenty-first-century notions of nation-states as more porous and globally connected entities. To assert American identity in the early twenty-first century, even in an official capacity on behalf of the government, requires recognizing the increased speed and prevalence of international communication and movement that puts people in touch with one another—regardless of where they live or what nation they are citizens of—in ways unprecedented even in the late twentieth century. While these trends have occurred unequally (not everyone has access to travel or the Internet, or financial access to international travel), possibilities for connecting with international communities have increased exponentially. Many of these connections arise from digital, rather than live, engagement. Given this, one significant aspect of DanceMotion is the program's insistence that live, in-person, physical engagement remains important to American foreign policy and to artistic and national development.

In workshops and performances, DanceMotion seeks to build new international connections, while also acknowledging preexisting cultural links, particularly in relation to the African diaspora. The importance the program places on recognizing the United States' place within African diasporic dance is most clear in the artists who have toured through the program. In the first four years of DanceMotion funding, each round included a company that explicitly labels itself as part of the African diaspora. In 2010, this was true for Evidence and Urban Bush Women (UBW); in 2012, for Rennie Harris Puremovement; in 2013, for Illstyle & Peace, and in 2014, for CONTRA-TIEMPO. Although companies chosen for twentieth-century tours, notably the Ailey company, had diasporic influences, few, if any, highlighted their diasporic connections as explicitly as the artists on DanceMotion's roster. For example, the Evidence repertory, all of it choreographed by Brown, overflows with African themes and movement influences. Brown builds a movement vocabulary from the dance forms of West Africa, Cuba, and the US house-dance scene, and Brown often invokes the spiritual in his work by blending references to moments of American struggle, particularly the civil rights movement, with the rituals of Santería and Yoruba. To watch Evidence perform means listening to Nina Simone sing of African American protest and

Nigerian high-life star Femi Koute sing of the power of African independence movements.

Even if audiences miss the diasporic elements within the work—movement and song, collaborators and costumes—the State Department ensures that audiences know that diasporic recognition is key. Many of the chosen companies, as noted earlier, describe themselves explicitly as part of the "African diaspora," and the State Department often highlights this term in the DanceMotion promotional materials.[4] In 2010, for instance, State Department press releases publicizing the UBW tour of Colombia, Venezuela, and Brazil always included multiple references to UBW as an African American company of the African diaspora.

Although DanceMotion highlighted the multiplicity of identities proliferating within an "official" American government program, it has intensely obscured the relationship among the various government forces, agencies, and private partners that created the program. DanceMotion in this way arises from the Information Age, slick in its branding and almost totalizing in its control of information about how the program is run and how artists come to be involved in it. Artists cannot apply to the program: they just one day get a phone call from Melillo inviting them to participate, as Brown did. What does circulate about the program are its ample promotional materials, mainly distributed through the program's website, though these are all consolidated in a way that somewhat obscures the State Department's role and, to a lesser degree, BAM's role. They are all authored by DanceMotion USA—the title the State Department gave the program years before it existed and the title that veils the public-private amalgam that,[5] more than any other program discussed in this book, constitutes DanceMotion. This intense consolidation of private and public makes careful scrutiny of artistic choices and what they might say about the meanings of contemporary cultural diplomacy all the more important.

Thinking back to my descriptions of the *Ife* performance that opened this chapter within the frame of twenty-first-century dance diplomacy means that to speak of some of its elements as American and others as African is misleading, at best. These elements are intertwined in the work and in the choreographer's and dancers' statements about what they do and who they are. Brown said he was incredibly excited to be going on the DanceMotion tour as an "African American man making dance from the perspective of being raised in Brooklyn and using vocabulary from Guinea, Senegal, and Cote d'Ivorie."[6] He described the complicated web of desire and origins that links American, African, and African American identity by borrowing the phrase "a twisted mirror" from African American artist-activist Bernice Reagon Johnson.[7] Brown said Johnson's phrase captures the cycles of recognition and misrecognition that flow between African Americans and Africans and between American art and African art—a complicated and generative web that Brown explores in his work.

This chapter focuses on how these cycles of recognition and misrecognition move through the world today as the United States uses dance to build relationships abroad. I begin this inquiry with an overview of DanceMotion's rise from the early twenty-first-century policy landscape. Next, I consider how the turn toward workshops and lecture-demonstrations rather than more traditional theatrical performances affected how the program took shape. What might be the difference between a setting in which Americans and non-Americans take turns teaching movement and a setting in which only Americans lead the assembled groups? (Both scenarios happened on the 2010 tours.) After discussing the workshops as the primary aspect of contemporary dance-in-diplomacy, I move back to the question of diaspora and how that might be another way of thinking Americans *with* non-Americans. In this discussion, I look specifically at performances of UBW's *Walking with Pearl: Africa Diaries* (2005; figure 4.1).

The chapter discusses all three of the tours funded through DanceMotion in its 2010 pilot year: the Evidence tour of Senegal, South

Figure 4.1
Jawole Willa Jo Zollar, founder and artistic director of Urban Bush Women, teaches a community workshop in Cali, Colombia, during the 2010 DanceMotion USA tour.
Source: Photograph by Paul Smith.

Africa, and Nigeria; the UBW tour of Colombia, Venezuela, and Brazil; and the ODC/Dance tour of Indonesia, Burma, and Thailand. Each company spent one month abroad, logging one week in each country visited. The pilot program's success helped make DanceMotion USA a permanent State Department program housed within the Bureau of Educational and Cultural Affairs (ECA) and administered by BAM.[8] The 2010 pilot became the blueprint for the ongoing program, so the 2010 tour provides the most public sense of how DanceMotion developed and how it continues.

Across all the queries about dance as a mode of moving with others in the twenty-first century looms the specter of the United States' other modes of moving with foreign bodies since the millennium: US soldiers toppling Saddam Hussein's statue in 2003; the horrific photographs of US soldiers torturing prisoners in the Iraqi prison Abu Ghraib in 2003 and 2004; and the many years of prisoner hunger strikes protesting perpetual imprisonment in Guantanamo Bay. These images, some easily recalled from the viral spread of photographs and videos, others only imagined by most Americans, tell a story of invasion (though some would say liberation), domination, and abjection. US foreign policy moves US bodies into the world to enforce an American vision of politics, pushing some out of the category of decision-maker and others out of the category of human. These larger political dynamics mean that the international relationships DanceMotion works to create and build happen in a world of unevenly distributed power and privilege. What has to be acknowledged for an American to truly move *with* someone of another national identity, which is the greatest potential (if not always the reality) for contemporary dance in American diplomacy?

While some of the artists I interviewed for this chapter said they were particularly eager to say yes to DanceMotion after President Barack Obama took office, it is important to see the program's genesis, impact, and administration as stretching across the administrations of President George W. Bush (the son, not the father) and President Obama. This chapter seeks to move away from a story of the Bush and Obama foreign policy eras as disconnected, with the Obama administration as the more progressive. While Bush created the Guantanamo Bay detention camp, Obama maintained its place in the history of the so-called War on Terror to some degree, reversing his early promises to close the prison in 2009, months before the DanceMotion program began. This is the world from which DanceMotion grew: the one in which the United States sought to reclaim its global power while also distancing itself from human rights abuses. As the following policy history demonstrates, cultural diplomacy returned to US attention not just because of the 2001 attacks on the

US, but also because of how the government responded to those attacks with military invasions. DanceMotion entered into a tense global dance between Americans and non-Americans that had already begun.

CULTURAL DIPLOMACY REBORN
IN THE TWENTY-FIRST CENTURY

Cultural diplomacy was a hot topic in the United States in the 2000s, on the left and the right of the political spectrum. Since the end of the Cold War, the federal government had paid much less attention to global opinion of the United States, a situation that changed dramatically after 9/11. Discussions about cultural diplomacy began in earnest immediately after 9/11 as Congress grasped for answers, and continued after the US invasion of Afghanistan and then the 2003 US invasion of Iraq, when polls reported that international opinion of the United States had turned extremely negative.[9] Congress and political think tanks alike focused urgent attention on the United States' global reputation. These early discussions, however, did not immediately bring dance (or any art form besides television or film) to the fore. Later in the decade, the Obama-Biden campaign platform pushed cultural diplomacy back into the national conversation, calling for a return to Cold War–era investment in the arts as a tool for global engagement. In contrast, some experts and legislators argued for a transformed cultural diplomacy. Instead of returning to a Cold War template, they favored listening over speaking, engagement over export.

Congressional hearings on cultural diplomacy, particularly those held immediately after 9/11, first envisioned this new approach. They emphasized the need for the United States to try to understand the rest of the world, rather than trying to convince the world to accept American culture and ideals. The House Committee on International Relations held hearings about diplomacy, including two titled The Role of Public Diplomacy in Support of the Antiterrorism Campaign and The Message Is America: Rethinking American Public Diplomacy. Whereas representatives from the performing and visual arts worlds had been key speakers in cultural diplomacy hearings during the Cold War—for example, the 1963 hearing focused on Martha Graham described in chapter 3—now entertainment industry executives and producers, alongside former American ambassadors and Foreign Service officers, populated witness lists. The emphasis had shifted, from exporting "highbrow" artwork to a more global strategy of engagement through pop culture.

Testimony in the 2001 hearings often offered a relatively nuanced conception of diplomacy focused on listening rather than speaking. For instance, in testimony at the hearing The Message Is America, Edward Walker Jr., former US ambassador to Egypt, Israel, and the United Arab Emirates, called for re-envisioning American global interactions as dialogue rather than "messaging," a one-way, advertising-oriented approach to diplomacy:

> Public diplomacy must be much more than a convenient packaging technique for our foreign policy. It should be a means of promoting a two-way communication between the diverse peoples of the world, of enhancing our foreign policy through a comprehensive understanding of the world around us. There is absolutely no substitute for listening.[10]

Walker rejected the political stance inherent in the hearing's title, The Message Is America, and instead said American public diplomacy needed to examine, even change, the power dynamics that structured American relationships with other nations and peoples. Walker's statement exemplified the hearing's unusually conciliatory tone. These early hearings seemed genuinely poised to guide the United States toward progressive, open policy in the realm of public and cultural diplomacy.

A variety of publications pushed for more cultural diplomacy, too. The 9/11 Commission Report, published in 2004, as well as reports from think tanks, from the conservative RAND Corporation to the more progressive, arts-related (now-defunct) Center for Arts and Culture, recommended greater funding for cultural programs. They all cited the lack of US investment in public and cultural diplomacy as part of the reason foreign populations held such negative opinions of the United States prior to 9/11.[11] According to these reports, the closing of American libraries in embassies, the ending of the substantial arts touring programs, and reduction in funding for English-language training programs—all results of cuts in federal funding—meant fewer people were learning about American culture beyond what circulated commercially. Cultural diplomacy was not just a way to address the current geopolitical situation; its absence post–Cold War had actually contributed to the world's current issues with the United States.

The first George W. Bush administration did not heed the research showing education and, to a lesser degree, the arts as crucial for diplomacy but instead embraced advertising as the field best suited to reimagining "America" for the world. The State Department's efforts resembled corporate marketing strategies. Charlotte Beers, the first Under Secretary for

Public Diplomacy under Bush, came from Madison Avenue, where she had headed the large advertising company J. Walter Thompson.[12] Beers's first public diplomacy campaign created inserts, to be placed in Middle Eastern newspapers, detailing the deaths and injuries that resulted from the 9/11 attacks. Another infamous example of public diplomacy under Beers was a State Department website with a section called "Muslim Life in America" that featured pictures of American mosques and smiling Muslim families.[13] The emphasis was on exporting a vision of American life as, if not superior, at least good and worthy of global sympathy, rather than considering how to change the way the United States related to the world.

Meanwhile, international opinion of the United States, largely sympathetic immediately after 9/11, drastically shifted, first after the United States invaded Afghanistan in 2001, and then Iraq in 2003. The introduction to the Pew Research Center's 2003 Global Attitudes Project Report noted that global support persisted for "the fundamental economic and political values that the US has long promoted" but that those polled now had "a mostly negative picture of the image of America, its people and policies."[14] Many in Europe and even the Middle East hoped the invasion of Iraq might speed democratic reform in the region but felt the United States had been too aggressive and cavalier about civilian casualties.[15] Respondents still supported democracy and other "American" ideals, but they characterized the United States' interactions with other nations as reprehensible.[16] How the United States engaged with the world, not what the United States represented, had prompted the negative opinions. American rhetoric did not match American practice.

Cultural diplomacy, with its emphasis on local, people-to-people interaction, seemed an avenue well suited for addressing the situation, yet funding remained low. Even bills to fund cultural diplomacy efforts targeting Muslim communities abroad, the population singled out in congressional hearings and reports as needing urgent attention, failed to garner support in the House or the Senate. In March 2002, Representative Henry Hyde introduced the Freedom Promotion Act, which would have expanded the role of public diplomacy in the State Department.[17] Two months later, Senator Edward Kennedy introduced a similar bill that proposed earmarking $95 million over five years to enhance exchange programs with the Islamic world.[18] The former bill passed the House, but neither bill made it through the Senate.

Funding for cultural diplomacy did rise; it just did so incrementally. In 2009, the ECA saw its greatest single funding increase of the century: the budget for cultural diplomacy rose from $8.5 million in 2008 to $11.5 million in 2009.[19] (As a point of historical comparison to the Cold War era, when President Dwight Eisenhower announced the creation of the 1954 fund most responsible for placing the performing arts in the cultural diplomacy arena, he dedicated $2,225,000 to the State Department for the tours, which would be more than $19 million dollars in 2013 when adjusted for inflation.) The ECA dedicated $1 million of this increase to DanceMotion USA.[20] How much of this money reaches the selected dance companies is unknown since BAM does not reveal artist fees.[21]

These funding increases happened, in part, because supporters of cultural diplomacy existed in both of the United States' main political parties, the Republican and Democratic parties. The Republican Bush administration had promoted the substantial 2009 increase; that budget was created and had passed under Bush leadership one year earlier. In the 2008 presidential campaign, the Democrats' Obama-Biden ticket signaled its support for cultural diplomacy, too. The campaign arts platform, written in a nostalgic tone, read,

> America's cultural leaders were deployed around the world during the Cold War as artistic ambassadors and helped win the war of ideas by demonstrating to the world the promise of America. Artists can be utilized again to help us win the war of ideas against Islamic extremism.[22]

While this statement must be read in the context of campaign rhetoric, which often trades nuance for boldness, it still smacks of Cold War debates predicated on binaries of "us" versus "them," merely substituting "Islamic extremism" for Soviet Communism. The statement, too, is surprising given the conversation in the United States about the complexity of cultural diplomacy in prior years.

Once in office, however, the Obama administration's foreign-policy efforts embraced some of the ideas discussed after 9/11, imagining the United States' role as that of a global partner that listened to others. In a 2009 speech in the Czech Republic, President Obama said the United States "must not lead in the spirit of a patron but the spirit of a partner."[23] In a speech to the Council on Foreign Affairs, also in 2009, Secretary of State Clinton eschewed polarizing Cold War language and offered a vision of international relationships as networks. She described the United States' role in the world as "inducing greater cooperation among a greater number of actors and reducing competition, tilting the balance away from a multi-polar world and toward a multi-partner world."[24] Both Obama and Clinton first asserted the United States as international leader, but then described that leadership not in terms of one leader guiding many, but as leaders participating in a network, a global system of cooperation.

Obama's election changed another conversation about partnership, as artists became particularly interested in working with the federal government. UBW artistic director Jawole Willa Jo Zollar said that when BAM's Melillo initially invited her to be part of the program, she immediately responded, "Of course I'm interested. It's the Obama administration." [25] UBW executive director Jana La Sorte joined UBW immediately after working for the Obama campaign, so she, too, remembered being excited about the tie between the new administration and dance. But she also felt it was important to make sure, as she put it, "everyone had the facts right" when UBW went on tour: DanceMotion USA had been green-lighted under President Bush. [26]

The State Department did not mark DanceMotion as particularly tied to the new administration; rather, it framed the program as important to "America" more generally. Under Secretary of State for Public Diplomacy Colombia Barrosse said,

> It's great for us [the State Department] to know that this administration [Obama] has been and will continue to be supportive of the work we do overseas. We look at our programming in cultural diplomacy as fitting within people-to-people, citizen-to-citizen exchange. The fact is that they [the dance companies] are representing the United States citizen [not just the Obama administration].[27]

Barosse distinguished between representing the United States as a citizen and representing the politics of a specific administration, marking the former as the officially sanctioned position of the companies tapped for DanceMotion. Many of the dancers recalled that the State Department employees who briefed them before tours emphasized the distinction the State Department saw between being a partisan political representative and an individual cultural ambassador. The artists were to be the latter. The dancers were not to speak of politics, only of culture, and the briefings treated the two as cleanly divided arenas. When UBW dancer Christine King talked with me about the DanceMotion tours, she frequently hesitated to use the word "political." I asked her why she kept almost saying the word, but then stopping herself:

> Because we were told not to [discuss politics]. We knew that people were going to . . . try to talk politics while we were there, and we weren't there on a political mission. . . . [W]e were there as cultural ambassadors. So, and it was hard [sic]. People always wanted to know about "We have a black president now." They wanted to get into discussions with us, and you can do that on a very light level, but then other things come up.[28]

King described how murky she felt the line was between politics and culture. A discussion about a major event, such as the election of the United States' first black president, could easily lead to, and the company feared would lead to, off-limits discussions of issues like anti-American sentiment in Venezuela.

Even if the dancers steered conversations away from blatant political topics, UBW's work still was political—just not always in ways obvious to government officials as it is possible to watch work like UBW's *Walking with Pearl*, which is discussed later in this chapter, and not attach it to a specific time, place, or political issue.[29] Even with DanceMotion's emphasis on supporting African diasporic work, a topic I discuss at the end of the chapter explicitly in relationship to UBW, the government framed the tours as apolitical. As Barosse said in our interview, "Cultural diplomacy is an excellent opportunity to dispel negative stereotypes and come together in a space where a lot of things that are differences, whether they are race or religion, are set aside because we're communicating as human beings on a different level."[30] As the artists moved into a discussion of American cultural diplomacy begun by policy makers, different perspectives on what the arts might do surfaced. But first DanceMotion had to be planned.

MOVING FROM RHETORIC TO PLANNING: MAKING DANCEMOTION USA HAPPEN

DanceMotion moved from idea to reality in two years—a very quick turnaround for a government program. In two years of planning, DanceMotion grew from the work of many partners: the private administrators BAM and Lisa Booth Management, Inc. (LBMI); host countries, including some where stages had to be built to create a space suitable for dance performances; and three dance companies. The speed of the planning process is notable. Unlike a music tour, where the artists can often carry their instruments into all kinds of spaces, dance tours involve notoriously difficult logistics. Touring dance companies require supporting groups of people (there were twelve people on each 2010 tour), and these groups usually cannot perform in just any space, on any surface. These difficulties were compounded in 2010 by the absence of embassy staff with experience supporting arts groups. Logistical obstacles like these shaped many choices in the early years of DanceMotion. Tracking the layers of decisions made by private and public partners clarifies how artistic and administrative choices sometimes stemmed from explicit political goals, while, at other times, logistical choices had political impact.

DanceMotion returned annual seasons of full dance company tours to State Department programming for the first time in decades, but DanceMotion did have more recent predecessors that influenced its structure. Rhythm Road: American Music Abroad is a State Department and Lincoln Center partnership that in 2006 began sending musicians abroad to perform and teach. In its first six years, Rhythm Road sent 180 musicians from forty-six ensembles to 116 countries.[31] The tours gave the ECA and, perhaps more importantly, embassy staff experience in being the primary presenter of live performance.[32] At the height of the Cold War, many USIA and embassy officers had significant experience working with artists. This meant that an experienced USIA officer like George West, who got the Limón Dance Company through the Soviet Union and the Martha Graham Dance Company through Saigon in 1974, became knowledgeable about dancers' needs. There is no government corollary to West today. The speed with which DanceMotion came together made these holes in experience obvious, but only by administrating a tour could embassy officials become comfortable with the logistics of presenting or identify the best partners for artists to work within local communities.

Before DanceMotion, embassy staff had only worked with artists already on tour, facilitating extra events during a privately sponsored tour. This had kept most of the logistical and financial burden of supporting live artists on private entities. For instance, individual embassies can apply to the State Department through the Performing Arts Initiative for up to $30,000 to present groups already on tour. This program allowed many embassies to participate in the Merce Cunningham Company's Legacy Tour in 2010 and 2011.[33] Piggybacking on existing tours, rather than planning their own tours, however, meant that the State Department could not align artists' visits with larger policy goals, as is now possible through DanceMotion.

DanceMotion's other primary predecessor among State Department programs—a small, one-time, 2003 program that sent American modern dance choreographers abroad to make work with Muslim communities—had an obvious political goal.[34] ECA staff member Kathryn Wainscott, a now-retired State Department employee described by BAM staff as instrumental in DanceMotion's creation, directed the 2003 program, with the national service organization Dance/USA as a private administrator. Five American modern dance choreographers traveled to Tunisia, Egypt, Turkey, Malaysia, and India.[35] Each artist spent one month in one of the target countries and either restaged or created a dance work. Sponsoring individual choreographers rather than entire companies made this program significantly different from DanceMotion, but the shared emphasis on Americans and non-Americans working together links the two State Department programs.

Although sponsored by the State Department and heavily involved with individual embassies, all these programs differ from Cold War programs because they are administered and, in many instances, designed not by the government but by private partners. Dance/USA administered the 2003 dance program. Lincoln Center leads Rhythm Road. In 2008 the State Department initially, in a closed process, chose BAM to administer DanceMotion's pilot year. (In an open competition in 2010, BAM won the contract to be the permanent State Department partner; its previous success with the pilot program must have made BAM a difficult applicant to beat.) In 2008, BAM contracted with LBMI to imagine the template that has become DanceMotion's structure: sending a small number of companies (three in 2010 and 2014; four in 2012 and 2013) to a region for a one-month trip that includes stops in three countries.[36]

Given embassy employees' relative lack of experience with large-scale performing-arts presenting, BAM fills a large gap in practical knowledge; BAM also heavily guides artist selection, which places tremendous power within one private organization. It is worth considering, then, how private concerns and priorities become publicly validated when a private organization leads a publicly funded program. Looking back on the State Department's dance programming during the Cold War reveals how institutional structures contributed to canon formation. The companies who most regularly received State Department support in the earlier era of dance-in-diplomacy now form the bulk of the twentieth-century American dance canon: those of José Limón, Martha Graham, Paul Taylor, Alvin Ailey, and Merce Cunningham, among others. Companies chosen for DanceMotion, if the lessons of mid-century funding apply, have a higher chance of enjoying relative financial stability in the coming years, even decades. Based on four years of announced DanceMotion artists, it seems that some of BAM's artist selection criteria from its own annual seasons are holding and others not. Strikingly, the DanceMotion series includes a broader range of artistic styles than the BAM seasons do, and include modern stalwarts, such as Mark Morris, a 2014 DanceMotion artist; but also contemporary ballet (Trey McIntyre, 2012), tap (Jazz Tap Ensemble, 2012), smaller postmodern companies (David Dorfman Dance, 2014), and, as noted earlier, many companies exploring African diasporic dance, including UBW, Evidence, Illstyle & Peace, Rennie Harris Puremovement, and CONTRA-TIEMPO.

In addition to the diversity of styles and genres among the selected artists, DanceMotion also represents a wide swath of American geography.

Although six of the fourteen companies chosen as of 2014 hail from New York City, DanceMotion has also presented companies from California, Idaho, Seattle, Philadelphia, and Chicago. During the Cold War, with very few exceptions, practically every company sent abroad called New York home.

Given the attention to stylistic, geographic, and racial diversity, it is striking that one characteristic of BAM's presenting history, a relative lack of the presentation of companies led by women, has passed directly into DanceMotion's artist selection. Both BAM and DanceMotion present very few dance companies led by women. In the dance world, BAM is best known for its Next Wave Festival, an annual festival of avant-garde performance suitable for BAM's larger proscenium theater spaces. Joseph Melillo, BAM's artistic director and the primary force behind artist selection for DanceMotion, came to BAM to work on Next Wave and has remained a vital part of the festival. In the years 2010–2014, for instance, BAM'S Next Wave Festival presented companies led by men twice as often as those led by women.[37] (That ratio gets worse if companies and productions with a man and woman as codirectors are excluded.) Similarly, of the fourteen companies DanceMotion has presented, only four have female leadership: UBW, ODC, Jazz Tap Ensemble, and CONTRA-TIEMPO. In the three nonpilot program years, only two of eleven companies have had female leadership. Given the potential for institutional support to create artistic longevity, this gender discrepancy is troubling. DanceMotion, if this pattern continues, will have no more progressive an impact on making women choreographers part of the American dance landscape than did the Cold War programs. Will we spend the next fifty years still pointing to Martha Graham as evidence that female choreographers can succeed in American dance enough to represent the US dance community abroad?

BAM does not, however, make all the artistic decisions and it does work with others on final decisions. Speaking about the 2010 artist selections, LBMI's Deirdre Valente said that three criteria structured the process: a company's reputation; its ability to work in workshop-oriented community settings; and, in a notable shift from the twentieth- century programs, a company's incorporation of dance styles and approaches with influences from beyond the United States' borders. The selection committee, which included representatives from BAM, LBMI, and, as an individual consultant, dance critic Chermaine Warren, drew the companies from a list of those awarded grants or fellowships from the National Endowment for the Arts, the MacArthur Foundation, US Artists, and larger state arts councils.[38] According to Valente, the State Department's only explicit request was that all artists chosen have "interpersonal skills,"[39] which the committee measured through companies' record of working with community partners.

The State Department's agenda for the program is more visible in the selection of the 2010 tour destinations. State Department regional directors chose the countries to be visited—in Latin America: Colombia, Brazil, and Venezuela; in Africa: Senegal, Nigeria, and South Africa; and in Asia: Indonesia, Burma, and Thailand. According to Under Secretary Barosse, the main criteria for choosing the countries were embassy interest and feasibility: was each site's embassy interested in and capable of presenting a dance company?

The fact that infrastructure needed to present dance did not exist in all the countries chosen and significant investments were made to create that infrastructure—a stage suitable for dance was built in Burma—suggests that some countries' political value superseded logistical feasibility. In the first four years of funding, some trends in country selection have surfaced. First, Asia is a clear priority. ODC traveled to Indonesia, Thailand, and Burma in 2010. Since then, five more tours have gone to Central, South, and Southeast Asia, for a total of six of the fourteen announced tours. The first collaborative project between American and non-American dancers also built American and Asian ties: the collaboration between the Trey McIntyre Project and the Korean National Contemporary Dance Company (see chapter 5). At the low end of DanceMotion's priorities sits Europe, as was the case in the Cold War, which hosted no tours between 2010 and 2014. After Asia, the next target destination has been South America, which American companies visited in 2010, 2013, and 2014, including Doug Varone's 2013 collaboration with the Argentinian dance company Brenda Angiel Aerial Dance Company.

The only 2010 tour that did not begin a clear pattern in the DanceMotion tours was Evidence's work in sub-Saharan Africa. Jazz Tap Ensemble went to Mozambique, the Democratic Republic of the Congo, and Zimbabwe in 2012, but other tours have focused on North Africa and the Middle East. It is tempting to describe this approach to Africa as evidence of a reaction to the pro-democratic protests in the Middle East from 2010 to 2012, often grouped together under the title "the Arab Spring." As of 2014, however, I have not found sufficient evidence to support this claim. Other trends regarding the political strategy behind tour destinations will take time to surface.

Looking at the 2010 tours, it does seem that one aim of DanceMotion is to put dance diplomacy in countries where the United States lacks more traditional diplomatic avenues. On the 2010 tour, each company visited one country with limited diplomatic channels open to the United

States: Venezuela, Burma, and, to a lesser degree, Nigeria. Venezuela's President Chávez had been an outspoken critic of the United States since being elected in 1998. In 2008, Chávez intensified his critique of the United States, and then withdrew the diplomatic status of the American ambassador to Venezuela, which led the United States to do the same to the Venezuelan ambassador in Washington. The United States has not had open diplomatic relations with Burma for many decades because a military dictatorship ruled the country until recently. (The dictatorship called the country Myanmar; Burma is the country's former name and the name recognized by the United States.) In 2009, the State Department reviewed its policy on Burma, resulting in an assessment that neither the use of sanctions nor disengagement had led to progress. Burma then became one of the countries with which the Obama administration reopened diplomatic conversations.[40] As in Venezuela, sending DanceMotion to Burma allowed a small American diplomacy project to engage people in a country where the United States was still tentative about the best diplomatic approach.

In comparison to Burma and Venezuela, in 2010 Nigeria had friendly relations with the United States. The annual Pew Global Attitudes Surveys record relatively high favorability ratings of the United States among Nigerians throughout the first decade of the twenty-first century. Yet the dancers said that State Department officials frequently described the country to them as "challenging."[41] US favorability ratings were much lower among Nigeria's Muslim population than among its non-Muslim population.[42] As was true in the cultural diplomacy discussions immediately following 9/11, reaching Muslim communities abroad most likely remained a priority. (Of the forty-two countries selected for DanceMotion's first four years of touring, one-third have Muslim populations of 45 percent or more.)[43]

Embassy staff, generally Foreign Service officers serving as public affairs officers (PAO) or cultural affairs officers (CAO), made decisions about the cities companies visited, often making choices related to either specific policy goals or logistical possibilities. For instance, in Colombia CAO Rex Moser chose the cities Cali and Cartagena for stops on the UBW tour because they had Colombia's most robust dance communities.[44] Doing workshops with artists required being in sites with multiple arts groups.

BAM's Melillo had the final say on the companies chosen, a task completed after the tour destinations had been tentatively set. In a *New York Times* article about DanceMotion, Melillo described the rationale behind the company-country matches. His explanation, perhaps taken out of context and therefore less nuanced than intended, replicated old stereotypes about non-American audiences, including some that stretched back to the

Cold War. For instance, Melillo said he chose ODC, which, of the 2010 companies' had the most modernist aesthetic—clean lines with a hint of balletic virtuosity—for Southeast Asia because he felt Asia required a certain "formalism and a certain kind of elegance and smartness."[45] The Dance Panels of the 1950s and 1960s discussed Asia in a similar way. Asian theatrical and dance forms are, however, diverse, and the idea that formality might be a characteristic seen across sites as diverse as Burma, Indonesia, and Thailand says more about the persistent blunting of American knowledge of Asian dance than it does about actual Asian performance.

Melillo's other explanations for the company-country matches, as reported in the *Times*, offered a sparse and potentially narrow rationale for Evidence's and UBW's placement as well. For Africa, Melillo said he wanted "an African American modern dance company [that] demonstrate[d] sensitivity to African traditions but also show[ed] advancements in contemporary sensibilities," so he chose Brown.[46] This comment could be understood to mean either that African dance artists do not have "contemporary sensibilities" or that an African interest in a hybrid of traditional and contemporary aesthetics might bring Brown and African artists into a similar orbit. Melillo said he felt UBW's "very physical" choreography would work well in South America.[47] The comment about a need for "very physical" dance in South America perhaps suggests a less thoughtful approach to dance in South America, but, in all fairness, the quotation is too brief to mine for deep meaning. Nonetheless, it is interesting to note that Melillo associated Asia with formality and intellect; whereas South America occupied the embodied end of the mind-body split.[48]

Once the sites and artists were chosen, BAM and the LBMI staff spent 2009 researching and scheduling each tour, ensuring that the tour stops were not formulaic, a key aspect of programming insisted on by Melillo.[49] To find the best partners in each city, Melillo and LBMI staff traveled to each site to work with embassies to forge connections with local artists and community organizations and to identify suitable performance and workshop venues. During this period, BAM development staff raised the additional $370,000 needed to finance the program, furthering private influence on the public program. The funds came largely from the Robert Sterling Clark Foundation, a private endowment that supports relationships between the public and nonprofit sectors, and the pharmaceutical company Pfizer. (In subsequent years, the investment and banking firm J. P. Morgan has also been a private funder of DanceMotion.) This additional money primarily went toward creating a dance library of books and DVDs, mostly focused on American modern and postmodern dance companies and traditions.[50] The public-private funding structure behind

American cultural diplomacy that began in the early twentieth century with philanthropists, J.P. Morgan among them, supporting early visual art exchanges has continued into the twenty-first century.[51]

The companies had to prepare for the tours, too. Logistical issues often bled into the repertory selections. LBMI worked with each group on logistics, suggesting that companies avoid working with cumbersome sets or costumes that needed dry cleaning.[52] Only ODC had to explicitly consider the politics of their programming, and then only in Burma, where the State Department knew that censorship would be an issue. After two-day briefings in Washington, with repertory selected and rehearsed, the companies left on their tours. Evidence went first, then ODC, and finally, UBW. Dance-in-diplomacy international tours had arrived in the twenty-first century.

RELATIONSHIP-BUILDING BEYOND THE THEATER

Under Secretary Barosse described twenty-first-century dance-in-diplomacy as happening "far beyond the theater walls."[53] Compared to the Cold War–era tours, DanceMotion created situations in which American artists and non-Americans, including people with all kinds of dance backgrounds, could gather in workshops, as well as participate in community conversations, lecture-demonstrations, and master classes. Looking at how interactions did and, more often, did not happen during the Cold War programs and at how the twenty-first-century context demanded different things from cultural diplomacy offers lessons about DanceMotion's shift to nontheatrical settings. Theories of arts-in-community, from both sociological and artistic perspectives, demonstrate that moving from theaters to less spatially divided spaces does not magically foster "community" or, to put it in cultural diplomacy terms, "mutual exchange." The artists chosen for the 2010 tours brought with them decades of experience grappling with notions of community and exchange, the impenetrability of some cultural differences, and the possibilities of connecting across those differences. The strategies artists used in DanceMotion offer sophisticated approaches to the demands of working interculturally while also officially representing the United States. The situation demanded constant self-reflexivity, recognition of cross-cultural understanding as always partial, and vigilance toward the limits and possibilities of embodiment. Finally, even though DanceMotion was new, all the dancers involved in the 2010 tours lamented the same thing artists in cultural diplomacy always have: the limits of time.

Twentieth-century State Department dance-in-diplomacy programs emphasized theater performances, generally marginalizing interactions between local people (beyond those who sat in the theater) and the visiting Americans, leaving any meetings with locals to the individual companies or dancers to arrange. Dancers on the Cold War tours talked about wanting more opportunities for interaction, but their lack of familiarity with new cities and heavy performance schedules prevented them from being able to explore new places on their own. On a larger level, many of the countries the Cold War tours visited had barely allowed the dance companies into the country in the first place, so arranging time to dance and talk with local artists seemed an impossible task for both embassy staff and artists. Any scheduled interactive events, beyond formal embassy receptions, usually involved situations that replicated the dynamics of a theater with an audience and a set of performers—for instance, the New York City Ballet's visits to the famous Soviet ballet schools in Moscow and Leningrad to watch ballet classes.

DanceMotion's shift toward active engagement for all parties has required embassy staff to be the connective tissue between the visiting American artists and local communities. DanceMotion's website describes the engagement aspect of the program as consisting of "embassies partner[ing] with leading cultural, social service, and community-based organizations and educational institutions to create unique residencies that allow for exchange and engagement."[54] Rex Moser, the CAO in Colombia who helped organize the 2010 UBW tour, making him one of the first embassy staff members to move DanceMotion's mission into practice, described how he approached organizing performances versus workshops. Performances, he said, are "formal interactions where the dancers are onstage behind the curtain: they [the dancers] perform and they disappear. In workshops they can ask questions and do all kinds of activities that are much more impactful in the long term."[55] Both DanceMotion's mission statement and Moser emphasized the importance of building connections. Hopefully, these connections then lead to changes in perception, the key goal of the DanceMotion program. The emphasis on connection as the impetus for changing perceptions comes from a twenty-first-century mindset that assumes that a more networked world is a more equitable one. This, as stated earlier, was the foundation of the Obama/Clinton articulation of American foreign policy. But the question remains: who is expected to change in these exchanges?

Community-engaged cultural diplomacy risks presupposing a community with which visiting Americans can engage—and, even more so, a community that *wants* to engage with Americans. As sociologist Miranda

Joseph writes, "community" can become a point of fetishization, idealized as a "utopian state of human relatedness."[56] Looking at the types of and approaches to community interactions that the State Department, American artists, and non-American participants offered not only creates a space in which to study the premises undergirding the programmatic choices, but also, to again borrow from Joseph, to attend to how people invoke "community" as a way to "raise questions of belonging and power"—or to obscure unequal power.[57] To what do American-sponsored arts workshops abroad ask people to belong? What might be the difference between asking people to belong to a preexisting community of an idea imagined as already shared and asking people to share from whence they come and to consider what they want to make together?

While these questions were somewhat new to American arts diplomacy in the twenty-first century, they were not new to the artists selected for the 2010 program, all of whom had ample experience working with outside groups on a regular basis. Evidence's work in Brooklyn and on tour includes the traditional dance-company fare: master classes, a one-time event at which Brown or one of the dancers teaches the company's style, and lecture-demonstrations, which unfold like informal performances, often with as much space for talking as for dancing. Evidence's programs, though, also include Brown's self-designed all-male workshops focused on relationships among men, and company-led regular workshops focused on dance and disability. ODC's community engagement, like that of Evidence, includes the standard roster of teaching and workshops, but the company is also invested in making itself a hub of the San Francisco arts scene. ODC opens its space in San Francisco's Mission district to a wider public, hosting arts meetings and performances in its classrooms, studios, and theaters, which has given the company ample experience in building partnerships.

UBW has a long history of working in communities, in its home in Brooklyn and in its annual leadership program, now based in New Orleans, as well as in a myriad of workshops the company conducts on tour. UBW has worked extensively to reshape the larger arts conversation about what it means to work with communities. For instance, UBW publicly defines its methodologies, terminology, and practices, eschewing the term "community outreach" in favor of "community engagement." The company favors the latter term because it forwards "community-identified change," actions and conversations a community wants, rather than "a method of interacting with a community where there is an assumption of a powerful and knowledgeable center . . . that 'reaches out' to an assumed less powerful and knowledgeable community."[58] UBW's language speaks to community engagement as a negotiation of power and respect, rather than as an imposition of knowledge of the arts from an imagined "outside" space. These distinctions become important in considering how Americans and non-Americans work together through the DanceMotion program, since the artists had so much complex knowledge about how to recognize power differences and work together ethically.

Just being together in community settings was not enough to facilitate deep cultural exchange on a tour. The American artists were also mindful of how they represented the United States: the specter of the Ugly American—the stereotype of the arrogant, insensitive American traveling abroad popularized in mid-twentieth-century popular culture—loomed large. UBW artistic director Zollar and the other UBW artists drew upon their community work experiences in the United States and also from practices they had learned internationally to imagine other ways of being. UBW, for instance, had recently completed a long-term collaboration with the Senegalese company JANT-BI. Zollar explained the company's ethos, which she felt had deepened during the recent international collaboration, with a metaphor: "When you enter someone's house you don't walk in and go to the refrigerator and start changing the channels on the [TV] remote."[59] Zollar foregrounded respect for difference—different practices and different desires. On DanceMotion tours, the stakes for considering the ethics of such interactions are high, not just because the American dancers do not want to activate a decades-old stereotype of American arrogance, but because traveling with the presumption of being able to do whatever one wants prevents sensing and feeling one's surroundings. As Zollar said, "When we assume superiority, we see everything as wrong with where we are and we don't get the benefits." Humility and thoughtfulness must structure any entrance into an unfamiliar community.

While being mindful of American privilege and difference remained important throughout the 2010 tours, the companies also reckoned with the fact that contemporary dance today unfolds in a transnational community. DanceMotion was not necessarily doing something artists were not already doing; it just created a funding structure that helped American artists do this international work in multiple countries. On all three tours, the companies met their contemporary dance peers: highly trained, professional dancers working in, in some cases, internationally-known companies. The American dancers visited with Flatfoot Dance Company in South Africa, JANT-BI in Senegal, El Colegio del Cuerpo and the Incolballet in Colombia, and the Mariupi Ballet Academy in Jakarta, among others. In these settings, the truly transnational quality of the dance world was evident. Before joining DanceMotion, Brown had met and worked with

JANT-BI (which, as noted earlier, had also collaborated with UBW). And as ODC met with teachers and students at the Mairupi Ballet, they were not surprised to find that the main teacher, the school's founder and namesake, had a daughter currently dancing with an American ballet company.

All the companies said that, while they had some things in common with their partners, flexibility remained a key asset. Assuming what would and could happen in the many workshops before meeting face-to-face would have served no one. All the groups said they constantly reimagined what they were doing, entering every experience with a plan they had to be willing to abandon. If the company arrived prepared to teach a modern dance master class, but found that there was no dance floor and that all the participants were wearing jeans and sneakers, then no modern class. Flexibility was required at the macro and micro levels of the tour. BAM director Melillo has called DanceMotion an "artisanal" program because it avoids a formulaic approach.[60] Wisely, BAM designs specific programs for each country DanceMotion visits, rather than imposing a uniform structure across each tour. The dancers took this approach to the everyday level. ODC director Brenda Way said she often found herself asking, when the company arrived at a new site, "What could happen now, with *this* group of people?"[61] What worked yesterday would not, and perhaps should not, be the strategy for today. Zollar said it was only through "face-to-face exchange" that UBW knew what was really the best approach in any given setting.[62]

In embodied interactions, sometimes with translators, but sometimes not, companies fashioned ways to engage one another physically: teaching one another dances from their repertories—Americans learning from non-Americans, and vice versa. They practiced different ways to compose and arrange movement and sometimes just danced together. The different workshop arrangements around embodiment and face-to-face exchange demonstrated that dance offers something to intercultural engagement sometimes less reliant on spoken or written language.

The dancers, however, also experienced the limitations of embodiment—even the trap of relying too much on embodiment. Emphasizing movement practices over talking could backfire. ODC dancer Yayoi Kambara said she did not want to ask any questions that could be seen as offensive, which meant some conversations never happened. An East Asian studies major in college, Kambara knew a bit more about the countries ODC visited than some of her colleagues. During one workshop in Indonesia, Kambara recognized the name of a region near Java, when the teacher identified it as the source of the dance he was about to teach. She knew that the region was one with strict penal punishment, including stoning people to death. Kambara wanted to ask about that aspect of the culture, but, because she was there in the role of dance student and the attention was only on how to do the physical part of the choreography, she felt that it would be inappropriate.[63] As she "submitted" her body (and Kambara said learning dances from older master teachers in strict settings did often feel like "submitting"), she set many questions aside, leaving misperceptions or misunderstandings in place. In addition to demonstrating that dance and embodiment cannot do all the work of cultural exchange, her story also highlighted the pitfalls of asserting that the tours be only physical experiences, marginalizing the relationship among the physical, verbal, and political.

Still, if embodiment sometimes proved more limiting than the DanceMotion promotion materials suggest, the shift to workshop settings broadened what could be categorized as a "dance experience." The companies sometimes taught higher-level dance technique and composition dance classes, particularly when they were in university settings. In other instances, however, the line between workshop and performance blurred as the American company visited a local dance company, and the two groups took turns performing for one another and then learning phrases from one another's repertory. Other workshops invited diversity, from young to old and from trained dancer to people simply interested in moving. UBW dancer Bennalldra Williams, one of the co-leaders of UBW's intergenerational How We Got the Funk workshop, described the hours the company spent teaching African American social dances from the 1950s to the present as a way to "walk through the history of what's going on in the US," while also connecting through the shared experiences of social dance and popular music. The moonwalk may have started in the United States, but it is now a global phenomenon, and other social dances had the opposite migration pattern.[64] In other situations, UBW began workshops with a short performance, and then used that to introduce conversation topics. UBW's "Batty Raps" involves each company member introducing herself with a short rap and movement phrase drawn from the company's Batty Moves (2005), a sassy, feminist meditation on the female butt.[65] The piece, which draws its name from a Caribbean slang term for "butt," reclaims the female body and projects a sense of incredible power and individuality, which also lives in the workshop's structure. UBW executive director Jana La Sorte said the "Batty Raps" workshop often made an excellent departure point for community conversations in which UBW and participants were able to talk about broader social issues.[66]

Of the three companies, ODC had the most traditional community engagement activities: icebreakers followed by technique or composition workshops. But the company also made perhaps the riskiest engagement choice. In Rangoon, ODC learned a few movements of classical Burmese dance (figure 4.2), and then performed the phrase and introduced themselves in the local language at the end of their performance. Dancer Dennis Adams said the audience went crazy, even as the dancers fumbled with the spoken and danced languages foreign to them.[67] Company artistic director Brenda Way says she wanted to include the brief segment in the performance to emphasize that "We value what you do, and we tried to learn it."[68]

In all their descriptions of the workshops, the performers placed a high value on the American artists not just being teachers but trying to be students, too. The dancers' very public struggle to learn the new dance form displayed the Americans artistic limits, though even that bears interrogation: who can afford to look silly or unskilled in public?

Moving into different roles in the workshops led Americans to self-reflexively confront their desires and assumptions about the cultures they visited. Ronald Brown found himself constantly recognizing that a recurring lesson of his work in Africa has been that what is often imagined as the primary source of African diasporic dance is not necessarily the home of traditional African dance today. In one workshop setting in Nigeria, Brown asked a group of teenage dancers to show him some of their dances.

Figure 4.2
ODC dancers learn Burmese dance vocabulary onstage at the conclusion of the company's performance in Rangoon, Burma. *Left to right*: Yayoi Kambara, Vanessa Thiessen, Corey Brady, Anne Zivolich, Elizabeth Farotte Heenan
Source: Photograph by U Kyi Saw.

They immediately started doing dances that Brown recognized were from the house music scene in the United States.[69] Yet, returning to his interest in the relationship between Africa and African Americans being a "twisted mirror," Brown found himself confronting the fact that he might have more interest in traditional African dances than did his African counterparts, and they might have more interest in the dances of American (and African) clubs than he did. Performance ethnographer Joni Jones calls this recognition a "relinquishing [of] desire for authenticity" that she says "does not give up some vital aspect of blackness or spirituality, but [that] opens up blackness and spirituality to greater variety, ambiguity, and therefore possibility."[70] By moving away from the search for some stable, traditional, "authentic" African form, Jones says, artists working in the African diaspora no longer have to work in "bounded isolation," but instead can recognize their "shared humanity" and intertwined desires.[71] Dance steps can be shared, but the more potent conversation and artistic material grows from considering reciprocal desires to know another's culture.

In other situations, dancers confronted not only that they had made faulty assumptions about the places they visited, but also that visiting the countries and working with locals did not mean they could discern the meanings of what they experienced. Understanding was always partial. This realization was most present in relationship to the ODC dancers' ideas of what would be appropriate for women in the majority-Muslim countries they visited. In the Washington DC briefing, State Department officials told the company's women to wear modest clothing, such as long skirts, and to be mindful of physical interactions with the people they met. Dancer Quilet Rarang worried about this; she often hugs people as a greeting but did not want to make a cultural faux pas.[72] Dancer Anne Zivolich said the admonishments about the strict gender codes made her nervous, too, an anxiety that abated relatively quickly when an Indonesian woman sitting next to her on a plane gave Zivolich her phone number when she learned that ODC would be performing in her hometown of Surabaya.[73] The dancers had to learn that a different set of gender codes around dress and physicality did not mean people would be less friendly or open. ODC dancer Kambara said the superficiality of her ability to understand gender performance abroad surfaced for her as she watched women perform at the Mairupi Dance Academy in Indonesia. The women's bodies were almost entirely covered, but they were dancing in what seemed to Kambara to be a "kind of sexy or at least flirtatious" manner.[74] Watching that rehearsal, she realized that she really did not know where the line was between modesty and using the body to express oneself in Indonesian culture.[75]

These moments of cultural confusion might have lessened if the dancers had more time in each country and city they visited, or if they had had more time to interact with local artists outside the scheduled workshops. Most of the artists I interviewed agreed that the priority in DanceMotion seemed to be that the American artists meet as many local people as could possibly be packed into one month of touring. UBW dancer Marjani Forte found this intense scheduling very American:

> In the States, there's a strong value system around quantity, but quality is where art lies, I think. And so I think that you know when we, as we revisit these State Department exchanges—where the impact—or where the connections can be made, I think, *should* be made are in the quality of the exchanges between groups so that we're able to connect as human beings. That's where we're able to see each other then as human beings when it comes to policy forming and nation building or whatever you want to call it.[76]

What Forte said is not simply a request for longer workshops with any given group, but instead enough time with the groups to engage with them on several levels: as dancers, as people, and as citizens of another country with a whole host of experiences and backgrounds. She then argued that more time would allow greater resonance of individuals and nation in her own mind, seeing the people involved as part of larger communities, including national communities.

Dance so shaped the tours that time for other modes of interaction fell away. ODC dancer Daniel Santos, like Forte, noted a similar emphasis on quantity on the ODC tour, not just in the number of workshops that were scheduled, but also in the emphasis on dancing only, not talking or socializing, in the studio:

> It felt like we just touched the surface of something that could have been great and fulfilling. It's just the time constraints didn't lead in that direction. If we had spent more time—maybe another week or two in each place—to really get in there and have a conversation, because it was pretty much, "Let's teach class, take a picture, and leave." There was not the exchange that happens when we [ODC] spend so much time together on a piece. [When we're creating a piece] we also spend a lot of time talking outside of this [studio] environment. I feel like we kind of missed that part—to spend time outside the classroom environment.[77]

Santos made several points. First he expressed a desire to move from monologue to dialogue to potential collaboration, the same path policy analysts writing about cultural diplomacy have been advocating for since the early 2000s.[78] But, these policy analysts generally consider the arts, particularly performance, to be only monologic, not paths to dialogue or collaboration. Santos explained his feeling that making work with non-American artists might be the best way to create both dialogue and collaboration, but noted that that kind of interaction takes time. (His estimation of one or two weeks for creating a piece is quite short.) When the State Department funded individual choreographers to work abroad in 2003 and set work from their repertoires, each artist spent one month in one location. As of 2012, DanceMotion has indeed moved toward creating longer-term collaborative projects for at least one of the American companies selected to tour (see chapter 5).

The State Department deemed the emphasis on community engagement an overwhelming success, especially in evaluations written by embassy staff.[79] Chris Miner at the ECA said that the workshops were the piece of the program that would definitely remain in place as long as DanceMotion USA continues.[80] In subsequent years, the ratio of time between performances and interactive sessions has continued to lean toward the latter.

Performances, though, have their own forms of interaction—audiences are not passive vessels receiving information from the stage. The dancers felt the workshops primed audiences to get more out of the performances they saw later. The ODC performance of the classical Burmese dance choreography is the best example of how a workshop could affect performance, but there were others, too. The UBW dancers felt that the most successful performances they had were those where a large number of audience members had already interacted with the company in a dance workshop or community conversation. Bennalldra Williams felt the workshops served as a bridge to the performances, since people could sit in the audience and think, "'Oh, this is the person I had the class with. This is the person I talked to earlier this week.' . . . People had a connection, so they could really bring their full selves into the theater."[81] UBW dancer Christine King felt the greatest response from audiences in Venezuela, where there was the largest number of workshop participants in the audience. UBW, too, felt the deep, historical bonds of African diaspora performing in the theater, a connection not forged just in a workshop but also through bringing centuries of history into the present, public moment.

DANCING DIASPORA ON BEHALF OF THE UNITED STATES

On every stop of their DanceMotion tour, Urban Bush Women performed *Walking with Pearl: Africa Diaries*, choreographed by artistic director Jawole

Willa Jo Zollar in collaboration with the UBW dancers. Originally, UBW was set to perform *Walking with Pearl: Southern Diaries* (2005), a piece about African American dance anthropologist Pearl Primus's work in the American South, but an injury led the company to substitute *Walking with Pearl: Africa Diaries*," about Primus's work in Africa. The piece makes explicit UBW's commitment to African diasporic practices, embodying a hybridity of vocabularies to political ends. The work intertwines a range of movements and those dance forms' histories, naming not just multiplicity but also resistance as essential to African American dance practice. The piece's movement vocabulary includes African, Afro-Caribbean, and American modern dance. For instance, in one brief moment in *Africa Diaries*, there is an exchange among three dancers that weaves together the high-knee stepping of the Senegalese sabar; the inverted cartwheels and lunging stances of capoeira, the Afro-Brazilian dance–martial art based in the history of Afro-Brazilian resistance; and feet positions clearly recognizable as ballet's fifth position, perhaps the most Euro-American of all dance forms. The hybrid vocabulary rearranges the hierarchy of dancing, putting ballet and capoeira on the same plane, in the same bodies.

Africa Diaries revolves around an onstage narrator who reads selections from Primus's writing about the time she spent studying and performing in Africa in the late fifties. As she reads, an all-female ensemble dances.[82] The layers of text and movement, with the text's references to experiences that have already happened and the dancers' motion in the present moment create a temporal paradox. Primus seems to be with the dancers as they move; at times she even seems to be setting them into motion through her words. Performances of *Africa Diaries* have a mystical sheen to them, almost as though they bring Primus, and the conceptions of African diaspora she championed through her dancing and choreography, back from the dead.

As *Africa Diaries* draws the audience into its layered world, the audience joins the performers in crossing time and space. The piece lives simultaneously in the 1950s when Primus traveled in Africa and in the present moment, and it takes place in a diasporic world stretching between Africa and the United States and, as the DanceMotion tour made explicit, into Latin America. When I asked about the tour, Bennalldra Williams immediately described her experience dancing *Africa Diaries*, calling the piece a "meeting ground." Asked to explain what she meant by this phrase, she said, "While [Primus's] writings are the subject matter [of *Africa Diaries*] . . . the best part of that is finding how you can . . . put your own sense of opinion in it and live in that moment for yourself" (figure 4.3).[83]

With so many coexisting layers of temporality, geography, and corporeal technique, the UBW dancers must weave their physicality and personal stories from a complicated collage. To dance and to watch *Africa Diaries* is to experience something of how Primus felt about meeting people and a place both familiar and unfamiliar to her, to commune with sentiments from another time and place, and to question what people owe one another in those moments of encounter.

The opening moments of *Africa Diaries* highlight these meetings of people and places—of audience and performer, past and present, dancer and writer, African American and African. First, the narrator enters, walking across the stage in a soft blue light, circling her neck, hands, and spine in a calm, serpentine motion. Just before taking her seat to begin reading Primus's words, the dancer raises her right hand, palm open and active, as though touching or perhaps conjuring Primus's presence. Then, as the narrator sits and begins introducing the text, noting that all the words are

Figure 4.3
Bennalldra Williams, Urban Bush Women dancer, in Jawole Willa Jo Zollar's *Walking with Pearl: Africa Diaries*.
Source: Photograph by Rose Eichenbaum.

from Primus's unpublished journals and collected writings, the ensemble enters, then stands still. The narrator on the DanceMotion tour, longtime company dancer Christine King, reads Primus's statement: "My life has been like traveling up a river. Now and then I hear singing around the bend and around the bend I would go." As though answering Primus's call to investigate what is "around the bend," the women begin to move. They dance, at first, with internal focus. They are a group dancing together, but everyone is alone. But then, on one side of the stage, one dancer loops behind another, and halfway through her circling, shifts her eyes to the other woman. The soft stare says, "I see you." Next, two women (Williams often danced one of these roles) circle one another, then walk toward one another. They do not touch, but it seems as though the energy that rises from each woman's chest meets that of the other. "I do not touch you, but I can feel you." Thus connected, both dancers open their arms and make a calm gesture, almost a bow, that looks softly reverent and like a deep exhalation of breath. They are equals, sharing space.

Africa Diaries models a variety of ways people come together. In the foregoing description, the dancers meet as equals, as in the moment the two dancers first make eye contact. In its larger historical context, the piece models how people come together through shared histories and goals. Onstage, UBW, a company that is, among other things, one of the heirs to Primus's legacy, crosses space and time to bring Primus's work into the present moment. Finally, the piece creates space for the meeting of American, Latin American, and African cultural forms and connections, celebrating diaspora in the contemporary moment of performance. As a multilayered "meeting ground," to return to Williams's phrase, *Africa Diaries* offers ways of thinking about the transnational and trans-temporal relationships embodied in dance and what those relationships might mean within twenty-first-century US foreign policy.

In reflecting on the 2010 tour, Williams used *Africa Diaries* as a recurring touchstone to think about the tour's importance. She felt an even greater responsibility to communicate the work's ideas through dance, since the text, written and spoken in English, created a language barrier for the Latin American audiences.[84] When *Africa Diaries* "really worked" on the DanceMotion tour, Williams felt it caused "both the audience to feel something, as well as the performer to really go."[85] When all parties involved came together, open to the possibility of being changed, "*Africa Diaries* became a true meeting ground" where it was "not about the performer or the audience watching the performer, but it's [sic] about this reciprocal kind of action that hopefully everyone is experiencing as you [are] going through that journey."[86]

The piece, for dancers and for spectators, emphasizes how and why people come together. Rebekah Kowal has described *Africa Diaries* as centered on "recollection, commemoration, and reconsideration,"[87] as it returns Primus's legacy to public view, but also as it asks what it means to embody diaspora. Kowal argues that *Africa Diaries* adopts Primus's "position as cultural mediator." (Kowal, too, notes that positioning the American Primus, rather than an African voice, as mediator/spokesperson is not without complication.)[88] The writing read aloud in *Africa Diaries* chronicles a trip Primus took hoping to learn about Africa, not from books, but from physical experience. The dance piece, notably, uses dance, not just text, to embrace the idea of diaspora "to make it politically and artistically efficacious" through embodiment.[89]

The work did not just bring these ideas to DanceMotion and the contemporary moment; it returned ideas and an artist once marginalized and rejected by the State Department to national and international attention. In the 1950s and 1960s, when Primus was at the height of her artistic career, the State Department refused to present her work on its tours, in part because of her interest in diaspora. In considering whether Primus should receive State Department support in the early sixties, the artist selection panel took considerable notice of a memo from the American embassy in Nigeria, in which a staff member said that he feared presenting Primus would make it seem that the United States thought American artists could do African dance better than Africans could.[90] Primus's dance work, which drew upon her anthropological research in West Africa, put choreography onstage that she meant to be seen as "African" rather than "universal" at a time when the latter category was seen as a better fit for Cold War cultural diplomacy (see chapter 2). To properly represent the United States onstage required dancing in a manner that could be seen as somehow essentially American, or "only" American. The Cold War–approved American aesthetic was not one that embodied transnational, diasporic relationships.

Africa Diaries is an example of the State Department taking a wider view of African diaspora as part of American culture. The recognition of diaspora as a powerful contemporary practice and politics is by no means a radical assertion in nongovernmental circles or in transnational artistic and scholarly discourse today. Still it is an unusual statement for the American government to make given the general tone of American policy statements in the early twenty-first century.[91] In the wake of 9/11 and the declaration of the so-called War on Terror, President George W. Bush took a hard line, separating the United States from all other national cultures: nations and groups are either "with us or against us" as he said in a

2001 address to Congress.⁹² Bush's statements of absolute binaries separating the United States from other nations intertwine the domestic and
the foreign, but always from a premise of stark national difference and
American exceptionalism.

In contrast, the UBW performance of diaspora emphasized the feedback loops and cultural flows that make national identity porous, always
intersecting with an individual's multiple affiliations and communities.
As Williams said about what it feels like to dance *Africa Diaries*, each person stands in the midst of a variety of times, places, and histories, and
must find her personal way to navigate those intersecting forces. UBW
describes "celebrating the movement and culture of the African diaspora"
as one of its "core values."⁹³ In the interviews, the UBW dancers frequently
cited diaspora as a key source of inspiration. Keisha Turner, for example,
described herself as a "perpetual student of what it means to be a person
of the diaspora."⁹⁴ In dance, UBW encapsulates the from/with paradox of
diaspora, embodying at once an acknowledged and shared set of origins
in the past and a contemporary desire to connect—to dance and imagine
diaspora anew across geographic and political divides. American identity
and African diaspora exist in productive friction and overlap in an ongoing, shifting relationship in the present.

Performing African diaspora in 2010 on a State Department–sponsored tour, UBW functioned as an official trumpet for the United States as
a nation and made clear that "nation" is a porous frame. Sociologist Arjun
Appadurai has described these kinds of public moments and the creation
of diasporic communities as the "diasporic public sphere," a categorization that "confound[s] theories that depend on the continued salience of
the nation-state as the key arbiter of important social changes."⁹⁵ For a
nation-state to recognize, even celebrate, diaspora challenges the prominence of the nation-state as the primary organizing category of global
power. The United States' embrace of diaspora through DanceMotion,
then, seems to undercut US power to some degree. Yet the celebration of
diaspora through DanceMotion also manifests one possible model of what
President Obama and Secretary Clinton might have meant when, in 2009,
they spoke publicly about the United States being not just a leader, but
also a partner in the international community. Whereas on the Cold War
tours, the artistic excess that refused the boundaries of national identity
largely came from the artists' practices of resistance, in 2010 the United
States embraced and even fostered these challenges.

The American embassies presented *Africa Diaries* in ways that emphasized the triangulated diasporic connections among the United States,
Africa, and Latin America. All three of the countries visited—Brazil,

Venezuela, and Colombia—are located in the Afro-Caribbean coastal region and have large populations of African descent. And, as is the case with the United States, much of that population resulted from the transatlantic slave trade. Embassy staff were openly keen on UBW interacting with Afro-descendant populations in every city and country the company visited. At these American embassies, particularly the US embassy in Brazil, there is an ongoing programmatic emphasis on the fact that Latin America and the United States share in the African diaspora. In Brazil, for instance, the embassy sponsors a celebration known as Black Consciousness Day.

While the US government seems to be using diaspora to celebrate international connection and partnership, the theories and artistic practices of diaspora also attend to the power dynamics, forced exiles, and violence that form diasporic communities. In the now-iconic essay in which anthropologist James Clifford described diaspora as invested in "roots and routes," he further described "transnational connections linking diasporas" as forged from people's "shared, ongoing history of displacement, suffering, adaptation, or resistance."[96] It is not just UBW's interest in the dance practices of the African diaspora in the United States, the Afro-Caribbean, and Africa that make DanceMotion USA programming a fertile "meeting ground" for African American and Afro-Caribbean artists and audiences. It is also the violent legacy of slavery's history that connects these sites and populations.

Including *Africa Diaries* on the DanceMotion tour recognized diaspora as part of American experience and thus shifted other marginalized aspects of American history to center stage—namely, slavery. In the 1960s, the USIA materials, as discussed in chapter 2, cited slavery to make the claim that there had been great racial progress in the United States. In pamphlets distributed throughout Africa, the USIA placed images of slavery alongside images of nascent efforts toward racial integration, visually recognizing slavery, but rhetorically using it only to argue "but look how far we've come!"[97] In contrast, the choreographic embodiment of slavery's pain and trauma, circulated via State Department programs that included such works as Alvin Ailey's *Revelations*, which closed so many State Department programs in the sixties and seventies, showed slavery and racism to be still affecting African American life.

Africa Diaries extended this commentary. Like *Revelations*, the piece embodies the experience of slavery, but instead of the abstract sense of pain seen in *Revelations*' "I Been 'Buked" or in the jerky, agonizing gestures of slaves laboring in "Didn't My Lord Deliver Daniel" (also from *Revelations*), *Africa Diaries* explicitly references the Middle Passage, the horrific experiences of African people being shipped to a life of enslavement in the Americas, which is, literally, the event and experience that ties together the Afro-descendant populations on both sides of the Atlantic and in North and South America. In preparing for the *Africa Diaries* section "Blood Ocean," the cast had many discussions about "being on slave ships and what that meant—the smell, the sea."[98] The choreography of "Blood Ocean" bears these ideas out as the ensemble hurls one woman forward again and again, while pinning her arms back. The group comes closer and closer together, as though the dimming light presses the women into an ever-shrinking space. "Blood Ocean" re-creates the tightness of a slave ship's underbelly, but, more than that, this section of *Africa Diaries* makes palpable the claustrophobic trauma of a body not allowed to control its own motion in a world with few possibilities for escape.

As Zollar put it in an interview, choreography, in this case dealing with the history of slavery, allows her to put "hyper-literality and abstraction" together. Her choreography for "Blood Ocean" offered an image or a sensation both recognizable—the text, read aloud, literally names the section as "Blood Ocean" and the arrangement of dancers conjures a boat's close quarters—while the dancing also gestures to something bigger, something felt, which tapped a history of trauma that possibly united the Latin American audiences and American artists on DanceMotion's Latin American tour. As performance historian Nadine George-Graves has said of *Africa Diaries*, the piece "evokes a baptism by blood, through dance, so that she [Zollar] may connect with her ancestors in order to find herself."[99] Christine King said that after performances of *Africa Diaries* in all three of the countries, but particularly in Venezuela, audience members always wanted to discuss the way they felt connected to Africa as Latin Americans. They told King that they connected to Primus's phrase, the feeling of being "soaked in the tears of my people," and felt "proud of the people and the journey and the energy that comes from [the experience] of slavery and racial oppression."[100] King remembered the comments after the Venezuelan performances with obvious warmth. It is hard to place the anecdotes in a larger Venezuelan context, since all newspapers focused on previewing rather than reviewing the performances.

Keisha Turner, the dancer who described herself as a "perpetual" student of diaspora, extended the idea that connections cross not just time but space in *Africa Diaries*. The use of Primus's journals in the piece focused, in Turner's estimation, on how Primus grappled with "the becoming of herself . . . as a woman and also connecting with what it means to be a woman of African descent."[101] Turner felt that the section of *Africa Diaries* she called the "African sunset" embodied the way diaspora lives in the present day through the company's dancing of the piece. Dance critic Susan Reiter has described this portion of *Africa Diaries*, which occurs near the end, as a moment when the idealization of "Africa" in Primus's writing becomes visceral—no longer an ideal of Africa but rather the practice of Africanness—as Primus's description of the sunset suddenly brings forth the deep red of the women's costumes and the women's ability to embody "larger-than-life essence" in their "sensual, curving undulations and earthy energy."[102] Turner's experience of dancing this choreography was to feel "knowledge as being passed from woman to woman . . . embracing your sensuality and validity and learning what it is to be a woman. Standing in that power, firmly rooted in the coming of oneself."[103] Self is manifested in the piece as the dancers move through a range of interconnected identities: being African American, being of African descent, and being women, and all these related selves live in concert with the work of being American.

MOVING TOWARD ENGAGEMENT

Turner narrated dancing in "Africa Diaries" as a sense of personal becoming and change. The State Department and those who planned DanceMotion clearly hoped this sense of transformation would extend beyond the individual to the level of community. The emphasis on workshops and, as CAO Rex Moser said, "interactions" outside the theater were DanceMotion's primary goal.

The scenes many of the 2010 DanceMotion artists described do echo earlier scenes in American dance-in-diplomacy when Americans and non-Americans showed physical and affective exchanges that sometimes challenged the narratives of difference unfolding in the mainstream political sphere. In DanceMotion's pilot year, the State Department put Americans and non-Americans in the same room. In 2012, the State Department put them in the same dance.

CHAPTER 5

Never a Solo

I n 2012, American dance-in-diplomacy made a huge shift. The State Department funded the collaborative creation of a new dance piece by American and non-American artists. As was the case in the 2010 DanceMotion pilot tours described in chapter 4, American companies traveled abroad to tour on behalf of the United States. But now one American company also chose a foreign company to invite to the US, create a dance work together, and then perform together at New York's Brooklyn Academy of Music (BAM).

In the first iteration of the new collaborative endeavor, the contemporary ballet company Trey McIntyre Project (TMP), based in Boise, Idaho, spent three weeks rehearsing with the Korea National Contemporary Dance Company (KNCDC). Trey McIntyre, TMP's artistic director, chose KNCDC as a partner a few months earlier during his company's DanceMotion tour of China, Vietnam, the Philippines, and South Korea. In fall 2012 McIntyre choreographed *The Unkindness of Ravens*, a twenty-minute work for two TMP dancers and three KNCDC dancers. The Korean and American artists devoted three weeks to rehearsals at TMP's studios in Boise, and then over a month to touring *Ravens* in the United States. The State Department funded the rehearsals and the companies' performance in New York at the Brooklyn Academy of Music (BAM), and TMP funded the national tour through private sponsorship. By tracking the rehearsal and tour, this chapter considers the possibilities and limitations of what I call the "collaborative turn" in cultural diplomacy.

The recent developments in dance-in-diplomacy programs have changed my relationship to this book's topic, too. I began this project as a historian, but I arrived at the 2012 tour of *Ravens* as a historian increasingly drawing upon tools of critical ethnography—I was enmeshed in the tour as it unfolded, and I had to reckon with my perspective in a new way.[1] Although critical distance is always a partially fictive scholarly possibility, temporal distance does make it an easier illusion to maintain. When I interviewed the dancers whose work on behalf of the State Department had been completed, as was the case in all of the preceding chapters, we were both—the narrators and myself—looking back, reflecting, considering how the tours would be remembered just as much as we were discussing what actually happened on the tours. As I began to work on DanceMotion, the interviews had already changed a bit, particularly since I was now speaking with people who hoped to receive State Department funding again.

In 2012, I began speaking with dancers who were still enmeshed in their moment of national representation, and I was no longer imagining the tours' audiences. I *was* the tour's audience. I followed TMP and KNCDC across the United States: to TMP's home in Boise, to New York (a performance I "attended" via a livestream platform facilitated by DanceMotion), and to Chicago, where the Korean and American dancers had their final performance. I witnessed these performances as a kinesthetically interested spectator and also felt the full weight of this book and the research behind it informing my performance viewing and the interviews. My lived, embodied experience felt explicitly part of the process of description and analysis; therefore, I have written myself into this chapter far more than I did in the preceding chapters. This methodological choice allows me to ask a series of questions. How were we all—dancers, both the Koreans and Americans, and myself—moving in and out of the frame of the nation-state, whether we were onstage or off? And how did those moments of sharing space, the weight of cultural capital, and national representation shape what we understood of one another?

This is how I came to stand in the lobby of Chicago's Harris Theatre on the first day of December in 2012. TMP and KNCDC had just finished their final performance of *The Unkindness of Ravens* (figure 5.1). I stood watching, waiting to interview the dancers, while they signed autographs for children who had just seen the performance as part of the theater's family matinee series. KNCDC dancer Chang An-lee and TMP dancer Ryan Redmond, both part of *Ravens* cast, sat side-by-side, awaiting the next pint-sized fan seeking an autograph. As the line slowed, Chang and Redmond passed the time by bouncing their heads lightly against one another. The scene, as I recognized it as a former dancer myself, revealed a physical intimacy between dancers who have worked together and sweated together, felt the rush of adrenaline onstage together, and also felt the tedium of touring—waiting in line at airports, checking in and out of hotels—together. Redmond and Chang did not speak to one another. (All the dancers said the language barrier had been a challenge throughout the tour.) The brief playful physical interaction, a quick glimpse of a private connection in a public space, communicated the bond the two had made, even if they remained very different people, still largely incapable of having a conversation in the same spoken language.

When the dancers finished signing autographs, they came to the green room, the lounge area backstage, to speak with me—first the American men from the cast, Brett Perry and Redmond, and then the Korean women, Chang, Lee So-jin, and Kim Tae-hee. In all the interviews, the dancers told stories of their fear that the process would not work and would be too hard, and also said they were surprised that the moments in the collaborative process, over time, upended their initial anxieties and expectations. Lee had been concerned that the arrangement would be a purely professional encounter with another choreographer, who was already accustomed to a way of working with his dancers. She had worried she would be expected to adhere to a preexisting formula:

> When I was in Korea, what I had heard was, usually if you go to a foreign country they absolutely won't take care of you, won't look out for you. Everyone

Figure 5.1
The full cast of *The Unkindness of Ravens* in rehearsal. *Left to right*: Chang An-lee, Ryan Redmond, Lee So-jin, Brett Perry, Kim Tae-hee.
Source: Photograph by Kyle Morck.

will just have to take care of themselves. But when we got here they took care of us with such a family-like atmosphere, and watched out for us—spoke very slowly for us. I was really thankful and moved beyond words because of all the things they did for us.[2]

Lee said that her ideas about how Americans treat others had changed through the work in Boise and on the subsequent national tour. A bond formed among the dancers that surprised the American and Korean dancers alike.

The time the dancers spent together changed their minds and—as I noticed watching the performances of *Ravens* over time—their bodies. The process also allowed the dancers to play with what can happen (and what can be recognized) in the act of cultural exchange. The dancers had time together to recognize what could be understood and what might be productively recognized as a misunderstanding—a misunderstanding that might not be overcome, but rather seen as an important cultural difference.

This chapter considers what happens when cultural exchange is a practice, albeit a fraught one, rather than an imagined ideal. Whereas American cultural diplomacy has always unfolded within a rhetoric of "mutual understanding," the 2012 shift in process allowed, for the first time, a dance-in-diplomacy program to bring people together for longer periods of time in the space of creation—an environment that offered some new possibilities for dance-in-diplomacy, while also revealing the persistent dynamics of power and difference in international collaborations. Partially as historian, partially as ethnographer, I explore the TMP/ KNCDC collaboration as an example of the entanglement of globalization, nation-states, individuals, and groups.

In this examination, I take heed of cultural critic Rustom Bharucha's warning about imagining individual autonomy overcoming the power of the nation-state in the space of intercultural artistic work:

> In short, there should be no false euphoria about the celebration of autonomy in interculturalism. The autonomy exists, but I believe it has to be negotiated, tested, and protected against any number of censoring, administrative, and funding agencies that circumscribe the ostensibly good faith of cultural exchange itself.[3]

The 2012 dancers participated in cultural diplomacy within a globally interconnected world in which various entities, particularly the United States, work to reassert the power of the nation-state. This agenda follows the

1990s fantasy that increased globalization meant the end of nation-states as they had been understood since World War II—the primary organizing force of global power. American cultural diplomacy in the twenty-first century is, indeed, both part of global cultural circulation that exceeds national identifications and part of the resilient power of nation-states. The dance and dancers involved in the 2012 collaboration came together in an environment in which globalization and dance frame and reframe the dynamics of corporeal encounter—the dancers' encounters with one another and, on occasion, their encounters with me as an audience member and scholar (figure 5.2).

The chapter begins with the meetings prior to my arrival on the scene: the rehearsals in Boise. I then move across the three performance sites where I met, watched, and interacted with the dancers: the premiere of *Ravens* in Boise; the livestream broadcasts of the performance at BAM and complementary program elements in New York; and the group's final appearances together in Chicago, where I conducted the balance of my interviews.

Figure 5.2
Benjamin Behrends, a Trey McIntyre Project dancer, teaches a dance class at the Department of Dance of the Sichuan Art Professional College in Chengdu, China, during the company's 2012 DanceMotion USA tour.
Source: Photograph by Trey McIntyre.

DanceMotion described KNCDC's visit to Boise as a way for the two companies to "continue their work;"[4] yet the two groups were practically strangers when KNCDC stepped off a plane at the Boise airport in October 2012. TMP had toured Asia—China, the Philippines, Vietnam, and South Korea the previous May and June—but on that trip TMP only saw KNCDC perform briefly, in a dance competition setting in Seoul, where the two groups had little interaction. Later that summer McIntyre and costume designer Sandra Woodall had met the three dancers from KNCDC, when McIntyre and Woodall returned to Korea to confirm that KNCDC would be the collaborating company.

Logistics made McIntyre's choice of KNCDC complicated and simple all at once. The State Department kept the exchange aspect of the Asia tour shrouded in secrecy to prevent foreign companies from lobbying for a spot in the project.[5] This meant that McIntyre could ask few questions of companies about their working styles and could only rely on what he saw in performances and workshops on most of the tour. Yet, after seeing KNCDC perform during the Korean leg of the Asia tour and then after a twenty-minute visit with the company's then–artistic director Sung-yop Hong, McIntyre felt he had enough to (and had to) "go on instinct that this was the right company."[6] KNCDC then chose the three dancers to make the trip: the three women who happened to not be involved in the company's already scheduled fall project.

Beyond the logistics behind the choice of KNCDC, the selection was, according to McIntyre, the culmination of moving past what he called his "romantic fantasy" about partnering with a "traditional" dance company. (As was true in my interviews with all the TMP dancers, McIntyre augmented his use of the term "traditional dance" by making scare quotes with his fingers, a gesture that seemed to further symbolize the end of his "romantic fantasy" about the "traditional.") McIntyre said he recognized that, even if he were to find such a company, he "didn't have anything to contribute" to another dance tradition that was, literally, foreign to him. Traveling, as well as watching dance in Asia, McIntyre also realized that, with the exception of what many TMP dancers called their day of Filipino dance "boot camp" in a rural region, the tour mainly took them to what McIntyre called "some of the biggest cities on the planet."[7] In the end, McIntyre felt drawn to KNCDC because it had a similar aesthetic to TMP's, a contemporary dance sensibility heavily influenced by the dancers' backgrounds in ballet and a balletic emphasis on line. In addition to this stylistic similarity, both companies were young—TMP celebrated its tenth anniversary in 2012 and KNCDC, its second. Finally, McIntyre said he found KNCDC's status as South Korea's first state-recognized contemporary dance company remarkable. The imprimatur of the nation-state made impressions in both directions.

McIntyre said the enormity of his role in a creation process labeled as an international collaboration made him proceed cautiously as he conceptualized the work. He knew what he did not want to do: "I knew I could not help but acknowledge this was a collaboration with an entirely different culture . . . and no way did I want to make some big, sweeping journey into the history of our two cultures and pretend that I had anything of significance to [add to] that." Once McIntyre had abandoned his "romantic fantasy" of intercultural collaboration, he moved toward an idea he had already been considering: a fascination with ravens. The idea of focusing on a raven arose from two serendipitous events—costume designer Woodall wanting a crow for a pet and seeing a birdlike image in a work performed by KNCDC in Seoul. The idea came to fruition when McIntyre became interested in ravens (which in a group are known as an "unkindness") because they are the only animal, besides humans, known to have a sense of humor. The difficulty of translating humor across cultures then became a way to think about the visual and kinetic symbol of the raven and also the ideas of humor, communication, and the limits of translation that eventually propelled *The Unkindness of Ravens*.

This mix of logistical concerns, changing artistic vision, shared physical sensibilities, desire, and curiosity are what brought Chang, Lee, and Kim to the top of the escalator in the Boise, Idaho, airport on a Sunday afternoon in October 2012. In the YouTube video produced by TMP that documents the women's arrival, the camera first shows only McIntyre with the women as they exit the airplane.[8] The music of K-pop rapper PSY's hit "Gangnam Style" plays, seemingly as back-up music for the video. Then we see the women get on the escalator, and Lee begins to laugh. The TMP artists dance in the baggage claim area, greeting the new arrivals with the bouncing, lassoing choreography of the "Gangnam Style" viral video. TMP, dancing in lines and facing the women as they come down the escalator, seemingly invite the women to join them. The three women, and their translator Ben Shawn, briefly do join the American dancers, bouncing along, face-to-face, in a complicated feedback loop of mimicry, greeting, and exchange that spans the 5,000-plus miles the Korean dancers have just traveled.

This encounter in the Idaho airport, with the US dancers welcoming the Korean dancers using "Gangnam Style," embodies the way the dancers are already connected via global technology and culture, even as it also notes, if not actual national difference, then perceived national difference. Although the online communities that popularized "Gangnam Style" may, at times, have seemed to transcend national borders, national identity remains central in this anecdote at the airport. The TMP dancers chose "Gangnam Style," in part, because it signified "Korea" to them, and because it was a signifier they knew both they and the visiting dancers would recognize. The global circulation of pop culture and national exportation facilitates the exchange at the airport, making clear that the Korean-American exchange began long before this live meeting.

If anything, though, it was Korean government funding, not American, that facilitated the airport dancing since K-pop, the larger musical genre that includes "Gangnam Style" as well as the Korean film and television industry, has received ample government support in recent years. The Korean government's funding of artistic export through changing national policies has created what popular culture scholar Jeongsuk Joo calls the "Korean Wave." The phenomenal circulation of "Gangnam Style" is "one of the latest examples refuting the view that equates globalization with an undisrupted advance of American popular culture."[9] Korea, too, like the US, funds cultural exports through official and commercial channels, and the appearance of "Gangnam Style," as well as the dancers of the government-funded KNCDC, in the Boise airport is an example of the success of those exports. The same government ministry that has supported the Korean Wave also provided the initial funding for KNCDC to form in 2010. McIntyre's "gut instinct" may have brought the two companies together artistically, but both are part of the curious intertwinement of nationalism and globalization that Joo aptly describes as a contemporary form of nationalism that boasts of the "continued significance of the nation-state and nationalism in shaping globalization," even as what constitutes national identity is reworked by ongoing globalization.[10]

The scene in the airport, however, smacks of an American phenomenon that is not new. The choice of "Gangnam Style" verges on Orientalism, a flattened representation of an Asian culture seen from a Western perspective, rather than from the perspective of the Korean dancers.[11] The Korean dancers arrived in Boise and were greeted by a misrepresentation, or, at least, a limited representation, of their own culture. This, too, is complicated; in the video the TMP dancers move in an almost too earnest way through the "Gangnam Style" video choreography, suggesting that the moment is a greeting but also a joke. The Korean dancers dance along and laugh—a laugh that could be one of discomfort or a more genuine response. How humor plays in this instance is hard to understand, but it seems worth noting given that humor being translatable (or not) became a central theme in *Ravens*.

While TMP's "Gangnam Style" video deserves to be critiqued, it also bears consideration as a sincere act. The fact remains that the dancers greet one another, laughing together and literally touching one another for the first time. The American dancers said they thought hard about how to greet their guests, because they felt so elaborately welcomed at every stop on the Asian tour with red carpets and gifts.[12] Dancer Ryan Redmond learned the "Gangnam Style" video choreography from YouTube and taught it to the company, and everyone agreed to perform it at the airport on a Sunday afternoon, even though Sunday was the dancers only day off, and they, like the Korean dancers, were heading into a grueling three-week rehearsal process.[13]

The moment in the airport laid the groundwork for the head bump I saw in Chicago. Rehearsals seemed to have truly built a connection between the Korean and American dancers, as the two groups learned how to work together across significant cultural barriers and as the casting of the piece disturbed the power dynamics between the companies.

The gendered division of McIntyre's casting of *Ravens*—pairing two American men with the three Korean women—makes sense within a balletic structure of generally strict gender divisions. The casting also presented something to negotiate in rehearsals.[14] In ballet, men generally lift women, not vice versa. The TMP dancers were accustomed to making eye contact prior to a lift, a nonverbal cue TMP dancer Ashley Werhun explained as communicating "You have me?"[15] As she described how this cue works, she said her partner's eyes meet hers, and then she knows his answer is "yes." The dancers said the Americans' expectation that there would be this kind of eye contact in *Ravens* made the rehearsals awkward, because the Korean women and the American men negotiated non-verbal communication styles that were not part of the women's physical repertoires. Werhun recalled the Korean dancers explaining their repeated resistance to the pre-lift moment of eye contact: "We don't do that. It's not part of our nature as dancers in our company."[16] Yet one afternoon as Perry and Chang struggled with a lift, Perry stopped for a moment and spoke to Chang, as the other dancers watched: "I promise I am not going to drop you. I got you; you're going to be safe."[17] After a long pause, Chang said, significantly, in English so Perry could understand, "I know. I trust you."[18]

In the back-and-forth of the rehearsal studio, it was not only the Korean dancers who had to adjust their artistic practices and ways of working with others. Lee made a huge impression in one studio interaction—so much so that every TMP dancer I interviewed told the story as evidence that he or she had made a naïve assumption about the visitors. *Ravens* begins with Lee at a microphone, lit in a spotlight, telling a joke to the audience. "How many dancers does it take to change a light-bulb?" she asks. (The answer: "5, 6, 7, 8.") In rehearsals, the American dancers and McIntyre kept explaining the joke to Lee again and again, assuming she could not tell the joke in the way that the stand-up comedy frame demanded because she did not understand the joke. Only after many such explanations did Lee finally say, "I understand the joke; I just don't think it's funny." The Americans, so sure the Korean woman did not understand the joke, had overexplained it, initially ignoring the possibility of a shared understanding of content but not a shared sense of humor. The American dancer joke was simply not funny to the Korean dancer. This was not an example of a partiality of understanding or a site where the Korean dancers needed to change to fit into the American formula—Lee did that gracefully and effectively in telling the joke in performances. The time spent in rehearsals explaining something Lee already understood was simply a case of not asking another artist what she knew and how she wanted to weigh in on a performance choice.

The role of understudies in *Ravens* led to an even more complicated layering of what it meant to be Korean and American together in a creative space. Although TMP has an egalitarian structure, with no dancer named as above another, Chanel DaSilva had a longer artistic relationship with McIntyre than other dancers and almost always performed solos in the company's repertory. So, on one hand, she was a natural choice to understudy Lee in *Ravens* main role, but, on the other hand, she had rarely been second-cast in anything TMP had ever done. Yet that was where DaSilva found herself in *Ravens* rehearsals. As she described the process from the perspective of understudy, her admiration for Lee was clear:

> I have my way of doing what comes out of Trey's body, but So-jin processed it [McIntyre's movement] and danced it completely different[ly] than I ever would. And, instead of me saying to myself, "No, that's not how Trey would want to do it," and kind of taking on an egotistical point of view, I danced it how So-jin danced it. "A" because it's being created on her and "B" because I want to broaden my vocabulary. I think that So-jin is such an artist. How she danced it I still think is fantastic to this day and I was like, "Oh, I want to dance it like So-jin." I don't want to be up there and do the same "Chanel moves" that Trey is used to. I want to bring something different. And I feel like So-jin—having been her understudy—that gave me a really good opportunity

to expand on my own dancing and take a step back and, you know, if she didn't do it on the count of 2, she did it on the count of 3, then it's on 3 and it's not on 2 because I saw 2. But whatever So-jin did is what it's going to be.[19]

DaSilva narrates the complexities of taking on what another's body does. She excels in TMP, in part, because she can do "what comes out of Trey's body," but she had another task in the *Ravens* rehearsals. She became, not the dancer who does "the same Chanel moves that Trey is used to," but actually one who took on Lee's ways of moving. Likely, given DaSilva's skill, she adopted that way of moving with some degree of exactitude. *Ravens* did not result from a structural combination of American and Korean dance at the choreographic level, but from the individual Korean dancers making choices within McIntyre's creation about where to put the emphasis or how to dance a particular step that had been given to them. This approach then required the American dancers, especially the understudies learning the Korean women's roles, to take into their bodies a Korean interpretation of an American choreographer's imagination. As was the case with the "Gangnam Style" interaction, national identities did not disappear; they were re-mixed through multiple crossings of embodiment and imagination.

Both TMP and KNCDC dancers said that another reason the the collaboration worked was that both companies were new to a choreographic process of working together to create movement, rather than having an artistic director tell the dancers what to do. Because of this, everyone in the more collaborative process of *Ravens* was learning other ways of making dance. As DaSilva said of the usual TMP process, "Trey choreographs every single step, every single count." Lee said that KNCDC's work develops in the same way: "The choreographer shows every movement, from beginning to end, and we have to match that and move in that way. [In both TMP and with KNCDC director Hong] every single movement and rhythm is choreographed."[20] The new way of working, generating movement together in the studio, coupled with the language barrier, meant that everything slowed down. The dancers said that McIntyre notoriously makes work extremely quickly and, with three new dancers, a translator, and a language barrier, that was not possible. TMP dancer Ashley Werhun described the slowed-down rehearsals as "kind of a blessing . . . slowed down and picked apart a little bit more, and I think you see that in the work."[21] Yet speed is relative and, while the Americans had to work differently, they did so in their native language. In the short documentary film that TMP showed before *Ravens'* Boise premiere, Chang, when asked to describe the process of working with McIntyre, simply said, "Fast, fast,

fast." What felt slow to the Americans felt quite fast for their Korean guests. Indeed, speed was necessitated, not just by creative processes, but by the performance schedule. After three weeks of rehearsal, TMP and KNCDC brought *Ravens* to the public.

BOISE PART I: THE "WORLD" COMES TO BOISE

As an introduction to the Boise program on which *Ravens* premiered, TMP screened a short documentary film about the company's DanceMotion tour of Asia and the collaboration with KNCDC, outlining how the company had taught and performed on tour, as well as the rehearsal process for *Ravens*. The film ended with McIntyre floating in front of a wide shot of Boise in its autumnal glory, saying that TMP usually "brings Boise to the world," but today TMP "bring[s] the world to Boise." The quip gets at the multidirectional nature of the collaboration and the fact that Boise, not a coastal cosmopolitan city, stands in for the United States in this moment in DanceMotion's history. The film, however, does not fully capture the swirl of the multidirectional flows when bodies trained to incorporate one person's way of moving use that skill to create a mélange of ways of dancing and communicating. Too, the local and the global connection, "Boise" and "the world," lacks specificity. Boise stands in for the United States and "the world" for South Korea, a side-by-side pairing that elevates Boise and subsumes South Korea.

On my flight into Boise for the premiere of *The Unkindness of Ravens*, I could not help but think about the oddity of Boise representing not just the United States, but American dance today. Of the dance companies discussed in this book, only one other company, ODC, calls a city other than New York home. *Ravens'* premiere in Idaho (although the "official" premiere took place in New York two weeks later) reconfigured the "America" of American dance in DanceMotion. By incorporating Idaho, the program expanded the geographical recognition of where Americans dance and, too, through the pairing with the Korean company, redefined on what terms "America" must be defined internationally. Rather than defining "American dance" in relationship to a specific form, mainly dance modernism, or against a political ideology, communism—as was the case during the Cold War—what counts as "American" never becomes stable in the context of DanceMotion's collaboration in 2012. In these nascent years of touring, DanceMotion seems to offer a more flexible space for defining America as it encompasses a variety of dance styles, dance company geographies, and different international partners—even though those partners always risk being defined as "the world," rather than also retaining both flexibility and cultural specificity.

These productive challenges to any one definition of "America" arose in DanceMotion; other challenges arose in larger contexts as *Ravens* moved from rehearsal to the stage. Two temporal political contexts pressed on the performances I flew to Boise to see: the 2012 presidential election and the 9/11 terrorist attacks. As the plane began its descent into Boise, I saw both the region's rolling mountains and, in my mind's eye, Idaho's outline, cut in deep red, the televised image I knew from five nights earlier, when cable news fixated on each state's role in reelecting Barack Obama as the US president. Though Obama won with a clear majority, the coverage of the election depicted a United States deeply divided, largely over the debate about public and private support for national good. Against an increasingly neoliberal backdrop in which all public goods become increasingly privatized, the existence of an international arts exchange funded by the American government seems remarkable. The mere existence of DanceMotion was a radical political possibility in the recent history of American cultural diplomacy, as I landed in the beautiful red state benefiting from federal support for the arts.

DanceMotion did not, however, as explained in the chapter 4, arise from an interest in public investment in the arts as a more amorphous public good. Rather, the program arose from policy objectives formed in a post–9/11 moment focused on persuading foreign publics of the United States' altruistic international aims. Though this policy was at its most explicit over a decade ago, the TMP-KNCDC collaboration nonetheless highlighted 9/11 as its reason for being, albeit implicitly. Though the State Department had confirmed the TMP/KNCDC project in August, the company announced the collaboration through a press release on September 11, 2012.[22] Whether intentional or not, the date meant that articles announcing the collaboration and the State Department as the key funder appeared nationally on September 11. Articles about the project ran in print and online that day in newspapers from Illinois to Florida and in a variety of New York–based arts publications.[23] Though the articles do not mention 9/11, the coincidence of their arrival in the public eye on that date connected the new work with the catalyst behind the second era of cultural diplomacy.

The imprimatur of "American" preceded the press announcement from TMP that formally tied TMP and the State Department. Being selected for the State Department tour and, even more so, being selected as the first American company to participate in a DanceMotion-funded collaboration, sutured TMP to the category of "American." The nature of the selection process—there was no application, just a phone call from BAM executive producer Joseph Melillo inviting TMP to tour—seemed the first indication that the company had reached a rarefied level in American dance. Company dancer and executive director John Michael Schert said the invitation "validated" what the company had "internally for a long time been saying":

> Trey's work is very American. And we don't mean that in the worst possible sense: that could mean stars and stripes and saluting. We mean it in that it's [McIntyre's] work is earnest. . . . [It's] very honest. It's very human. It's very personal. It's exuberant. It's also very entrepreneurial.

Schert began by noting that the label "American," perhaps even more so in an international context, could be imagined as superficially patriotic: "stars and stripes." He then listed several descriptors for "American" that draw (somewhat) on the qualities of modernism that were so important to the exportation of American work in the twentieth century—namely, "human"—even as he does not mention any descriptors that would fit the formal qualities of abstraction also key to American modernism. He trades the cold formalism of ballet's American past for the earnest and the personal. [24]

Schert's final descriptor, "entrepeneurial," bears greater consideration as marking the company as American. To be an American arts entrepreneur is to make one's own way and to do so creatively: traits that the American dance community has very much attached to TMP because it chose Boise as its home; created a national, rather than local, board of directors; and partnered with local organizations, namely, the City of Boise and local hospitals, to create a year-long calendar of work for the company. In fact, among the first things I saw when as I disembarked from the plane at the Boise airport was a bright blue "Welcome" banner celebrating TMP as the city's Economic Development Cultural Ambassador. The designation, bestowed on TMP in 2010 and again every year since (until the company closed in 2014 just months before the publication of this book), stems from the now familiar argument for public support for the arts, which Boise mayor David Bieter described as an argument centered on "how powerful our arts organizations are at driving our local economy."[25]

American cities of all sizes now champion the arts—not as spaces for thinking, enacting the public good, or even proving local or national cultural superiority—but for their economic value. The value of the arts in this formula arises from the exchange of money: audience members go out to dinner and stay in hotel rooms on the way to and from arts events.

(I spent $225.17 on my hotel, performance tickets, and food before I passed back underneath the "Welcome" sign featuring TMP the next day.) The banner in the Boise airport made clear the ascendancy of the arts-as-economic-engine argument; the banner and the coupling of the words "American" and "entrepreneur" mark TMP as one of the most successful business models for dance. Yet this coupling of the economic and the cultural, too, raises a larger question, not just about how the arts are valued, but about what is being exchanged in, through, and on behalf of dance.

Part of TMP's success—its "Americanness" even—was predicated on its ability to leverage minimal public support to build private support in a world of diminishing financial public support for the arts. Although the State Department funded TMP's Asia tour, the two companies' rehearsal time in Boise, and the New York performances of *Ravens*, TMP funded the rest of the national tour, mainly through private sources. It is important to compare this to how the United States supported its artists in earlier decades. When the New York City Ballet was preparing to go to the Soviet Union in 1962, the State Department funded eight weeks of rehearsal prior to the tour, and then the entire two-month tour. That kind of financial support demonstrated a government belief in the arts as a public good and a tool of cultural diplomacy. Today DanceMotion supports American dance, but it works with a miniscule budget compared to those of the Cold War–era tours.

BOISE PART II: PERFORMANCE

When KNCDC dancer Lee So-jin stepped to the microphone to tell the light-bulb joke in the first performance of *Ravens*, she delivered the line, "How many dancers does it take to change a light-bulb," somewhat awkwardly. In the afternoon show, the theatre audience sat silent after she asked her question. In the evening performance, when Lee's delivery included a more pronounced upward vocal inflection than it had at the earlier performance, the line landed as a joke, and several audience members yelled out responses: "1!" "4!" In *Ravens'* opening scene, Lee's slight tentativeness and the awkward silence that followed—even when the joke landed—immediately acknowledged, even accentuated, that what people say is often misunderstood. The change in the performance of the piece, separated by only a few hours, highlighted that performance changes, too. Degrees of understanding or misunderstanding can shift very quickly.

The inevitability of misunderstanding arises as a theme in *The Unkindness of Ravens*. Several times during the work, the pop-music collage goes silent, and one of the five-member cast steps to the microphone to tell a joke, often in a language most of the American audience members cannot understand. The recurring motif climaxes when TMP dancer Ryan Redmond goes to the microphone. He approaches with a squeaking ball in his mouth. At the microphone, he squeezes the ball in a rhythmic manner, making a sound that suggests speech, though what he says is unintelligible and heard only as an irritating series of squeaks amplified by the microphone. What the audience hears is an intent to communicate, and, at the same time, nonsense.

The emphasis on the partiality of understanding despite intentions otherwise has become a nascent theme in the State Department sponsorship of international arts collaborations. While DanceMotion began in 2010, as mentioned in chapter 4, the State Department had funded a smaller dance residency in 2003 that sent American modern dance choreographers to make work in countries with large Muslim populations.[26] Of the five residencies, one created a particularly strong bond, resulting in a multiyear collaboration between the San Francisco–based choreographer Margaret Jenkins and the Kolkata–based choreographer Tanusree Shankar. As a result of the State Department program, the two women and their companies eventually created the evening-length work *A Slipping Glimpse* (2007), which toured the United States with private funding and then received some State Department funding for a tour of India. Jenkins's title *A Slipping Glimpse* referenced the painter Willem de Kooning's observation, "Reality is a slipping glimpse." For Jenkins, the process of working internationally and interculturally underscored that her understanding of another dance culture, even one she got to know quite well over a long period of time, was always a partial understanding. She was drawn to the phrase "a slipping glimpse" because "it kind of seemed like what we [Jenkins and Shankar] were talking about in a way [in the piece]: that one only gets a slipping glimpse of each other's culture no matter how deeply one becomes embedded in the study of another way."[27] Too, the gerund, the "–ing," in the title references how gaps in understanding shift over time. Intercultural work is a process of perpetual translation; exchanges of meaning that never quite land in the way intended or in a manner than can be fully grasped.

The Unkindness of Ravens follows in this thematic trajectory but also offers the insight that commenting upon partial understanding and miscommunication often relies upon a shared sensibility or training system—from a site of commonality difference becomes visible. As was the case with the Jenkins-Shankar collaboration, KNCDC and TMP shared a similar physical training, since both groups mostly hire dancers who have come to contemporary dance via ballet. Even in the first Boise performances, when the cast still seemed to be figuring out how to dance together, the American and Korean dancers looked remarkably well paired. All five dancers extended through their limbs with elegance, displaying an ability to draw shapes and lines, especially with their lower bodies. They achieved a sense of linearity and, at times, angularity, without sacrificing kinetic propulsion, though the Korean women's energy diffused in space, whereas the TMP men danced with a more focused, frenetic energy.

During *Ravens*, the energetic difference makes it difficult to tell whether the stylistic variation has to do with the dancers' dance-training backgrounds or the gender norms embedded in dance, since the Americans in the piece are men and the women in the piece are Korean. After watching the TMP company in the rest of the program (in Boise TMP performed two other pieces—the Korean women only appeared again at the evening's final bow), the sense of extremely forceful energy bore out as a style that stretched across TMP, regardless of dancers' gender. It was not vocabulary, but style that registered a national difference among the dancers. Both groups of dancers inflect modern/contemporary dance with a balletic approach, though one company (KNCDC) describes itself as a "contemporary dance company" and the other (TMP) describes itself as a "contemporary ballet company."

While the companies meshed onstage in some respects, difference remained stark between the Korean guests and the Boise audience. At both performances, the lobby overflowed with white people, with the exception of a few Asian people who had arrived with the company's translator (while, of course, race is not always apparent through the visual alone, the overwhelming sea of whiteness is a strong hypothesis given Idaho's 93.8 percent white status in the 2010 US Census). DanceMotion's shift away from the New York dance community as exclusively representing the United States had clear demographic ramifications. While the KNCDC dancers might not stand out in a New York theater, in Boise the presence of anyone who looks at all not white is difficult to ignore. The performances might have connected with a less racially diverse audience, but they did connect with a different population than they would have if a New York company had done this collaboration. To reach a more diverse audience, the piece had to tour and/or take advantage of DanceMotion's new investment in technology. I left Boise the morning after the performance, and the company followed later that day. We would meet again a week later, except that meeting would happen on the Internet, as I watched TMP and

KNCDC in the official New York premiere of *Ravens*, which happened in BAM'S theater and online.

NEW YORK: FANTASIES OF GLOBAL CONNECTION?

Although the primary locations of the 2012 "exchange" were anywhere the American and Korean dancers worked together, DanceMotion also turned to technology to expand the possibilities of exchange beyond the local. With the Boise performances behind them, TMP and KNCDC—the three dancers from *Ravens* as well as the rest of the Korean company—met in New York to perform at BAM, where they also conducted a variety of complementary program elements.

DanceMotion has embraced technology as a cultural diplomacy tool, and the 2012 collaborative addition increased the possibilities of the program. The main technology in DanceMotion's 2010 pilot was a blog that BAM maintained, which included photographs, short videos, and posts from dancers. During the 2012 TMP/KNCDC stop in New York, there was a master class with Lim Yi-jo, a master teacher of Korean traditional dance, who led a class through distance-learning technology with students from New York's Korean Traditional Music and Dance Institute and from Seoul's Gukak National High School. BAM also live-streamed the TMP/KNCDC performance to a special audience gathered in Korea to watch the show together and then participate in a post-show online discussion with the artists and audience in New York. The livestream of the performance and post-show discussion was also public, which is how I was able to watch the events while traveling for work in Puerto Rico.

In addition to the State Department's technology-oriented efforts, technology entered DanceMotion through the already techno-centered lives of young people. In interviews, the TMP and KNCDC dancers and the artists participating in the 2010 pilot program all named Facebook as a way they planned to stay in touch. How deep these connections will be remains to be seen, but compared with what was available to the artists in the Cold War programs, it is striking that there are so many relatively easy online tools that may help Americans and non-Americans stay connected. On those earlier tours, some of the dancers imagined they would write letters to people they met but most said they did not. Of course, the question lingers of whether posting a status on Facebook that a former artistic collaborator in another country might see was what the writers of the 1961 Fulbright-Hays legislation meant when they imagined culture diplomacy as a way to promote long-term relationships.

Yet comparing DanceMotion's use of technology only to the lack of technology during the Cold War is not the most important comparison between past and present. Since 9/11, various thinkers, in the government and beyond, have pondered how technology might be part of twenty-first-century cultural diplomacy. During the George W. Bush administration, the State Department's efforts to use technology as a form of public diplomacy focused on sending messages about the United States to the world, rather than building a global network of exchange and cooperation. The Broadcasting Board of Governors (BBG) employed the Internet and satellite broadcasting in American cultural diplomacy efforts.[28] The most famous post-9/11 BBG program has been Radio Sawa, a radio station that tried to reach Middle Eastern youth with programming that blended music and news. In a 2006 speech to the Council on Foreign Relations, Karen Hughes, the last Bush appointee to the office of under secretary of state for public diplomacy, highlighted technology as an important, but largely underused, aspect of public diplomacy. Hughes discussed the possibility of text messaging and of creating podcasts as avenues for bringing information about US policies and values to the world.[29] The Council on Foreign Relations report "Finding America's Voice" critiqued efforts like those Hughes suggested as examples of still thinking of technology in the "one-to-many broadcasting model," rather than as a "more complex array of push-and-pull interactions."[30] A networked world did not necessarily lead to networked thinking.

Writing about the role of international broadcasting and of newly available technologies in public diplomacy, policy analysts Monroe Price, Susan Haas, and Drew Margolin write that the Internet and broadband could move cultural diplomacy into "the culture of interaction and user-originated content. 'New technologies' means far more than reaching more people, reaching faster, penetrating through great barriers. It means. . . altered modes of thinking . . ."[31] The early twenty-first century Shankar/Jenkins collaboration used low-cost technology to forge one possible version of how technology might facilitate longer-term exchange. After working together in person doing a State Department–sponsored residency in 2003, the two companies sent choreographic prompts back-and-forth through e-mail and exchanged videos of short sections of choreography for the other company to learn over the course of more than a year. The Shankar/Jenkins collaboration did not fully move beyond the power dynamics that often privilege American over non-American partners, but the back-and-forth between the two companies made a first (and inexpensive) step toward the kind of "push-and-pull" feedback loop the

Council on Foreign Relations imagined would foster deeper conversation and connection.

DanceMotion, in contrast to Shankar/Jenkins, has so far focused on how technology might benefit audiences, rather than artists. For example, I watched the BAM performances online via a livestream from a hotel room in Puerto Rico. I wondered who my fellow online audience members might be as I saw the online audience member count climb on the right side of my screen—reaching a high of fifty-eight people. I got my answer during the intermission, when several online viewers took advantage of the comment section embedded in the website design. All those who posted comments identified themselves as TMP fans; most of them lived in Boise. The note on the screen during intermission, "Next up, the pride of Boise," likely prompted the Boise audience to comment. The chat board filled with comments from viewers clearly familiar with TMP, McIntyre's choreography and the dancers, and most offered congratulations to McIntyre and the company. While it was enthusiastic, the comment strand was decidedly not an exchange that offered possibilities for American and non-American audiences to come together, especially since everything posted relied on knowledge of individual dancers (the online platform had no program information). Not a single commenter during the almost two-hour broadcast mentioned the Korean dancers in *Ravens* or the performances by KNCDC.

The comment board also drew my attention to the frames through which the live versus online audience watched the performance. The programs for the live American audiences identified the evening as part of DanceMotion, though it is difficult to know how many audience members actually read those programs. The live audience had in their programs details about choreographers, piece titles, and dancers' names, which the online audience did not have. Online, we only had the DanceMotion banner across the top of the screen, and the banner, a mix of bright green, pink, yellow, and blue, did not indicate a patriotic or governmental frame, even though the logo featured the full program name, including the "USA."

The lack of program information made the online viewing of the Korean company's portion of the performance confusing since KNCDC presented a series of excerpts strung together as though they were one piece. It was hard to know when one work began and another ended, making it difficult to sense the dramaturgical shape of any individual work. This obstacle to understanding new work had been addressed by the time DanceMotion presented the next American and non-American collaboration a year later. When the New York–based company Doug Varone and Dancers and the Argentinian Brenda Angiel Aerial Dance Company appeared together in the fall of 2013, each company presented a work of its own, and then together premiered their collaborative piece *Bilingua* (2013).

I did not realize while I watched TMP and KNCDC that a group of twenty people had gathered in Seoul to watch the live-streamed performance, or that this audience was not included among the fifty-eight indexed on my computer screen (that, or the whole group was counted as one). The Seoul audience members suddenly appeared online as the post-show discussion began in New York. The post-show panel included the moderator, dance writer Chermaine Warren; Sung-yop Hong, KNCDC artistic director; Hong's translator; John Michael Schert, the TMP executive director; and dancer Chanel DaSilva.

The arrangement for the post-show discussion seemed not so much a metaphor of the difficulties of transnational, multidirectional conversation, but an actual enactment of those challenges. No one knew how to move between the live audience, the panel, and the Korean audience. Neither the online community that I was part of nor the audience in Korea were really included, although we could see and hear. (Again, this problem had been addressed by 2013. In the following year's performance, an online moderator encouraged those watching via livestream to pose questions to the artists and then funneled the questions into the discussion via the panel moderator, dance critic Deborah Jowitt.) In both 2012 and 2013, however, there was great confusion about where to look when questions were posed and when the panel should answer. The panel faced its live New York audience, and the New York audience could see both the panel and the Korean audience, hovering on a screen behind the panel. The panelists kept turning away from the American audience to look at the Korean audience, but then realized that meant that both the Americans in the live audience and those watching online were seeing the backs of their heads.

Language, too, created a barrier, although it was more a question of not adequately thinking through how to have a discussion in multiple languages than it was a problem of people speaking in multiple languages. Sung-yop, KNCDC's artistic director, spoke at length in the Q&A and, with the help of his translator, moved between Korean and English. He discussed the choice of choreography, explained the reasoning behind presenting the excerpts, and told the stories that had inspired some of the works. The conversation was disjointed because there was no system for dealing with translation in an equally inclusive manner. No one translated anything spoken in English for the audience members who only spoke Korean, but almost everything spoken in Korean was translated into English. The Korean-speaking audience had to catch whatever parts of the discussion it could.

As the conversation opened to the audience, another layer of multidirectionality emerged. Many of those wanting to ask questions in the live New York audience were of Korean descent (many had prominent Korean accents) and many of those in the Korean audience were American. A woman in the American audience, speaking with a Korean accent, asked about the particular word choice in the joke told in Korean during *Ravens*. She understood the joke told in Korean and, it seemed, the English-language joke, too. When the Korean moderator chose someone in the Seoul audience to ask a question, it was an American costume designer studying in Seoul on a Fulbright. Throughout the conversation, and throughout the entire simulcast, there were always multiple audiences, and those audiences did not often fit the assumptions I had made about what various groups could understand or where they were located— Americans asked questions from Korea and vice versa. To say a program addresses multiple audiences is one thing; to actually address and engage multiple audiences is another.

NATIONAL TOUR: MORE AUDIENCES, MORE FACES OF THE CHOREOGRAPHY EMERGE

Things are coming to an end. As I watch the final iteration of *Ravens* in Chicago several weeks after seeing the simulcast of the New York show, I am struck by how much the KNCDC dancers have become the center of the piece. They are much bolder presences now. In the Boise performances and the New York simulcast, the two American men had driven the work, even when the entire cast shared the stage. In the earlier performances, the entire piece climaxed with the two men's athletic duet.

Now in Chicago, the companies' last tour stop together, Lee So-jin has assumed the work's central role. The choreography has not changed (at least not much), but the piece now seems driven by her energy. Structurally this was perhaps inevitable: Lee tells the opening joke and has more solo material than any of the other dancers, especially in the first half. The difference now is that whereas she seemed softer, lacking the edges of the movements in Boise, she now seems angular and more confrontational toward the audience. She goads the audience as she tells us her joke and as she dances. Her voice is louder.

The companies discussed in this book often performed choreographic works more than twenty, even thirty times on just one State

Department–sponsored tour. The problem with treating a premiere or a first-cast performance as *the piece* when really that is just where a work begins is clearly one of the lessons for dance historiography embedded in the study of dance tours. On tour, dancers are in motion and in process, and so are choreographic works. Over time, with different audiences—a more boisterous one here, a quieter one there—dancers make changes both subtle and grand. Landing that opening joke in English to the audience in Chicago meant that Lee, the Korean dancer, became the primary point of connection for the audience. Later in the piece, it was Ryan Redmond, the American man who spoke first in Korean and then squeaked the ball into the microphone, who could not be understood.

After the performance, I first interview the cast's men, Brett Perry and Ryan Redmond, and then, later, the three Korean women: Lee So-jin, Chang An-lee, and Kim Tae-hee. The men speak about the tour in a way I cannot help but find moving. I have never been an objective bystander in this research, but I find myself increasingly rooting for dance to be a way for people to come together in a fractious world. Redmond and Perry have to say good-bye to the KNCDC dancers the next day and are visibly sad about their imminent departure. Redmond tells me that working with the Korean dancers made him realize how closed he had been to the idea of working across national and cultural differences, even within the tiny, often inward-gazing world of elite dance. A former student at Juilliard, a school with a large international student population, Redmond says he now realizes that he missed opportunities to grow from that environment:

> I went to Juilliard where there were a lot of foreign students and I think it was a shame looking back on it because I didn't really engage with a lot of them as much as I could have because I felt like there was a barrier just because of the cultural differences. I never disliked them. . . . It was never that. It was just the underlying concept of me not investigating it and instigating it and initiating a conversation.[32]

Redmond's experiences on the tour made him look back on his past experiences, and to see how xenophobia becomes an "underlying," if under-scrutinized, American stance. He realizes that he wants to move forward in his artistic life differently. It takes a daily practice, or at least a regular practice, to arrive at a place where people of different backgrounds can say to one another "I trust you," as Kim said to Perry in that early *Ravens* rehearsal.

I then speak with the Korean dancers. The company no longer has a translator traveling with them, and has not for several weeks, so I am left—with no knowledge of Korean—to figure out how to do the interview. This is my last interview for the book. I cannot stop thinking about this fact. I am somewhat stunned that the last interview is going to be in Korean. Inae Chung, a recent graduate of the University of Michigan where I work, has translated my list of questions into Korean, and the Korean dancers have agreed to respond in Korean. Only later, when another Michigan graduate student has completed the transcription will I know what the KNCDC dancers said. I'm pleased, even relieved, to be able to speak with non-Americans about one of the tours, as my access to those perspectives has been limited throughout this process. But I am also aware that doing the interview in Korean will offer me only fraught material in a less than ideal circumstance.

It seems just right that my last interview of this project about international dance exchanges sponsored by the American government has me sitting at a table with three dancers speaking to me in a language I don't understand. I have written about their dancing and find all three to be extraordinarily talented, particularly Lee, who so transformed her role in *Ravens* (figure 5.3) in just a few weeks of performance. She has a way of moving the side of her head that adds a sly comment to an otherwise balletically fluid approach to modern dance. She dances and comments on her dancing at the same time.

When Lee answers the written questions into my phone, which is recording the interview on the table between us, she looks at me and speaks Korean to me, as though I will understand her. She knows I understand absolutely nothing. I know I understand nothing she says. But I nod my head as though I do, an unconscious reaction to having someone speak to me directly. I really want to understand her, and I hope my odd, furious head-bobbing communicates this. Although the three women initially balked at doing an interview, they speak quite a bit now that we're here. They tell me (I find out later) how much they will miss the TMP dancers, how surprised they were by the American hospitality, and many other things, all quoted in the preceding pages.

But in the moment of the interview it is our desire to understand one another that moves between us, even though I can't, at this moment, know what the Korean women want me to know. I can't answer them. So I nod, using my body to acknowledge they are speaking to me, even as I fail in my gesture. My nod suggests that I understand them, but I do not. I will need others to help me understand what is happening, what has happened. The body offers up no essential knowledge, but it gives me a way to communicate desire and affect, if not always, or ever, direct meaning.

Figure 5.3
Lee So-jin, dancer from the Korea National Contemporary Dance Company, in the opening moment of Trey McIntyre's *The Unkindness of Ravens*.
Source: Photograph by Drew A. Kelley.

My work is coming to an end, but these tours continue. In each iteration, there are fits and starts, logistical details that could have been imagined better and earlier, artistic choices that seem strange, while others feel somewhat perfect, as I've come to think the fit between TMP and KNCDC was. Mainly, it seems clear these tours will continue to change as American identity is refashioned and reimagined in reaction to events abroad and at home. Dance will be part of that performance of international communication, not in some transcendental mode of imagined "universality," but in public moments of exchange. Feet and sweat, politics and art will dance along the edges of the nation-state, even as they also exceed it.

List of Interviewees by Company and Tour

DANCERS

New York City Ballet, Soviet Union tour, 1962
Gloria Govrin
Allegra Kent
Sally Leland
Robert Maiorano
Kay Mazzo
Arthur Mitchell
Karen Morrell
Mimi Paul
Nadine Revene
Suki Schorer
Bettijane Sills
Victoria Simon
Kent Stowell
Carol Sumner
Violette Verdy
Edward Villella

Carmen de Lavallade/Alvin Ailey American Dance Theater tour, Asia, 1962
Carmen de Lavallade
Dudley Williams

Alvin Ailey American Dance Theater tour, Africa, 1967
George Faison
Judith Jamison

Sharron Miller
Lynne Taylor-Corbett
Dudley Williams

Martha Graham Dance Company, Asia tour, 1974
Takako Asakawa
David Chase
Janet Eilber
Diane Gray
Diana Hart Johnson
Bonnie Oda Homsey
Peggy Lyman Hayes
Lucinda Mitchell
Elisa Monte
Eric Newton
Carl Paris
Peter Sparling

Margaret Jenkins / Tanusree Shankar Collaboration, United States and India, 2003–2007
Debjit Burman, TSDC
Mary Carbonara, MJDC
Joseph Copley, MJDC
Steffany Ferroni, MJDC
Varshaa Ghosh, TSDC
Jaydip Guha, TSDC
Matthew Holland, MJDC
Margaret Jenkins, MJDC
Katie Moremen, MJDC
Sumana Roy, TSDC
Tanusree Shankar, TSDC
Ryan Smith, MJDC

Individual Choreographers, 2003 US State Department Program*
Ruth Andrien
Loretta Livingston
Wendy Rogers

* These interviews were conducted as part of prior research, but are not directly cited in this book. I note them here to acknowledge their time and to note their involvement in the program that eventually led to the Jenkins/Shankar collaboration from 2003 to 2007.

ODC/Dance, Asia tour, 2010
Dennis Adams
Corey Brady
Yayoi Kambara
Quilet Rarang
Daniel Santos
Jeremy Smith
Vanessa Thiessen
Brenda Way
Anne Zivolich

Ronald K. Brown's Evidence, Africa tour, 2010
Ronald K. Brown
Lilli-Ann Tai
Clarice Young

Urban Bush Women, Latin America tour, 2010
Marjani Forte
Christine King
Jana LaSorte
Keisha Turner
Bennalldra Williams
Jawole Willa Jo Zollar

Korea National Contemporary Dance Company/Trey McIntyre Project, Korea and United States, 2012
Chang An-lee, KNCDC
Lee So-jin, KNCDC
Kim Tae-hee, KNCDC
Chanel DaSilva, TMP
Trey McIntyre, TMP
Brett Perry, TMP
Ryan Redmond, TMP
John Michael Schert, TMP
Ashley Werhun, TMP

ADMINISTRATORS

DanceMotion USA

Colombia Barrosse, US State Department

Joseph Melillo, Brooklyn Academy of Music

Chris Miner, US State Department

Rex Moser, US Foreign Service

Deirdre Valente, Lisa Booth Management, Inc.

2003 US State Department Program for Individual Choreographers

Rebecca Rorke, Dance/USA

Andrea Snyder, Dance/USA

International Dance Tours Described in *Dancers as Diplomats**

US STATE DEPARTMENT PROGRAM FORERUNNERS

American Ballet Caravan, 1941, Latin America. Sponsored by the Office of Inter-American Affairs

New York City Ballet, 1952, France. Sponsored by the Congress for Cultural Freedom

President's Special Emergency Fund, 1954–1955

José Limón Dance Company, 1954, Latin America

Martha Graham Dance Company, 1955, Asia

CULTURAL PRESENTATIONS PROGRAM: 1956–1978

José Limón Dance Company, 1957, Europe

Moiseyev Dance Company, 1958, United States

Bolshoi Ballet, 1959, United States

American Ballet Theatre, 1960, Soviet Union

Carmen de Lavallade /Alvin Ailey American Dance Theater, 1962, Asia

Martha Graham Dance Company, 1962, Europe

Bolshoi Ballet, 1962, United States

New York City Ballet, 1962, Europe and the Soviet Union

Alvin Ailey American Dance Theater, 1966, Senegal

Alvin Ailey American Dance Theater, 1967, Africa

Alvin Ailey American Dance Theater, 1970, Soviet Union

New York City Ballet, 1972, Soviet Union

---

* This list is not a comprehensive listing of all international dance tours sponsored in part by the US State Department. This list only includes US State Department-sponsored dancers tours mentioned in *Dancers as Diplomats*.

José Limón Dance Company, 1973, Soviet Union
Alvin Ailey American Dance Theater, 1974, Eastern Europe
Martha Graham Dance Company, 1974, Asia
Joffrey Ballet, 1975, Soviet Union

US State Department sponsorship, Independent Programs
Ruth Andrien, Margaret Jenkins, Loretta Livingston, Wendy Rogers, Kwame Ross, 2003, Tunisia, India, Turkey, Malaysia, Egypt
Margaret Jenkins Dance Company and Tanusree Shankar Dance collaboration, 2003–2007, India and the United States
Merce Cunningham Dance Company's Legacy Tour, 2010–2011, worldwide

DanceMotion USA: 2010–present
ODC/Dance, 2010, Asia (Indonesia, Burma, Thailand)
Evidence, 2010, Africa (Senegal, South Africa, Nigeria)
Urban Bush Women, 2010, Latin America (Brazil, Colombia, Venezuela)
Jazz Tap Ensemble, 2012, Africa (Democratic Republic of the Congo, Mozambique, Zimbabwe)
Rennie Harris Puremovement, 2012, Middle East (Egypt, Israel, the Palestinian Territories)
Seán Curran Company, 2012, Asia (Kazakhstan, Kyrgyz Republic, Turkmenistan)
Trey McIntyre Project, 2012, Asia (China, Korea, the Philippines, Vietnam)
Korea National Dance Company and Trey McIntyre Project, 2012, United States
Doug Varone and Dancers, 2013, Latin America (Argentina, Paraguay, Peru)
Hubbard Street Dance Chicago, 2013, Europe/North Africa (Algeria, Morocco, Spain)
Illstyle & Peace Productions, 2013, the former Soviet Union (Belarus, Russia, Ukraine)
Spectrum Dance Theater, 2013, Asia (Bangladesh, Nepal, Sri Lanka)
Brenda Angiel Aerial Dance Company and Doug Varone and Dancers, 2013, United States
David Dorfman Dance, 2014, Asia/Middle East (Armenia, Tajikistan, Turkey)
Jazz Tap Ensemble, 2012, Africa (Mozambique, Democratic Republic of the Congo, Zimbabwe)
Mark Morris Dance Group, 2014, Asia (Cambodia, China, Taiwan, Timor-Leste)
CONTRA-TIEMPO, 2014, Latin America (Bolivia, Chile, Ecuador)
David Dorfman Dance and Korhan Basaran Company, 2014, United States

NOTES

INTRODUCTION

1. Dennis Adams, Corey Brady, Jeremy Smith, and Anne Zivolich, interview by author, San Francisco, June 28, 2011.
2. For more on the possibility of state support, leftist critique, and public good not being mutually exclusive possibilities, see Shannon Jackson, *Social Works: Performing Arts, Supporting Publics* (London, New York: Routledge, 2011).
3. Yayoi Kambara and Daniel Santos, interview by author, San Francisco, June 29, 2011.
4. DanceMotion USA, "ODC/Dance: Brenda Way Artistic Director," promotional material, DanceMotionUSA.org, http://www.dancemotionusa.org/media/6488/odc%20one-sheet.pdf, accessed June 1, 2014.
5. Dennis Adams, Corey Brady, Jeremy Smith, and Anne Zivolich, interview by author, San Francisco, June 28, 2011.
6. Chris Miner, telephone interview by author, September 30, 2010.
7. Quilet Rarang and Vanessa Thiessen, interview by author, San Francisco, June 28, 2011.
8. Rarang and Thiessen, interview.
9. Milton Cummings has defined cultural diplomacy broadly as the "exchange of ideas, information, art and other aspects of culture among nations and their peoples in order to foster mutual understandings." See "Cultural Diplomacy and the United States Government: A Survey," in *Cultural Diplomacy: Recommendations and Research* (Washington, DC: Center for Arts and Culture, 2003), 1. For a comprehensive study of international cultural diplomacy over centuries, see Richard T. Arndt, *The First Resort of Kings: American Cultural Diplomacy in the Twentieth Century* (Washington, DC: Potomac, 2005).
10. Secretary of State Clinton had announced earlier that year (2010) a review of US policy toward Burma. See Michael F. Martin, "U.S. Policy towards Burma: Issues for the 113th Congress," Report to Congress by the Congressional Research Service, March 12, 2013, http://www.fas.org/sgp/crs/row/R43035.pdf, accessed November 25, 2013.
11. "Statement by President Obama on Burma," White House, November 18, 2011, http://www.whitehouse.gov/the-press-office/2011/11/18/statement-president-obama-burma, accessed November 26, 2013.
12. For more on the historical triangulation of Burmese, Chinese, and US policy, see Wayne Bert, "Burma, China and the U.S.A.," *Pacific Affairs* 77, no. 2 (2004): 263–282. For more on the effect of American policy shifts on US/China/Burma relationships, see David I. Steinberg. "Myanmar-China-US: The Potential for

Triangular Cooperation," *Asia Pacific Bulletin*, no. 271, EastWestCenter.org, November 15, 2013, http://www.eastwestcenter.org/sites/default/files/private/apb241.pdf, accessed November 26, 2013.

13. See Serge Guilbaut, *How New York Stole the Idea of Modern Art: Abstract Expressionism, Freedom, and the Cold War*, trans. Arthur Goldhammer (Chicago: University of Chicago Press, 1983).

14. Penny Von Eschen, *Satchmo Blows Up the World: Jazz Ambassadors Play the Cold War* (Cambridge, MA: Harvard University Press, 2004), 63–64.

15. Susan Foster, "Choreographing History," in *Choreographing History*, ed. Susan Foster (Bloomington: Indiana University Press, 1995), 15.

16. Bonnie Oda Homsey, interview by author, Los Angeles, June 27, 2011.

17. Randy Martin has argued for dance studies as political theory because dance is "a social process that foregrounds the very means through which bodies gather." See *Critical Moves: Dance Studies in Theory and Politics* (Durham, NC: Duke University Press, 1998), 6.

18. Jean Graham-Jones, "Editorial Comment: Theorizing Globalization through Theatre," *Theatre Journal* 57, no. 3 (2005): 2.

19. Carbonara et al., interview.

20. Marxist theorist Raymond Williams elaborates on his term "structures of feeling" in *Marxism and Literature* (New York: Oxford University Press, 1978).

21. Christina Klein, *Cold War Orientalism: Asia in the Middlebrow Imagination, 1945-1961* (Berkeley: University of California Press, 2003), 53, 14.

22. Klein, *Cold War Orientalism*, 14–15.

23. For more discussion of sentimental sympathy as a form of American neo-imperialism, see Mary Louise Pratt, "Arts of the Contact Zone," in *Profession* 91 (1991), 33–40. Also see Lilie Chouliaraki, *The Ironic Spectator: Solidarity in the Age of Post-Humanitarianism* (Malden, MA: Polity, 2013).

24. Naima Prevots, *Dance for Export: Cultural Diplomacy and the Cold War* (Middletown, CT: Wesleyan University Press, 1998), 12.

25. Calculation done using the US Bureau of Labor Consumer Price Inflation Calculator on November 26, 2013.

26. Susan Foster, *Choreographing Empathy: Kinesthesia in Performance* (London and New York: Routledge, 2011), 11.

27. Foster, *Choreographing Empathy*, 11.

28. Unknown author, Untitled, 1955, regular feature, *Dance Magazine*. Records, New York Public Library for the Performing Arts, New York, NY.

29. Victoria Geduld, "Dancing Diplomacy: Martha Graham and the Strange Commodity of Cold-War Cultural Exchange in Asia, 1955 and 1974," *Dance Chronicle*, 33, no. 1 (2010): 44–81.

30. Thomas Borstelmann, *The Cold War and the Color Line: American Race Relations in the Global Arena* (Cambridge, MA: Harvard University Press, 2001). Also see Mary Dudziak, *Cold War Civil Rights: Race and the Image of American Democracy* (Princeton, NJ: Princeton University Press, 2000).

31. Von Eschen, *Satchmo*, 17.

32. National Commission on Terrorist Attacks Upon the United States, *The 9/11 Commission Report: Final Report of the National Commission on Terrorist Attacks Upon the United States* (Washington, DC: National Commission on Terrorist Attacks Upon the United States, 2004), 377. The additional reports include Center for Arts and Culture, *Cultural Diplomacy: Recommendations and Research* (Washington, DC: Center for Arts and Culture, 2004); The Curb Center for

Art, Enterprise and Public Policy, *Cultural Diplomacy and the National Interest: In Search of a 21st-Century Perspective* (Nashville, TN: Vanderbilt University, 2007).

33. "Remarks by President Barack Obama," Prague, the Czech Republic, White House, Washington, DC, April 5, 2009. Accessed June 1, 2012. http://www.whitehouse.gov/the_press_office/Remarks-By-President-Barack-Obama-In-Prague-As-Delivered.

34. Patrice Pavis has coined the term "corporeal-cultural check-up" in arguing that intercultural collaborations offer the possibility of a collaborator "confront[ing] his/her technique and professional identity with those of the others." For Pavis, the "greater the concern with the exchange of corporeal techniques, the more political and economic it [intercultural collaboration] becomes . . . inconceivable outside of political and economic structures, but . . . realized in an individual exchange of bodies and organic reference points." Pavis's argument for corporeality as tense, deep, and confrontational provides a frame for evaluating twenty-first-century dance-in-diplomacy, judging where American power is maintained and where it is contested. See the introduction to *The Intercultural Performance Reader*, ed. Patrice Pavis (New York: Routledge, 1996), 14–15.

35. Pauline Koner, *Solitary Song* (Durham, NC: Duke University Press, 1989), 223.

36. Harvey Feigenbaum, "Globalization and Cultural Diplomacy," in *Cultural Diplomacy: Recommendations and Research* (Washington, DC: Center for Arts and Culture: 2004), 9.

37. Joseph Nye, "Public Diplomacy and Soft Power," *Annals of the American Academy of Political and Social Science* 616, no. 1 (March 2008): 94.

38. Von Eschen, *Satchmo*, 281.

39. "Mutual Educational and Cultural Exchange Program," United States Code, Title 22: Chapter 33, Government Printing Office, http://www.gpo.gov/fdsys/pkg/USCODE-2012-title22/html/USCODE-2012-title22-chap33.htm; Bureau of Educational and Cultural Affairs, US Department of State, "Cultural and Arts Programs: Goals, Authority, and Program Descriptions," last updated November 24, 2005, www.state.gov/r/whconf/index.html.

40. Frances Stonor Saunders, *The Cultural Cold War: The CIA and the World of Arts and Letters* (New York: The New Press, 1999), 115-116.

41. Saunders, *Cultural Cold War*, 379–383.

42. Political theorist Joseph Nye most fully explains what he means by "smart power" in "Public Diplomacy and Soft Power," 94–109. Hillary Clinton championed "smart power" beginning with her 2009 confirmation speech, "Statement Before the Senate Foreign Relations Committee." Washington, DC. January 13, 2009, http://www.state.gov/secretary/rm/2009a/01/115196.htm, accessed November 25, 2013.

43. Charlotte M. Canning, "Teaching Theatre as Diplomacy: A US *Hamlet* in the European Court," *Theatre Topics* 21, no. 2 (2011): 153.

44. Frank A. Ninkovich, *The Diplomacy of Ideas: U.S. Foreign Policy and Cultural Relations, 1938-1950* (Cambridge, UK: Cambridge University Press, 1981).

45. Situating American efforts in a global context reveals other distinguishing aspects of American approaches to cultural diplomacy. European cultural efforts have always outpaced those of the United States, in part because the tradition of investing in culture—even seeing a national culture not just a national public good but as a "potential global public good"—has been a Continental project since the nineteenth century. Europe, too, tends to use cultural diplomacy

to build on preexisting, often tense relationships, whereas the United States has generally used cultural diplomacy to begin relationships. See Margaret Wyszomirski, *International Cultural Relations: A Multi-Country Comparison* (Washington, DC: Center for Arts and Culture, 2003).

46. Nicholas Cull, *The Cold War and the United States Information Agency: American Propaganda and Public Diplomacy, 1945-1989* (Cambridge, UK: Cambridge University Press, 2009): 81–82.

47. Prevots, *Dance for Export*, 40.

48. ANTA Dance Panel minutes, September 25, 1958, Bureau of Educational and Cultural Affairs Collection, Collection 468, box 101, folder 15, University of Arkansas Special Collections, Fayetteville (hereafter cited as Collection 468).

49. ANTA began as a federally charted organization in 1935, created to nurture American drama and dramatic training. Theater historians have often overlooked ANTA in favor of studying the Federal Theatre Project, which was founded in the same year and received more government funding. See "National Theatre is Authorized by Congress to Advance the Drama," *New York Times*, June 30, 1935, 1.

50. ANTA Dance Panel minutes, February 21, 1963, Bureau of Educational and Cultural Affairs Collection, Collection 468, box 101, folder 16.

51. "Contact Info," DanceMotion USA website, http://www.dancemotionusa.org/contact/, accessed November 25, 2013.

52. Juliet Sablosky, "Reinvention, Reorganization, Retreat: American Cultural Diplomacy at Century's End, 1978-1998," *Journal of Arts Management, Law and Society* (March 1999): 30–34.

53. Sablosky, "Reinvention, Reorganization, Retreat," 36.

54. "Gallup Poll of the Islamic World," Gallup.com, February 26, 2002, http://www.gallup.com/poll/5380/gallup-poll-islamic-world.aspx, accessed (November 25, 2013); Pew Global Attitudes Project. *Views of Changing World 2003: War with Iraq Further Divides Global Publics*, (Washington, DC: Pew Research Center, 2003).

55. Judith Hamera, *Dancing Communities: Performance, Difference and Connection in the Global City* (London: Routledge, 2007), 5.

56. Jeff Friedman, "Muscle Memory: Performing Embodied Knowledge," in *Art and the Performance of Memory: Sounds and Gestures of Recollection*, ed. Richard C. Smith (London: Routledge, 2002), 160.

57. Diana Taylor, *The Archive and the Repertoire: Performing Cultural Memory in the Americas* (Durham, NC: Duke University Press, 2003).

58. Rebecca Schneider, *Performing Remains: Art and War in Times of Theatrical Reenactment* (New York: Routledge, 2011), 100.

59. Taylor, *Archive*, 17; Friedman, "Muscle Memory," 160.

60. Judith Jamison, *Dancing Spirit: An Autobiography* (New York: Doubleday, 1993); Allegra Kent, *Once a Dancer* (New York: St. Martin's Press, 1997); Edward Villella, *Prodigal Son: Dancing for Balanchine in a World of Pain and Magic* (New York: Simon & Schuster, 1992).

61. Michael Frisch, *A Shared Authority: Essays on the Craft and Meaning of Oral and Public History* (Albany: State University of New York Press, 1990), 161.

62. Frisch, *Shared Authority*, 160.

63. J. L. Austin, *How to Do Things with Words* (Cambridge, MA: Harvard University Press, 1962), 6–7.

64. Rebekah Kowal, *How to Do Things with Dance: Performing Change in Postwar America* (Middletown, CT: Wesleyan University Press, 2012), 6–8.
65. Paul Gilbert, *The Philosophy of Nationalism* (Boulder, CO: Westview Press, 1998), 6.
66. Anthony Shay, *Choreographic Politics: State Folk Dance Companies, Representation, and Power* (Middletown, CT: Wesleyan University Press, 2002), 2.
67. David Román, *Performance in America: Contemporary US Culture and the Performing Arts* (Durham, NC: Duke University Press, 2005), 269.
68. Clifford Geertz, "Thick Description: Toward an Interpretive Theory of Culture," in *The Interpretation of Cultures: Selected Essays* (New York: Basic Books, 1973), 3–30; Thomas DeFrantz, *Dancing Revelations* (Oxford: Oxford University Press, 2004), xi.
69. Richard Schechner, *Performance Theory* (London: Routledge, 2003): 394.
70. Michel De Certeau, *The Practice of Everyday Life*, trans. Steven Rendell (Berkeley: University of California Press, 1984), 97.
71. Elin Diamond, *Introduction to Performance and Cultural Politics*, ed. Elin Diamond (London, New York: Routledge, 1996), 1.
72. Bruce McConachie, *American Theater in the Culture of the Cold War: Producing and Contesting Containment, 1947-1962* (Iowa City: University of Iowa Press, 2003), 9–10.
73. While that tour and, even more so Limón's work, appear repeatedly throughout this book, not enough dancers remained available to include it more fully in the book *Diplomats*. For more on US–Latin American cultural diplomacy efforts during the Cold War, see Darlene J. Sadlier, *Americans All: Good Neighbor Cultural Diplomacy in World War II* (Austin: University of Texas Press, 2012).
74. David K. Johnson, *The Lavender Scare: The Cold War Persecution of Gays and Lesbians in the Federal Government* (Chicago: University of Chicago Press, 2004).

CHAPTER 1

1. This description relies on available recordings of performances closest to the tour's time period. See *Western Symphony*, DVD, directed by Thomas Rowe (Monitor Productions, 1957).
2. John Martin, "Ballet: Visit to Bolshoi," *New York Times*, October 10, 1962, 59.
3. *Spartacus,* choreographed to music by Aram Khachaturian, was reincarnated several times through the fifties and sixties (Leningrad: Leonid Yakobson, 1956 and 1962 tours; Moscow: Igor Moiseyev, 1958 tour; Yakobson revised, 1962). On the 1962 tour, the Bolshoi performed Yakobson's revised version.
4. John Martin, "Ballet: Adieu to Moscow," *New York Times*, October 31, 1962, 34.
5. Christina Ezrahi, *Swans of the Kremlin: Ballet and Power in Soviet Russia* (Pittsburgh, PA: University of Pittsburgh Press, 2012), 166.
6. Ezrahi, *Swans*, 133.
7. Sally Leland, telephone interview by author, August 4, 2008.
8. Edward Villella, telephone interview by author, June 10, 2008.
9. Gloria Govrin, interview by author, Minneapolis, June 8, 2008.
10. Government officials, including Khrushchev, had attended the opening night one week earlier.
11. See Nancy Fraser, "Rethinking the Public Sphere: A Contribution to the Critique of Actually Existing Democracy," in *Habermas and the Public Sphere*, ed. Craig

Calhoun (Cambridge, MA: MIT Press, 1992). Also see Román, *Performance in America*, 269.

12. ANTA Dance Panel minutes, September 18, 1962, Bureau of Educational and Cultural Affairs Collection, Collection 468, box 101, folder 17.

13. Ezrahi, *Swans*, 133.

14. Balanchine made the bulk of his choreography in the United States, but choreographed ballets in Russia and Europe prior to his arrival in the United States in 1933.

15. Michel de Certeau, *The Writing of History* (New York: Columbia University Press, 1992), 96.

16. Yale Richmond, *Cultural Exchange and the Cold War: Raising the Iron Curtain* (University Park: Pennsylvania State University Press, 2003), 123.

17. ANTA Dance Panel minutes, February 10, 1955, Collection 468, box 101, folder 14.

18. Dana Adams Schmidt, "Fingerprint Rule," *New York Times*, October 20, 1957, 23.

19. Richmond, *Cultural Exchange*, 16–19.

20. "Review of Exchanges," US State Department internal memo, April 4, 1963, New York City Ballet Archives, New York, NY.

21. Richmond, *Cultural Exchange*, 19. Through this public-private arrangement, the United States continued its hallmark policy of using private philanthropy, in addition to public funding, to fund cultural diplomacy. See Frank Ninkovich, *The Diplomacy of Ideas: US Foreign Policy and Cultural Relations, 1938-1950* (Cambridge, UK: Cambridge University Press, 1981).

22. Harlow Robinson, *The Last Impresario: The Life, Times, and Legacy of Sol Hurok* (New York: Penguin, 1994), 258.

23. For more on popular reception of the Moiseyev, see Victoria Hallinan, "The 1958 Tour of the Moiseyev Dance Company: A Window into American Perception," *Journal of History and Cultures* 1 (2012): 51–64.

24. ANTA Dance Panel minutes, October 17, 1957, Collection 468, box 101, folder 13.

25. ANTA Dance Panel minutes, February 18, 1960, Collection 468, box 101, folder 15.

26. ANTA Dance Panel minutes, October 2, 1958, Collection 468, box 101, folder 15.

27. ANTA Dance Panel minutes, September 25, 1958, Collection 468, box 101, folder 15.

28. ANTA Dance Panel minutes, May 21, 1959, Collection 468, box 101, folder 15.

29. ANTA Dance Panel minutes, April 21, 1960, Collection 468, box 101, folder 15.

30. ANTA Dance Panel minutes, December 19, 1957, Collection 468, box 101, folder 13. All the material attributed to Chase and Kirstein in this paragraph is from this document.

31. ANTA Dance Panel minutes, May 11, 1960, Collection 468, box 101, folder 15.

32. ANTA Dance Panel minutes, May 11, 1960.

33. ANTA Dance Panel minutes, May 11, 1960.

34. ANTA Dance Panel minutes, January 13, 1955, Collection 468, box 101, folder 14.

35. ANTA Dance Panel minutes, November 17, 1960, Collection 468, box 101, folder 15.

36. The Gostkoncert initially proposed the Palace of Congresses Theatre rather than the Bolshoi. Correspondence between company manager Betty Cage and tour manager Leonidoff does not mention the theater Gostkoncert proposed in Leningrad.

37. ANTA Dance Panel minutes, February 20, 1962, Collection 468, box 101, folder 17.

38. ANTA Dance Panel minutes, February 20, 1962.

39. Catherine Gunther Kodat, "Dancing through the Cold War: The Case of *The Nutcracker*," *Mosaic* 33, no. 3 (2000): 7.

40. Richard T. Arndt, *The First Resort of Kings: American Cultural Diplomacy in the Twentieth Century* (Washington, DC: Potomac, 2005), 82–83; Martin B. Duberman, *The Worlds of Lincoln Kirstein* (New York: Knopf, 2007), 354–369.

41. Saunders, *The Cultural Cold War*, 115–116.

42. Lincoln Kirstein, *Thirty Years: Lincoln Kirstein's the New York City Ballet* (New York: Knopf, 1978), 127.

43. Betty Cage letter to Gertrude Macy, July 13, 1962, New York City Ballet Archives, New York, NY.

44. ANTA Dance Panel minutes, June 19, 1962, 468, box 101, folder 17, Collection 468.

45. Gloria Govrin, interview by author, Minneapolis, June 8, 2008; Arthur Mitchell, interview by author, New York, June 16, 2008.

46. L. Leonidoff to Betty Cage, July 9, 1962, New York City Ballet Archives, New York, NY.

47. Betty Cage to Robert Schaskin, Gostkoncert representative, October 9, 1962, New York City Ballet Archives, New York, NY.

48. Allen Hughes, "Ballet: Bolshoi Stages US Premiere of 'Spartacus,'" *New York Times*, September 13, 1962, 32.

49. Maya Plisetskaya, *I, Maya Plisetskaya*, trans. Antonina W. Bouis (New Haven, CT: Yale University Press, 2001).

50. Manifest, 1962 Tour file, New York City Ballet Archives, New York, NY.

51. See Heath Bowman to Betty Cage, September 1962, New York City Ballet Archives, New York, NY.

52. Because most of the dancers referred to cities by their 1962 names, I use the proper names as they were designated during the Soviet era.

53. Robert Maiorano, interview by author, Saratoga Springs, June 13, 2008.

54. Deborah Jowitt, *Jerome Robbins: His Life, His Theater, His Dance* (New York: Simon and Schuster, 2004), 104.

55. Jowitt, *Jerome Robbins*, 103.

56. David Caute, *The Dancer Defects: The Struggle for Cultural Supremacy during the Cold War* (Oxford: Oxford University Press, 2003), 492–493.

57. Caute, *Dancer Defects*, 492–493.

58. Caute, *Dancer Defects*, 492–493.

59. See Richard Buckle, *George Balanchine, Ballet Master* (London: Hamilton, 1988), 237.

60. Michel de Certeau, *The Practice of Everyday Life* (Berkeley: University of California Press, 1984), 97.

61. Bettijane Sills, interview by author, New York, June 3, 2008.

62. Kay Mazzo, telephone interview by author, August 22, 2008.

63. Lincoln Kirstein, quoted in Buckle, *George Balanchine*, 236.

64. Govrin, interview.
65. Jack Raymond, "Big Force Masses to Blockade Cuba: Armada Is under Orders to Open Fire if Necessary—All Troops Are Alerted," *New York Times*, October 22, 1962, 1.
66. "Please Don't Call Times for Cuba Information," *New York Times*, October 25 1962, 20.
67. Mimi Paul, interview by author, Washington, DC, June 2, 2008. The two preceding quotations were made by Paul.
68. Suki Schorer, telephone interview by author, August 20, 2008; Govrin, interview.
69. Paul, interview.
70. Sills, interview.
71. Mitchell, interview. The three preceding quotations were all statements made by Mitchell.
72. Repeated requests to O'Brien to be interviewed for this book went unanswered. For more on the O'Brien incident, see Hans Tuchs, "Memorandum to the State Department: Soviet Evaluations," Bureau of Educational and Cultural Affairs Collection, Series 4, box 73, folder 28, Collection 468.
73. Mazzo, interview.
74. Kent Stowell, telephone interview by author, August 4, 2008.
75. Sills, interview.
76. Sills, interview.
77. Carol Sumner, interview by author, New York, June 3, 2008.
78. Victoria Simon, personal interview by author, New York, June 12, 2008.
79. Allegra Kent, interview by author, New York, June 10, 2008. All quotations in this paragraph are statements made by Kent.
80. Maiorano, interview. All quotations in this paragraph are statements made by Maiorano.
81. This description of *Serenade* is drawn from my attendance at several live performances of the ballet by New York City Ballet and from the public television broadcast on *Great Performances*. See *Great Performances: Dance in America*, "Serenade," directed by Judy Kinberg (Thirteen/WNET, 1990).
82. Nancy Goldner, *Balanchine Variations* (Gainesville: University Press of Florida, 2008), 21.
83. Schorer, interview.
84. Describing how bodies function as political agents in performance, Randy Martin writes, "Like any agent of social change, [the body] forges its own agenda and responds to a particular history. . . . It does not take shape simply as the consequence of control and domination but it also organizes experience beyond the quarters of social control." See *Performance as Political Act: The Embodied Self* (New York: Bergin & Garvey, 1990), 2.
85. Judith Hamera, *Dancing Communities: Performance, Difference and Connection in the Global City* (London: Routledge, 2007), 19.
86. Although some dancers remember seeing ballet performances in Moscow and Leningrad, including a performance of *Le Corsaire* at the Stanislavski Theatre, most of their exposure to Soviet ballet was in the schools rather than from professional performances. Given this, they were reticent to comment on the state of Soviet ballet in 1962. As dancer Karen Morrell said, "We knew their best dancers were in the West, so I don't like to judge based on that." Karen Morrell, telephone interview by author, July 21, 2008.

87. Schorer, interview.

88. Simon, interview. Simon was careful to point out that she saw this familiar position in just one class, where she assumed the teacher must have had a training lineage similar to Balanchine's. Ballet training had shifted in the schools since Balanchine's departure, largely through the development of Agrippina Vaganova's syllabus. For more on the transition from Russian Imperial ballet training to the Soviet approaches, see Vera Krasovskaya, *Vaganova: A Dance Journey from Petersburg to Leningrad* (Gainesville: University Press of Florida, 2005).

89. Simon, interview. All quotations in this paragraph are statements made by Simon.

90. Tim Scholl, *From Petipa to Balanchine: Classical Revival and the Modernisation of Ballet* (London: Routledge, 1994), 18.

91. Taper, *Balanchine*, 42.

92. Govrin, interview.

93. Not all the dancers who traveled on the tour were American citizens. Six, including the French Verdy, traveled on non-American passports. See Manifest, 1962 Tour file, New York City Ballet archives.

94. Violette Verdy, telephone interview by author, July 20, 2008.

95. Leningrad's ballet school had portraits of Pierre Vladimirov, Felia Doubrovska, and Anatole Obukhoff, all of whom had taught at SAB's Manhattan studios by 1962. See Kirstein, *Thirty Years*, 173. For more on the presence of Russian teachers in the United States, see Lynn Garafola, *Diaghilev's Ballets Russes* (New York: Oxford University Press, 1989), 377.

96. Maiorano, interview.

97. Nadine Revene, interview by author, Lancaster, PA, June 1, 2008.

98. Revene, interview.

99. Govrin, interview; Simon, interview.

100. Paul, interview.

101. Maiorano, interview.

102. Scholl, *Petipa*, 12.

103. Scholl, *Sleeping Beauty, a Legend in Progress*, (New Haven, CT: Yale University Press, 2004) 65.

104. Scholl, *Sleeping*, 79.

105. L. Leonidoff to Betty Cage, undated, New York City Ballet Archives, New York, NY.

106. Marvin Carlson, *The Haunted Stage: The Theatre as Memory Machine* (Ann Arbor: University of Michigan Press, 2001), 154.

107. Natalia Roslavleva, *Era of the Russian Ballet* (London: Da Capo Press, 1979), 271.

108. Alan Brinkley, "The Illusion of Unity in Cold War Culture," in *Rethinking Cold War Culture*, ed. Peter Kuznick and James Gilbert (Washington, DC: Smithsonian, 2001), 65, 72.

109. Peter Filene, "'Cold War Culture' Doesn't Say It All," in *Rethinking Cold War Culture*, ed. Peter Kuznick and James Gilbert (Washington, DC: Smithsonian, 2001), 157.

110. Taper, *Balanchine*, 278.

111. Taper, *Balanchine*, 278.

112. Taper, *Balanchine*, 25.

113. Thank you to Beth Genne for this point.

114. Balanchine, like many Russian émigrés, was vehemently anti-Communist. Several dancers said he rarely discussed his memories of the USSR other than telling them it was horrible, and they could see the strain he felt on returning to the Soviet Union.

115. Mitchell, interview.

116. John Martin, "Ballet: Americans in Kiev," *New York Times*, November 13, 1962, 42

117. Stowell, interview. All quotations in this paragraph are statements made by Stowell.

118. Schorer, interview.

119. Tuchs, *Memorandum*.

120. Tuchs, *Memorandum*.

121. Mitchell, interview.

122. Valery Panov, *To Dance* (New York: Knopf, 1978), 157.

CHAPTER 2

1. Clement Greenberg, *Forum Lectures* (Washington, DC: US Information Agency, 1960). Greenberg's ideas actually circulated with government support, when the Voice of America first published his lectures and then broadcast them on air in the 1960s.

2. John Martin, *The Modern Dance* (New York: A. S. Barnes and Co., 1933).

3. Rebekah Kowal, *How to Do Things with Dance: Performing Change in Postwar America* (Middletown, CT: Wesleyan University Press, 2010), 19–51.

4. Borstelmann, *The Cold War and the Color Line*, 140.

5. Jim Schwoch has argued that the increasing availability of television (and American satellite systems that broadcast American telecasts globally) shifted Cold War cultural wars of words to "multiple fronts . . . words, sights, sounds, and experiences," transforming "psychological warfare" into "early manifestations of . . . information diplomacy." See *Global TV: New Media and the Cold War: 1946-69* (Urbana: University of Illinois Press, 2009), 60.

6. Dudziak, *Cold War Civil Rights*, 235. Borstelmann, *Cold War*, 164.

7. Kenneth Heger, "Race Relations in the United States and the American Cultural and Informational Programs in Ghana, 1957-1966," *Prologue* 31, no. 4 (1999): 260–262.

8. Cultural theorist Richard Dyer describes the promise of American democracy as dependent on a narrative of increasing inclusion. See Dyer, *White: Essays on Race and Culture* (New York: Routledge, 1997), 53.

9. Von Eschen, *Satchmo*, 17.

10. As dance scholar Anthea Kraut has written, this interest in African art "valorized blackness as a vital, unfettered alternative to the alienation of modernity allegedly afflicting whites, the fantasy of the primitive only furthered racist assumptions that people of African origin were somehow outside of history." See "Between Primitivism and Diaspora: The Dance Performances of Josephine Baker, Zora Neale Hurston, and Katherine Dunham," *Theatre Journal* 55, no. 3 (2003): 435.

11. Robert Farris Thompson, *African Art in Motion* (Berkeley: University of California Press, 1974).

12. Brenda Dixon Gottschild, *Digging the Africanist Presence in American Performance: Dance and Other Contexts* (Westport, CT: Greenwood Publishing, 1996).

13. Susan Manning, *Modern Dance, Negro Dance: Race in Motion* (Minneapolis: University of Minnesota Press, 2004).

14. Anna Kisselgoff, "Ailey Dancers Set Russians Cheering," *New York Times*, January 21, 1971, 26.

15. Thomas DeFrantz, *Dancing Revelations: Alvin Ailey's Embodiment of African American Culture* (Oxford: Oxford University Press, 2004), 21.

16. Sharron Miller, interview by author, Montclair, NJ, March 4, 2009.

17. Mark Franko, *Dancing Modernism/Performing Politics* (Bloomington: Indiana University Press, 1995), ix.

18. Franko, *Dancing Modernism*, ix.

19. Guilbaut, *How New York Stole*.

20. Saunders, *The Cultural Cold War*, 254.

21. See Marilyn Kushner, "Exhibiting Art at the American National Exhibition in Moscow, 1959: Domestic Politics and Cultural Diplomacy," *Journal of Cold War Studies* 4, no. 1 (2002): 6–26.

22. Von Eschen, *Satchmo*, 63.

23. *Dancing for Mr. B: Six Balanchine Ballerinas*, DVD, directed by Anne Belle (1989, Kultur, International Films, 2008).

24. Dixon Gottschild, *Digging the Africanist Presence*, 66–68.

25. Arthur Mitchell, interview by author, New York, June 16, 2008.

26. Dixon Gottschild, *Digging the Africanist Presence*, 66–68.

27. Dixon Gottschild, *Digging the Africanist Presence*, 66–68.

28. *Arthur Mitchell Coaching the Pas de deux from "Agon,"* DVD, directed by Nancy Reynolds (1957, New York: George Balanchine Foundation, 2006).

29. *Arthur Mitchell Coaching*, DVD.

30. Stephanie Jordan, *Moving Music: Dialogues with Music in Twentieth-Century Ballet* (London: Dance Books, 2000), 151, 156–157.

31. Peggy Pascoe, "Miscegenation Law, Court Cases, and Ideologies of 'Race' in Twentieth-Century America," *Journal of American History* 83, no. 1 (1996): 48.

32. ANTA Dance Panel minutes, March 21, 1957, Bureau of Educational and Cultural Affairs Collection, Collection 468, box 101, folder 13.

33. ANTA Dance Panel minutes, January 19, 1956, box 101, folder 14, Collection 468.

34. ANTA Dance Panel minutes, January 19, 1956.

35. Mitchell, interview.

36. Allegra Kent, interview by author, New York, June 10, 2008.

37. Gloria Govrin, interview by author, Minneapolis, June 8, 2008.

38. Violette Verdy, interview by author, Bloomington, IN, December 27, 2010.

39. Preston Grover, "New York City Ballet Puzzles Official Moscow," *Montreal Star*, October 11, 1962, 7; David Miller, "New York Negro Wows Moscow Ballet Fans," *Calgary Herald*, October 10, 1962, 49.

40. John Martin, "Ballet: Visit to Bolshoi," *New York Times*, October 10, 1962, 59.

41. John Martin, "City Ballet Ends Leningrad Stand," *New York Times*, November 9, 1962, 32.

42. John Martin, "Ballet: Adieu to Moscow," *New York Times*, October 31, 1962, 34.

43. José Esteban Muñoz, "Feeling Brown: Ethnicity and Affect in Ricardo Bracho's *The Sweetest Hangover (and Other STDs)*," *Theatre Journal* 52, no. 1 (2000): 68.

44. Mitchell, interview.

45. Mitchell, interview.

46. Susan Manning has argued that *Revelations* is the preeminent example of a choreographic work that uses what she calls "mythic abstraction" and black self-determination in equal parts. See Manning, *Modern Dance*.

47. Kimberley Benston, *Performing Blackness: Enactments of African-American Modernism* (London: Routledge, 2000), 7.

48. Dudley Williams, interview by author, New York, March 5, 2009.

49. Lynne Taylor-Corbett, interview by author, New York, March 5, 2009.

50. Carmen de Lavallade and Dudley Williams, interview by author, Austin, November 9, 2005.

51. Martin Luther King Jr., "The Negro Is Your Brother," *Atlantic Monthly* 212, no. 2 (1963): 78–88.

52. Judith Jamison, telephone interview by author, October 4, 2010.

53. Airgram from Accra, Ghana, American Embassy to US Department of State, August 17, 1968, Series 16, box 317, folder 19, Collection 468; Taylor-Corbett, interview.

54. Other countries on the 1967 tour had concrete American political assets, for instance, the Malagasy Republic's NASA tracking station. See Karen Bell, "Developing a 'Sense of Community': US Cultural Diplomacy and the Place of Africa during the Early Cold War, 1953-64," in *The United States and West Africa: Interactions and Relations,* ed. Alusine Jalloh and Toyin Falola (Rochester, NY: University of Rochester Press, 2008), 139.

55. Von Eschen, *Satchmo,* 149.

56. Williams, interview.

57. Taylor-Corbett, interview.

58. Joni L. Jones, "Conversations with History: Sekou Sundiata, Craig Harris, and *Elijah,*" in *The Color of Theater: Race, Culture and Contemporary Performance,* ed. Roberta Uno and Lucy Mae San Pablo Burns (London: Continuum, 2002), 410.

59. Dudziak, *Cold War,* 49.

60. Dudziak, *Cold War,* 49.

61. Dudziak, *Cold War,* 49.

62. Dudziak, *Cold War,* 52.

63. USIS, "The Dignity of Man: America's Civil Rights Program," document 5a, box 135, folder USIA 1, Lyndon B. Johnson Library and Museum, Austin, TX.

64. Dudziak, *Cold War,* 238.

65. Dudziak, *Cold War,* 237.

66. USIS, "Dignity," 10.

67. USIS, "Dignity," 10.

68. USIS, "Dignity," 15.

69. USIS, "Dignity," 15–16.

70. Memo recording conversation among Beverly Gerstein, Martha Hill, Walter Terry, and William Bales, "Ailey Programs for Russia," July 6 and 7, 1970, Series 2, box 53, folder 13, Collection 468.

71. DeFrantz, *Dancing Revelations,* 23.

72. Judith Jamison, interview.

73. All descriptions of *Revelations* are drawn from a composite of viewings of chore-ography, including numerous personal viewings in Washington, DC, New York

City, and Austin, TX. Also see "Revelations," choreographed by Alvin Ailey, *An Evening with the Alvin Ailey American Dance Theater*, DVD, directed by Thomas Grimm (1986, Kultur, 2001).

74. "Revelations," choreographed by Alvin Ailey, DVD.
75. Judith Jamison, interview.
76. Alvin Ailey, quoted in Von Eschen, *Satchmo*, 153.
77. George Faison, interview by author, New York, March 4, 2009.
78. Susan, Foster. "Closets Full of Dances: Modern Dance's Performance of Masculinity and Sexuality," in *Dancing Desires: Choreographing Sexualities On and Off the Stage*, ed. Jane Desmond, 147–207. Madison: University of Wisconsin Press, 2001; Nadine Hubbs, *The Queer Composition of America's Sound: Gay Modernists, American Music, and National Identity* (Berkeley: University of California Press, 2004), 4.
79. Memo to Thomas Huff, "Security Information Regarding Three Members of Alvin Ailey Dance Theater," June 28, 1967, box 53, folder 7, Collection 468.
80. Enclosure, letter to Honorable Lee C. White, White House, Washington, DC, January 18, 1965, FBI File Subject: Alvin Ailey Jr. Record No. 116-74732-2, FOIPA Request No.: 1163795-000.
81. Letter to Alexander P. Butterfield, Washington, DC, July 7, 1970, FBI File Subject: Alvin Ailey Jr., FOIPA Request No.: 1163795-000.
82. See Memo to Thomas Huff, 28 June 1967, box 53, folder 7, Collection 468. All quotations in this paragraph are from this memo. This conversation may have precipitated further surveillance of Ailey. A 1970 letter in Ailey's FBI file says the FBI was advised in October 1967, four months after the State Department meeting with Ailey, by "another governmental agency which conducts personnel investigations," of Ailey's August 1967 arrest in Italy; see Letter to Alexander P. Butterfield, Washington, DC, July 7, 1970, FBI File Subject: Alvin Ailey Jr., FOIPA Request No.: 1163795-000.
83. Johnson, *The Lavender Scare*, 8.
84. Johnson, *Lavender*, 16.
85. Johnson, *Lavender*, 77.
86. Johnson, *Lavender*, 196–197.
87. "The Jose Limon Dance Company-Soviet Tour 1973: Note," undated, box 68, folder 10, Collection 468.
88. Johnson, *Lavender*, 210.
89. Airgram from American Embassy Moscow to Department of State, "Evaluation Report," February 24, 1975, box 58, folder 20, Collection 468.
90. Simon Karlinsky, "Russia's Gay Literature and Culture: The Impact of the October Revolution," in *Hidden from History: Reclaiming the Gay and Lesbian Past*, ed. Martin Duberman, Martha Vicinus, and George Chauncey Jr. (New York: Penguin, 1989), 363.
91. Johnson, *Lavender*, 199.
92. Bettijane Sills, interview by author, New York, June 3, 2008.
93. Jennifer Dunning, *Alvin Ailey: A Life in Dance* (Reading, MA: Addison-Wesley, 1996), 224.
94. Dunning, *Alvin Ailey*, 224.
95. "USSR Trip Report," undated, box 53, folder 15, Collection 468.
96. Unknown author, "Summary," June 22–July 14, 1974, box 53, folder 16, Collection 468.

97. DeFrantz, *Dancing Revelations*, 108–109.

98. Memo recording conversation among Beverly Gerstein, Martha Hill, Walter Terry, and William Bales, "Ailey Programs for Russia," July 6 and 7, 1970, Series 2, box 53, folder 13, Collection 468. All quotations in this paragraph are statements from this memo.

99. Thomas DeFrantz has persuasively argued that white dance critics' dismissal of Ailey, even as the company became extremely popular with audiences, reflected their lack of knowledge about African American artistic forms and left them feeling "left out" of audiences' reactions. See DeFrantz, *Dancing Revelations*, 109–111.

100. Program Draft, undated, Series 2, box 53, folder 14, Collections 468.

101. Unknown author, "Summary," June 22–July 14, 1974, box 53, folder 16, Collection 468.

102. "USSR Trip Report," undated, box 53, folder 15, Collection 468.

103. Memo from Joseph Pressel to Mark Lewis, October 15, 1970, box 53, folder 15, Collection 468.

104. Memo from Pressel to Lewis, October 15, 1070.

105. Anna Kisselgoff, "Ailey Dancers Set Russians Cheering," *New York Times*, January 21, 1971, 26.

106. Memorandum from Mark Lewis to Frederick Irving, January 23, 1971, box 53, folder 15, Collection 468.

107. Constance Valis Hill, "Katherine Dunham's *Southland: Protest in the Face of Oppression*," in *Dancing Many Drums Excavations in African American Dance*, ed. Thomas F. DeFrantz (Madison: University of Wisconsin Press, 2002), 304. I would also like to thank Joanna Dee Das for her insights regarding *Southland*.

108. Taylor-Corbett, interview.

109. Jamison, interview.

CHAPTER 3

1. Henry Kissinger to Gerald Ford, "White House Appearance by the Martha Graham Dance Company," undated, Bureau of Educational and Cultural Affairs Historical Collection, Special Collections, Collection 468, box 65, folder 2.

2. Tom Prinkley, "Is Martha Too Sexy for Export?" *Life* magazine, undated, Martha Graham Collection, Scrapbooks, box 355, Graham Scrapbooks, Library of Congress, Washington, DC (hereafter cited as LOC).

3. Peter Sparling, interview by author, Ann Arbor, MI, May 11, 2011.

4. Dwight Eisenhower, quoted in Nicholas Cull, *The Cold War and the United States Information Agency: American Propaganda and Public Diplomacy, 1945-1989* (Cambridge, UK: Cambridge University Press, 2009), 81.

5. "Winning the Cold War: The U.S. Ideological Offensive," part 4, Hearings Before the Subcommittee on International Organizations and Movements of the Committee on Foreign Affairs, House of Representatives, 88th Cong., 407 (1963), 392–396.

6. Marilyn S. Kushner, "Exhibiting Art at the American National Exhibition in Moscow, 1959: Domestic Politics and Cultural Diplomacy," *Journal of Cold War Studies* 4, no. 1 (2002): 6–26.

7. Eisenhower, quoted in Kushner, "Exhibiting," 13.

8. Susan Manning, *Modern Dance, Negro Dance: Race in Motion* (Minneapolis: University of Minnesota Press, 2004), 126–128.

9. Victoria Geduld, "Dancing Diplomacy: Martha Graham and the Strange Commodity of Cold-War Cultural Exchange in Asia, 1955 and 1974," *Dance Chronicle*, 33, no. 1 (2010): 53.

10. ANTA Dance Panel minutes, May 5, 1955, box 101, folder 14, Collection 468,

11. Unsigned memo from American Embassy-Warsaw to Department of State, undated, RG 306, box 12, folder 8, Records of the United States Information Agency, National Archives II, College Park, MD.

12. Martha Graham, *Blood Memory* (New York: Doubleday, 1991), 89.

13. Kowal, *How to Do Things*, 19–51.

14. For more on how John Martin theorized dance modernism, see Gay Morris, *A Game for Dancers: Performing Modernism in the Postwar Years, 1945-1960* (Middletown, CT: Wesleyan University Press, 2006); and Martin, *The Modern Dance.*

15. John Martin, "Dance as a Means of Communication," in *What Is Dance?* ed. Roger Copeland and Marshall Cohen (Oxford, UK: Oxford University Press, 1983), 23; John Martin, "Metakinesis," in Copeland and Cohen, *What Is Dance?*, 25.

16. Graham, *Blood*, 202.

17. Manning, *Modern Dance*, 127. Penny Von Eschen has noted a similar preference rooted in "color-blind liberalism and modernist aesthetics" in jazz tours. See Kowal, *How to Do Things*, 19–51.

18. Manning, *Modern Dance*, 127; Ellen Graff, *Stepping Left: Dance and Politics in New York City, 1928-1942* (Durham, NC: Duke University Press, 1997), 130.

19. Manning, *Modern Dance*, 134–135.

20. Ellen Graff, *Stepping Left*, 130.

21. ANTA Dance Panel minutes, December 7, 1954, box 101, folder 19, Collection 468.

22. Von Eschen, *Satchmo*, 17.

23. Anna Kisselgoff, "Martha Graham Dies at 96: A Revolutionary in Dance," *New York Times*, April 2, 1991, Proquest, accessed May 18, 2013. http://search.proquest.com.proxy.lib.umich.edu/docview/428029897/73BEFA600476423CPQ/15?accountid=14667.

24. ANTA Dance Panel minutes, May 5, 1955, box 101, folder 14, Collection 468.

25. Von Eschen, *Satchmo*, 20–22.

26. ANTA Dance Panel minutes, December 7, 1954, box 101, folder 14, Collection 468; ANTA Dance Panel minutes, March 20, 1958, box 101, folder 15, Collection 468.

27. ANTA Dance Panel minutes, March 21, 1957, box 101, folder 13, Collection 468; ANTA Dance Panel minutes, May 5, 1955, box 101, folder 14, Collection 468.

28. ANTA Dance Panel minutes, March 20, 1958, box 101, folder 15, Collection 468.

29. ANTA Dance Panel minutes, December 17, 1954, box 101, folder 14, Collection 468; ANTA Dance Panel minutes, September 17, 1955, box 101, folder 14, Collection 468; ANTA Dance Panel minutes, April 17, 1958, box 101, folder 15, Collection 468.

30. For more on the American reception to Moiseyev, see Victoria Hallinan, "The 1958 Tour of the Moiseyev Dance Company: A Window into American Perception," *Journal of History and Cultures* 1 (2012): 51–64.

31. Ramsay Burt, "Dance, Gender and Psychoanalysis: Martha Graham's *Night Journey*," *Dance Research Journal* 30, no. 1 (1998): 56.

32. ANTA Dance Panel minutes, September 17, 1963, box 101, folder 16, Collection 468.

33. ANTA Dance Panel minutes, September 17, 1963.

34. For more on the controversies surrounding Dunham, see Hill, *Katherine Dunham's Southland*, 289–316.

35. ANTA Dance Panel minutes, April 17, 1958, box 101, folder 15, Collection 468.

36. Penny Von Eschen, "Made on Stage: Transnational Performance and the Worlds of Katherine Dunham from London to Dakar," in *Transnational Lives: Biographies of Global Modernity, 1700-present*, ed. Desley Deacon, Penny Russell, and Angela Woollacott (London: Palgrave Macmillan, 2010), 158–160.

37. Von Eschen, "Made on Stage," 164.

38. ANTA Dance Panel minutes, February 19, 1959, box 101, folder 15, Collection 468.

39. ANTA Dance Panel minutes, May 11, 1960, box 101, folder 15, Collection 468.

40. ANTA Dance Panel minutes, May 21, 1959, box 101, folder 15, Collection 468.

41. ANTA Dance Panel minutes, October 17, 1961, box 101, folder 17, Collection 468.

42. ANTA Dance Panel minutes, June 23, 1963, box 101, folder 18, Collection 468.

43. ANTA Dance Panel minutes, December 22, 1955, box 101, folder 14, Collection 468; ANTA dance-panel minutes, September 19, 1961, box 101, folder 17, Collection 468.

44. Memorandum of Conversation, Shirley Gornitsky and Beverly Gerstein, February 12, 1964, box 144, folder 4, Collection 468.

45. Memorandum of conversation, Gornitsky and Gerstein, February 12, 1964.

46. Elaine Tyler May, *Homeward Bound: American Families in the Cold War Era* (1988; New York: Basic Books, 1999), 63.

47. Tracy Davis, *Stages of Emergency: Cold War Nuclear Civil Defense* (Durham, NC: Duke University Press, 2007).

48. Mire Koikari, *Pedagogy of Democracy: Feminism and the Cold War in the U.S. Occupation of Japan* (Philadelphia, PA: Temple University Press, 2008), 1–4.

49. Klein, *Cold War Orientalism*, 10–14.

50. Christina Klein, *Cold War Orientalism*, 192.

51. Kowal, *How to Do Things*, 22–24.

52. K. A. Cuordileone, *Manhood and American Political Culture in the Cold War* (New York: Routledge, 2005).

53. For more on the Cold War obsession with "penetration," see Frank Costigliola, "'Unceasing Pressure for Penetration': Gender, Pathology, and Emotion in George Kennan's Formation of the Cold War," *Journal of American History* 83, no. 4 (1997): 1309–1339.

54. K. A. Cuordileone, *Manhood*, 216.

55. Franko, *Martha*, 7.

56. Walter Terry, "Sex and Martha Graham," *New York Herald Tribune*, undated, Graham Scrapbooks, LOC. Walter Terry, *Frontiers of Dance: The Life of Martha Graham*. New York: Thomas Y. Crowell, 1975.

57. Susan J. Leonardi and Rebecca A. Pope, *The Diva's Mouth: Body, Voice, Prima Donna Politics* (New Brunswick, NJ: Rutgers University Press, 1996), 57.

58. Rebecca Schneider, *The Explicit Body in Performance* (New York: Routledge, 1997), 1–2.

59. Lauren Berlant, *The Queen of America Goes to Washington City: Essays on Sex and Citizenship* (Durham, NC: Duke University Press, 1997), 222–223.

60. Prinkley, "Is Martha," LOC.

61. "Winning the Cold War," hearings, 392–396.

62. "Winning the Cold War," hearings, 420.

63. "Winning the Cold War," hearings, 420.

64. "Winning the Cold War," hearings, 437.

65. Janet Eilber and Peter Sparling confirmed that the 1963 version of *Phaedra* did not include this choreography. Janet Eilber and Peter Sparling, personal e-mail, January 20, 2011.

66. Robert Tracy, *Goddess Martha Graham's Dancers Remember*, (New York: Limelight Editions, 1997), 163.

67. Andrea Friedman, "The Smearing of Joe McCarthy: The Lavender Scare, Gossip, and Cold War Politics," *American Quarterly* 57, no. 4 (2005): 1105–1106.

68. Whitney Strub, "The Clearly Obscene and the Queerly Obscene: Heteronormativity and Obscenity in Cold War Los Angeles," *American Quarterly* 60, no. 2 (2008): 373–398.

69. Johnson, *The Lavender Scare*, 8.

70. Memo to Thomas Huff, "Security Information Regarding Three Members of Alvin Ailey Dance Theater," 28 June 1967, Series 2, box 53, Folder 7, Collection 468.

71. Peter Frelinghuysen, "Ballet Held Shocking: Letter to the Editor," *New York Times*, September 23, 1963, Graham Scrapbooks, LOC; "Washington Letter by your Congressman Rep. Peter Frelinghuysen Jr.," *Peapack Somerset Hills News*, September 18, 1963, Graham Scrapbooks. LOC.

72. "Sense and Censorship," editorial, *Washington Star*, Graham Scrapbooks, LOC. A *New York Post* article compared Kelly's complaint with Vietnamese leader Madame Nhu's crackdown on all forms of social dancing in Vietnam. See "Rep. Kelly's Dancing Daze," *New York Post*, undated, Graham Scrapbooks, LOC.

73. Frelinghuysen, "Ballet Held Shocking"; "Washington Letter."

74. Richard Meyer, "'Have You Heard the One about the Lesbian Who Goes to the Supreme Court?': Holly Hughes and the Case Against Censorship," *Theatre Journal* 52, no. 4 (2000): 550.

75. "Sense and Censorship," editorial.

76. "Sense and Censorship," editorial.

77. "Guest Editorials Not Bubbles: Editorial," *Chicago Tribune*, September 24, 1963, Graham Scrapbooks, LOC.

78. For the fullest description and excusal of *Phaedra*, see Walter Terry, "To Martha Graham: Editorial," *New York Herald Tribune*, September 11, 1963, Graham Scrapbooks, LOC.

79. John Chamberlain, "These Days, Syndicated Column," *Peekskill Star*, October 22, 1963; *Cornellsville Courier, Cesborton Tribune, Elyria Ohio Chronicle Telegram, Iowa City Iowa Citizen, Fostoria Ohio Review Times, Huntington Indiana Herald Press, Lancaster Pennsylvania Intelligence-Journal, New York Journal American, New Haven Register, Kenton Ohio Times, New Castle Pennsylvania News, Manistee Michigan News Advocate, Marietta Ohio Times, Massillon Ohio Independent, Meriden Connecticut Journal, New Philadelphia Ohio Times, Boston Record American, Allentown Pennsylvania Call, Bozeman Montana Chronicle, Bellevue Ohio Gazette, Ansonia Connecticut Sentinel, Wichita Kansas Beacon, Xenia Ohio Gazette, Willimantic Conn Chronicle, Tamaqua Pennsylvania Courier, San Francisco News-Call Bulletin, San Antonio Light, Donora Pennsylvania Herald American*, October 24, 1963; *Montgomery Journal, Monogahela Republican, Athens Ohio Messenger, Los Angeles Herald Examiner, Circleville Ohio Herald, Middletown Ohio Journal*, October 25, 1963; *Little Rock Democrat*, October 26, 1963; Graham Scrapbooks, LOC.

80. "Guest Editorials Not Bubbles: Editorial," *Chicago Tribune*, Sept 24, 1963, Graham Scrapbooks, LOC.

81. Telegram from Edna Kelly to Roy Leatherman, September 11, 1963, Graham Scrapbooks, LOC.

82. Mark Franko has argued that Graham's choreographic approach to gender and sexuality anticipated the early seventies feminist arguments for female sexual revolution, see *Martha*, 177.

83. For more on different categories of feminism in American performance history, see Jill Dolan, *The Feminist Spectator as Critic* (Ann Arbor: University of Michigan Press, 1991), 3–8.

84. Telegram from USIS London to Charles Ellison, March 5, 1965, box 64, folder 28, Collection 468.

85. Airgram from American Embassy Bonn to Washington, DC office, US State Department, August 22, 1966, box 64, folder 28, Collection 468.

86. Eric Foner, *The Story of American Freedom* (New York, W. W. Norton, 1998), 275–276.

87. Diana Hart Johnson, interview by author, Kalamazoo, MI, June 19, 2011; Elisa Monte, interview by author, New York, May 6, 2011; Sparling, interview.

88. Johnson, interview.

89. Peggy Lyman Hayes, interview by author, New York, May 3, 2011.

90. Hayes, interview.

91. Bonnie Oda Homsey, interview by author, Los Angeles, June 27, 2011. Count Basie had actually been to Burma on a State Department tour as recently as 1971. See Von Eschen, *Satchmo*, 119.

92. Diane Gray, interview by author, Cleveland, May 10, 2011.

93. Robert Schulzinger, *A Time for Peace: The Legacy of the Vietnam War* (New York: Oxford University Press, 2006), 160.

94. Sparling, interview.

95. David Chase, interview by author, San Francisco, June 29, 2011.

96. Carl Paris, interview by author, New York, May 2, 2011.

97. Mitchell, interview.

98. Chase, interview.

99. Lucinda Mitchell, interview by author, Bethesda, MD, July 6, 2011.

100. Carl Paris, interview.

101. Lucinda Mitchell, interview.

102. Letter from William Batchelder to unknown recipient, undated, box 65, folder 1, Collection 468.

103. Letter from George West to Washington, DC office, US State Department, undated, box 65, folder 2, Collection 468.

104. *Martha Graham Dance Company's Dance in America*. Wea Corp: 1987.

105. Janet Eilber, interview by author, New York, May 3, 2011.

106. For more on this scenario of cross-racial compassion, see Lauren Berlant, *Compassion: The Culture and Politics of an Emotion* (New York: Routledge, 2004), 4; Linda Williams, *Playing the Race Card: Melodramas of Black and White from Uncle Tom to O. J. Simpson* (Princeton, NJ: Princeton University Press, 2001).

107. Judith Hamera, *Dancing Communities: Performance, Difference and Connection in the Global City* (London: Routledge, 2007), 25-30.

108. Sparling, interview.

109. Gray, interview.

110. Monte, interview.

111. Gray, interview.

112. Homsey, interview.

113. Chase, interview.
114. Monte, interview; Homsey, interview.
115. Eric Newton, telephone interview by author, September 8, 2011.
116. Von Eschen, *Satchmo*, 148–150.
117. "Saigon Applauds Graham Dancers: A Workshop for Students Is Also Given a Sudden Silence," *New York Times*, October 11, 1974, 30.
118. Gray, interview.

CHAPTER 4

1. Ronald K. Brown, interview by author, Brooklyn, May 5, 2011.
2. *Get to Know DanceMotion USA*, You Tube, video, accessed May 15, 2013, https://www.youtube.com/watch?v=dwvigD8rNtY&index=7&list=PL2B3CC870AA72 95F7.
3. *Get to Know DanceMotion*, You Tube.
4. *Get to Know DanceMotion*, You Tube.
5. Deirdre Valente, interview by author, New York, May 3, 2010.
6. Ronald K. Brown, telephone interview by author, October 9, 2009.
7. Brown, 2009, interview.
8. The 2010 tours were also administered by Lisa Booth Management, Inc. Subsequent years of touring were administered by BAM alone.
9. "Gallup Poll of the Islamic World," Gallup.com, http://www.gallup.com/poll/5380/gallup-poll-islamic-world.aspx; "Views of a Changing World," Pew Global Attitudes Project, accessed May 15, 2013, http://www.pewglobal.org/2003/06/03/views-of-a-changing-world-2003/.
10. The Message Is America: Hearing Before the Committee on International Relations, 107th Cong, 12 (2001), statement of Edward Walker Jr., former US ambassador to Egypt, Israel, and the United Arab Emirates.
11. 9/11 Commission, *The 9/11 Commission Report: Final Report of the National Commission on Terrorist Attacks Upon the United States* (Washington, DC: National Commission on Terrorist Attacks upon the United States, 2004), 377. The additional reports include Center for Arts and Culture, *Cultural Diplomacy: Recommendations and Research* (Washington, DC: Center for Arts and Culture, 2004); The Curb Center for Art, Enterprise and Public Policy, *Cultural Diplomacy and the National Interest: In Search of a 21st-Century Perspective* (Nashville, TN: Vanderbilt University, 2007); and Charles Wolf and Brian Rosen, *Public Diplomacy: How to Think about and Improve It.* (Santa Monica, CA: RAND Corporation, 2004), http://www.rand.org/pubs/occasional_papers/OP134.
12. Alexandra Starr, "Charlotte Beers' Toughest Sell," *Business Week,* December 17, 2001, 14.
13. Starr, "Charlotte Beers'," 14.
14. Pew Research, "Views," 1.
15. Pew Research, "Views," 25.
16. Pew Research, "Views," 2.
17. Center for Arts and Culture, *Cultural Diplomacy,* 23.
18. Center for Arts and Culture, *Cultural Diplomacy,* 24.
19. Roslyn Sulcas, "Soft Steps of Diplomacy," *New York Times,* website, May 19, 2010, accessed May 15, 2013, http://www.nytimes.com/2010/03/21/arts/dance/21evidence.html?pagewanted=all&_r=0.
20. Sulcas, "Soft Steps."

21. E-mail to author from Sandy Sawotka, Director of Publicity, Brooklyn Academy of Music (BAM), May 31, 2014.

22. "Barack Obama and Joe Biden: Champions for Arts and Culture," the Obama/Biden Arts Platform, accessed August 15, 2013, http://www.artsdel.org/advocacy/Obama_Arts.pdf.

23. Barack Obama, "Remarks by President Barack Obama" speech, Prague, Czech Republic, April 5, 2009 http://www.whitehouse.gov/the_press_office/Remarks-By-President-Barack-Obama-In-Prague-As-Delivered.

24. Hillary Clinton, "Foreign Policy Address at the Council on Foreign Affairs" speech given at the Council on Foreign Relations, Washington, DC, July 15, 2009.

25. Jawole Willa Jo Zollar, telephone interview by author, September 2, 2009.

26. Jana La Sorte, interview by author, New York, October 18, 2010.

27. Colombia Barosse, telephone interview by author, September 16, 2009.

28. Christine King, interview by author, Brooklyn, October 17, 2010.

29. I would like to thank Marcus White for helping me think through this distinction.

30. Barosse, interview.

31. "Rhythm Road," Jazz at Lincoln Center, accessed June 1, 2012, http://jalc.org/theroad/index.asp.

32. Chris Miner, telephone interview by author, September 30, 2010.

33. Rex Moser, Skype interview by author, October 4, 2010.

34. For more on the 2003 program, see Clare Croft, "Dance Returns to American Cultural Diplomacy: The US State Department's 2003 Dance Residency Program and Its After Effects," *Dance Research Journal* 45, no. 1 (2013): 22–39.

35. What constituted a significant Muslim population varied. According to the 2006 Indian census, Kolkata, the primary site of Jenkins' work in India, is 23 percent Muslim.

36. Valente, interview.

37. These numbers are based on my analysis of BAM's press materials as presented on its website, see "About Our Programs: Next Wave Festival," Brooklyn Academy of Music, accessed November 12, 2013, http://www.bam.org/backstage/programs/next-wave-festival/.

38. Valente, interview.

39. Barosse, interview.

40. "Remarks by President Obama at the University of Yangon," White House, accessed May 15, 2013, http://www.whitehouse.gov/the-press-office/2012/11/19/remarks-president-obama-university-yangon; Michael F. Martin, "U.S. Policy Towards Burma: Issues for the 113th Congress." Congressional Research Service. March 12, 2013. http://www.fas.org/sgp/crs/row/R43035.pdf. Accessed November 25, 2013.

41. Lily Ann Tai and Clarice Young, interview by author, Brooklyn, May 5, 2011.

42. "47 Nation Pew Global Attitudes Survey," Pew Research Global Attitudes Project, June 27, 2007, accessed November 12, 2013, http://www.pewglobal.org/files/pdf/2007%20Pew%20Global%20Attitudes%20Report%20-%20June%2027.pdf.

43. All figures based on CIA Factbook figures for 2003, accessed August 15, 2014, https://www.cia.gov/library/publications/the-world-factbook/

44. Moser, interview.

45. Sulcas, interview.

46. Sulcas, interview.

47. Sulcas, interview.
48. Valente, interview.
49. Joseph Melillo, telephone interview by author, September 30, 2009.
50. Melillo, interview.
51. For more on the roots of American arts diplomacy in a public/private hybrid, see Frank A. Ninkovich, *The Diplomacy of Ideas: U.S. Foreign Policy and Cultural Relations, 1938-1950* (Cambridge, UK: Cambridge University Press, 1981).
52. Valente, interview.
53. Barosse, interview.
54. "DanceMotion USA: About," DanceMotion USA, website, US Department of State, accessed November 12, 2013, http://www.dancemotionusa.org/about/.
55. Moser, interview.
56. Miranda Joseph, *Against the Romance of Community*, (Minneapolis: University of Minnesota Press, 2002), ix.
57. Joseph, *Against the Romance*, xxiii.
58. "Mission & Core Values," Urban Bush Women website, accessed November 12, 2013, http://www.urbanbushwomen.org/mission_values.php.
59. Jawole Willa Jo Zollar, interview by author, Brooklyn, May 4, 2010
60. Melillo, interview.
61. Brenda Way, telephone interview by author, October 8, 2009.
62. Zollar, 2009, interview.
63. Yayoi Kambara and Daniel Santos, interview by author, San Francisco, June 29, 2011.
64. Bennalldra Williams, interview by author, New York, October 17, 2010.
65. Moser, interview.
66. Jana La Sorte, interview by author, New York, October 18, 2010.
67. Dennis Adams, Corey Brady, Jeremy Smith, and Anne Zivolich, interview by author, San Francisco, June 28, 2011.
68. Way, interview.
69. Brown, 2011, interview.
70. Joni L. Jones, "Performance Ethnography: The Role of Embodiment in Cultural Authenticity," *Theatre Topics* 12, no. 1 (2002): 12.
71. Jones, "Performance Ethnography," 12.
72. Quilet Rarang and Vanessa Thiessen, interview by author, San Francisco, June 28, 2011.
73. Adams, et. al., interview.
74. Kambara, et. al., interview.
75. Kambara, et. al., interview.
76. Marjani Forte, interview by author, New York, October 16, 2010.
77. Kambara, et. al., interview.
78. Cowan, Geoffrey, and Amelia Arsenault, "Moving from Monologue to Dialogue to Collaboration: The Three Layers of Public Diplomacy," *Annals of the American Academy of Political and Social Science* 616, no. 1 (2008): 18.
79. The pilot program was evaluated by the State Department in a comprehensive effort led by dance community leader and artistic director of Washington, DC, dance community center Carla Perlo. I have made FOIA requests and contacted individual officials at the US State Department in an attempt to obtain that report and have been told it is private.
80. Miner, interview.

81. Williams, interview.
82. All movement descriptions are a composite, based on my seeing the work on two occasions and viewing a DVD of the performance provided by the company.
83. Williams, interview.
84. In Venezuela and Colombia, a brief introduction to the piece was read in Spanish, but during the work, the journals were read in English. In Brazil, the presenter demanded that the company project subtitles, although Zollar felt these were extremely distracting. From Zollar, interview 2010.
85. Williams, interview.
86. Williams, interview.
87. Rebekah J. Kowal, "Dance Travels: 'Walking with Pearl,'" *Performance Research* 12, no. 2 (2007): 85.
88. Kowal, "Dance Travels," 87.
89. Kowal, "Dance Travels," 92.
90. Naima Prevots, *Dance for Export: Cultural Diplomacy and the Cold War* (Middletown, CT: Wesleyan University Press, 1998): 303.
91. Shelley Fisher Fishkin, "Crossroads of Cultures: The Transnational Turn in American Studies—Presidential Address to the American Studies Association, November 12, 2004," *American Quarterly* 57, no. 1 (2005): 17–57.
92. Bush's most famous iteration of the sentiment was directed at governments believed to be harboring Al-Qaeda operatives. See George W. Bush, "Congressional Address," *Washington Post*, website, September 20, 2001, http://www.washingtonpost.com/wp-srv/nation/specials/attacked/transcripts/bushaddress_092001.html.
93. "Mission and Values," Urban Bush Women website, accessed June 1, 2012, http://www.urbanbushwomen.org/mission_values.php.
94. Keisha Turner, interview by author, Brooklyn, May 4, 2010.
95. Arjun Appadurai, *Modernity at Large: Cultural Dimensions of Globalization* (Minneapolis: University of Minnesota Press, 1996).
96. James Clifford, *Routes: Travel and Translation in the Late Twentieth Century,* (Cambridge, MA: Harvard University Press, 1997), 249–250.
97. Dudziak, *Cold War Civil Rights.*
98. Williams, interview.
99. Nadine George-Graves, *Urban Bush Women: Twenty Years of African American Dance Theater, Community Engagement, and Working It Out* (Madison: University of Wisconsin Press, 2010), 203.
100. King, interview.
101. Turner, interview.
102. Susan Reiter, "20th Anniversary Season," danceviewtimes.com, June 21, 2005, accessed November 13, 2013, http://danceviewtimes.com/2005/Summer/01/ubw.htm.
103. Turner, interview.

CHAPTER 5

1. D. Soyini Madison, *Critical Ethnography: Method, Ethics, and Performance* (Thousand Oaks, CA: SAGE, 2012).
2. Chang An-lee, Kim Tae-he, and Lee So-jin, interview by author, December 1, 2012, Chicago; translated by Nora Hauk.
3. Rustom Bharucha, *The Politics of Cultural Practice: Thinking through Theatre in an Age of Globalization* (Middletown, CT: Wesleyan University Press, 2000).

4. "DanceMotion USA: About," DanceMotion USA, US Department of State, accessed November 12, 2013, http://www.dancemotionusa.org/about/.
5. Trey McIntyre, interview by author, Chicago, December 1, 2012.
6. McIntyre, interview. (Ahn Ae-soon became artistic director in the summer of 2013.)
7. McIntyre, interview.
8. "Gangnam-Style Welcome," Trey McIntyre Project website, accessed November 18, 2013, http://www.treymcintyre.com/video/gangnam-style-welcome/.
9. Jeongsuk Joo, "Transnationalization of Korean Popular Culture and the Rise of 'Pop Nationalism' in Korea," *Journal of Popular Culture* 44, no. 3 (2011): 496.
10. Joo, "Transnationalization," 502.
11. "Orientalism" is a term coined in the now iconic book by Edward Said, *Orientalism* (New York: Vintage Books, 1970). Dance scholar Yutian Wong has done the most explicit work considering how Orientalism is embedded in American dance practice. See Yutian Wong, *Choreographing Asian America* (Middletown, CT: Wesleyan University Press, 2010).
12. Chanel DaSilva, Skype interview by author, December 10, 2012; Ashley Werhun, interview by author, Chicago, December 1, 2012; Brett Perry and Ryan Redmond, interview by author, Chicago, December 1, 2012.
13. Perry and Redmond, interview.
14. Not all of McIntyre's work works this way, so this was a choice.
15. Werhun, interview.
16. Werhun, interview.
17. Perry and Redmond, interview.
18. Perry and Redmond, interview.
19. DaSilva, interview.
20. DaSilva, interview; Lee, et al., interview.
21. Werhun, interview.
22. "Trey is in the Creative Cave," Trey McIntyre Project website, accessed November 18, 2013, http://www.treymcintyre.com/blog/3/.
23. "Trey McIntyre Project to Collaborate with Korea National Contemporary Dance Company," *Chicago Tribune*, September 11, 2012, http://articles.chicago tribune.com/2012-09-11/entertainment/chi-trey-mcintyre-project-20120910_1_new-work-troupe-symphony-center; "Segerstrom Center Co-Commissions New Multimedia Dance by Trey McIntyre," *Broadway World*, broadwayworld.com, accessed November 18, 2013, http://www.broad-wayworld.com/bwwdance/article/Segerstrom-Center-Co-Commissions-New-Multimedia-Dance-By-Trey-McIntyre-Project-1123-25-20120911; "Trey McIntyre Project to Collaborate with Korea National Contemporary Dance Company," *Orlando Sentinel* online, accessed November 18, 2013, http://articles.orlandosentinel.com/2012-09-11/news/chi-trey-mcintyre-project-20120910_1_new-work-troupe-symphony-center.
24. John Michael Schert, interview by author, Chicago, December 1, 2012. All statements in this paragraph were made by Schert.
25. "Arts and History Economic Grants Announced," City of Boise Idaho, website, accessed November 18, 2013, http://mayor.cityofboise.org/news-releases/2012/10/arts-history- economic-development-grants-announced/. Bieter, and many other local government officials, draw their rhetoric from the arts economic argument made popular by policy theorist Richard Florida in *The Rise of the*

Creative Class: And How It's Transforming Work, Leisure, Community and Everyday Life (New York: Basic Books, 2002).

26. For more on the 2003 program, see Clare Croft, "Dance Returns to American Cultural Diplomacy: The State Department's 2003 Dance Residency Program and Its After Effects," *Dance Research Journal* 45, no. 1 (2013): 22–39.

27. Margaret Jenkins, interview by author, College Park, MD, September 20, 2007.

28. For a more elaborate discussion of these communications efforts, see Susan Haas, Drew Margolin, and Monroe Price, "New Technologies and International Broadcasting: Reflections on Adaptations and Transformations," *Annals of the American Academy of Political and Social Science* 616, no. 1 (March 2008): 150–172.

29. Karen Hughes, quoted in Haas, et al., "New Technologies," 171.

30. Council 15. For a more extended discussion of the politics of Radio Sawa's efforts, see James Schwoch, *Global TV: New Media and the Cold War, 1946-1969* (Urbana: University of Illinois Press, 2009).

31. Haas, et al., "New Technologies," 156.

32. Redmond, interview.

BIBLIOGRAPHY

9/11 Commission. *The 9/11 Commission Report: Final Report of the National Commission on Terrorist Attacks Upon the United States.* Washington, DC: National Commission on Terrorist Attacks upon the United States, 2004.

Alvin Ailey American Dance Theater Archives, New York, NY.

An Evening with the Alvin Ailey American Dance Theater. DVD. Directed by Thomas Grimm. 1986. Kultur, 2001.

Appadurai, Arjun. *Modernity at Large: Cultural Dimensions of Globalization.* Minneapolis: University of Minnesota Press, 1996.

Arndt, Richard T. *The First Resort of Kings: American Cultural Diplomacy in the Twentieth Century.* Washington, DC: Potomac, 2005.

Arthur Mitchell Coaching the Pas de Deux from Agon. DVD. Directed by Nancy Reynolds. New York, George Balanchine Foundation, 2006.

Austin, J. L. *How to Do Things with Words.* Cambridge, MA: Harvard University Press, 1962.

Bannerman, Henrietta. "Martha Graham's House of the Pelvic Truth: The Figuration of Sexual Identities and Female Empowerment." *Dance Research Journal* 4, no. 1 (2010): 30–45.

Bell, Karen. "Developing a 'Sense of Community': US Cultural Diplomacy and the Place of Africa during the Early Cold War, 1953-64." In *The United States and West Africa: Interactions and Relations,* edited by Alusine Jalloh and Toyin Falola, 125–146. Rochester, NY: University of Rochester Press, 2008.

Benston, Kimberley. *Performing Blackness: Enactments of African-American Modernism.* London: Routledge, 2000.

Berlant, Lauren. *Compassion: The Culture and Politics of an Emotion.* New York: Routledge, 2004.

Berlant, Lauren. *The Queen of America Goes to Washington City: Essays on Sex and Citizenship.* Durham, NC: Duke University Press, 1997.

Bert, Wayne. "Burma, China and the U.S.A." *Pacific Affairs* 77, no. 2 (2004): 263–282.

Bharucha, Rustom. *The Politics of Cultural Practice: Thinking through Theatre in an Age of Globalization.* Middletown, CT: Wesleyan University Press, 2000.

Borstelmann, Thomas. *The Cold War and the Color Line: American Race Relations in the Global Arena.* Cambridge, MA: Harvard University Press, 2001.

Brinkley, Alan. "The Illusion of Unity in Cold War Culture." In *Rethinking Cold War Culture,* edited by Peter Kuznick and James Gilbert, 61–73. Washington, DC: Smithsonian Books, 2001.

Brooklyn Academy of Music. "About Our Programs: Next Wave Festival." BAM online. Accessed November 12, 2013. http://www.bam.org/backstage/programs/next-wave-festival/.

Brown, Lauren Erin. "'Cultural Czars': American Nationalism, Dance, and Cold War Arts Funding, 1945-1989." PhD diss., Harvard University, 2008.

Buckle, Richard. *George Balanchine, Ballet Master.* London: Hamilton, 1988.

Bureau of Educational and Cultural Affairs Historical Collection (CU). Special Collections. University of Arkansas Library.

Bureau of Educational and Cultural Affairs. US Department of State. "Cultural and Arts Programs: Goals, Authority, and Program Descriptions." www.state.gov/r/whconf/index.html. Last updated November 24, 2005.

Burt, Ramsay. "Dance, Gender and Psychoanalysis: Martha Graham's Night Journey." *Dance Research Journal* 30, no. 1 (1998): 34–53.

Canning, Charlotte M. "Teaching Theatre as Diplomacy: A US Hamlet in the European Court." *Theatre Topics* 21, no. 2 (2011): 151–162.

Carlson, Marvin. *The Haunted Stage: The Theatre as Memory Machine.* Ann Arbor: University of Michigan Press, 2001.

Caute, David. *The Dancer Defects: The Struggle for Cultural Supremacy during the Cold War.* Oxford: Oxford University Press, 2003.

Center for Arts and Culture. *Cultural Diplomacy: Recommendations and Research.* Washington, DC: Center for Arts and Culture, 2004.

Chouliaraki, Lilie. *The Ironic Spectator: Solidarity in the Age of Post-Humanitarianism.* Cambridge, UK: Polity, 2013.

City of Boise Idaho. "Arts and History Economic Grants Announced." Last modified October 11, 2012. http://mayor.cityofboise.org/news-releases/2012/10/arts-history-economic-development-grants-announced/.

Clifford, James. *Routes: Travel and Translation in the Late Twentieth Century.* Cambridge, MA: Harvard University Press, 1997.

Clinton, Hillary. "Foreign Policy Address at the Council on Foreign Affairs." Speech at the Council on Foreign Relations. Washington, DC, July 15, 2009.

Costigliola, Frank. "'Unceasing Pressure for Penetration': Gender, Pathology, and Emotion in George Kennan's Formation of the Cold War." *Journal of American History* 83, no. 4 (1997): 1309–1339.

Cowan, Geoffrey, and Amelia Arsenault, "Moving from Monologue to Dialogue to Collaboration: The Three Layers of Public Diplomacy." *Annals of the American Academy of Political and Social Science* 616, no. 1 (2008): 10–30.

Croft, Clare. "Dance Returns to American Cultural Diplomacy: The U.S. State Department's 2003 Dance Residency Program and Its After Effects." *Dance Research Journal* 45, no. 1 (2013): 22–39.

Cull, Nicholas. *The Cold War and the United States Information Agency: American Propaganda and Public Diplomacy, 1945-1989.* Cambridge, UK: Cambridge University Press, 2009.

Cummings, Milton. "Cultural Diplomacy and the United States Government: A Survey." In *Cultural Diplomacy: Recommendations and Research.* Washington, DC: Center for Arts and Culture, 2003: 1-9.

Cuordileone, K. A. *Manhood and American Political Culture in the Cold War.* New York: Routledge, 2005.

Curb Center for Art, Enterprise and Public Policy. *Cultural Diplomacy and the National Interest: In Search of a 21st-Century Perspective.* Nashville, TN: Vanderbilt University, 2007.

Dance Magazine Records. 1955. New York Public Library for the Performing Arts Archives. New York, NY.

DanceMotion USA. "DanceMotion USA: About." US Department of State. Accessed November 12, 2013. http://www.dancemotionusa.org/about/.

DanceMotion USA. *Get to Know DanceMotion USA*. YouTube video. Accessed June 4, 2014. http://www.youtube.com/watch?v=8hAwyjfqfJw&list=PL2B3CC870AA7295F7.

DanceMotionUSA. "Contact Info." Accessed June 2, 2014. http://www.dancemotionusa.org/contact/.

Dancing with Mr. B: Six Balanchine Ballerinas. DVD. Directed by Anne Belle. 1989. Kultur, International Films, 2008.

Davis, Tracy. *Stages of Emergency: Cold War Nuclear Civil Defense*. Durham, NC: Duke University Press, 2007.

de Certeau, Michel. *The Practice of Everyday Life*. Translated by Steven Rendell. Berkeley: University of California Press, 1984.

de Certeau, Michel. *The Writing of History*. New York: Columbia University Press, 1992.

DeFrantz, Thomas. *Dancing Revelations: Alvin Ailey's Embodiment of African American Culture*. Oxford: Oxford University Press, 2004.

Diamond, Elin. Introduction to *Performance and Cultural Politics*, edited by Elin Diamond. London, New York: Routledge, 1996.

Dolan, Jill. *The Feminist Spectator as Critic*. Ann Arbor: University of Michigan Press, 1991.

Duberman, Martin B. *The Worlds of Lincoln Kirstein*. New York: Alfred A. Knopf, 2007.

Dudziak, Mary L. *Cold War Civil Rights: Race and the Image of American Democracy*. Princeton, NJ: Princeton University Press, 2000.

Dunning, Jennifer. *Alvin Ailey: A Life in Dance*. Reading, MA: Addison-Wesley, 1996.

Dyer, Richard. *White: Essays on Race and Culture*. New York: Routledge, 1997.

Ezrahi, Christina. *Swans of the Kremlin: Ballet and Power in Soviet Russia*. Pittsburgh, PA: University of Pittsburgh Press, 2012.

Feigenbaum, Harvey. "Globalization and Cultural Diplomacy." In *Cultural Diplomacy: Recommendations and Research*. Washington, DC: Center for Arts and Culture, 2004.

Filene, Peter. "'Cold War Culture' Doesn't Say It All." In *Rethinking Cold War Culture*, edited by Peter Kulznick and James Gilbert, 156–174. Washington, DC: Smithsonian, 2001.

Fisher, Shelley. "Crossroads of Cultures: The Transnational Turn in American Studies: Presidential Address to the American Studies Association, November 12, 2004." *American Quarterly* 57, no. 1 (2005): 17–57.

Florida, Richard. *The Rise of the Creative Class: And How It's Transforming Work, Leisure, Community and Everyday Life*. New York: Basic Books, 2002.

Foner, Eric. *The Story of American Freedom*. New York: W. W. Norton, 1998.

Foster, Susan. "Choreographing History." In *Choreographing History*, edited by Susan Foster, 3–21. Bloomington: Indiana University Press, 1995.

Foster, Susan. "Closets Full of Dances: Modern Dance's Performance of Masculinity and Sexuality." In *Dancing Desires: Choreographing Sexualities On and Off the Stage*, edited by Jane Desmond, 147–207. Madison: University of Wisconsin Press, 2001.

Foster, Susan. *Choreographing Empathy: Kinesthesia in Performance*. London, New York: Routledge, 2011.

Franko, Mark. *Dancing Modernism / Performing Politics*. Bloomington: Indiana University Press, 1995.

Fraser, Nancy. "Rethinking the Public Sphere: A Contribution to the Critique of Actually Existing Democracy." In *Habermas and the Public Sphere*, edited by Craig Calhoun, 109–142. Cambridge, MA: MIT Press, 1992.

Friedman, Andrea. "The Smearing of Joe McCarthy: The Lavender Scare, Gossip, and Cold War Politics." *American Quarterly* 57, no. 4 (2005): 1105–1129.

Friedman, Jeff. "Muscle Memory: Performing Embodied Knowledge." In *Art and the Performance of Memory: Sounds and Gestures of Recollection*, edited by Richard C. Smith, 156–180. London: Routledge, 2002.

Frisch, Michael. *A Shared Authority: Essays on the Craft and Meaning of Oral and Public History*. Albany: State University of New York Press, 1990.

Gallup. "Gallup Poll of the Islamic World." Last updated February 26, 2002. http://www.gallup.com/poll/5380/gallup-poll-islamic-world.aspx.

Garafola, Lynn. *Diaghilev's Ballets Russes*. New York: Oxford University Press, 1989.

Geduld, Victoria. "Dancing Diplomacy: Martha Graham and the Strange Commodity of Cold-War Cultural Exchange in Asia, 1955 and 1974." *Dance Chronicle* 33, no. 1 (2010): 44–81.

Geertz, Clifford. *The Interpretation of Cultures: Selected Essays*. New York: Basic Books, 1973.

George-Graves, Nadine. *Urban Bush Women: Twenty Years of African American Dance Theater, Community Engagement, and Working It Out*. Madison: University of Wisconsin Press, 2010.

Gilbert, Paul. *The Philosophy of Nationalism*. Boulder, CO: Westview Press, 1998.

Goldner, Nancy. *Balanchine Variations*. Gainesville: University Press of Florida, 2008.

Gottschild, Brenda Dixon. *Digging the Africanist Presence in American Performance: Dance and Other Contexts*. Westport, CT: Greenwood Publishing, 1996.

Graff, Ellen. *Stepping Left: Dance and Politics in New York City, 1928-1942*. Durham, NC: Duke University Press, 1997.

Graham-Jones, Jean. "Editorial Comment: Theorizing Globalization through Theatre." *Theatre Journal* 57, no. 3 (2005): viii–xvi.

Graham, Martha. *Blood Memory*. New York: Doubleday, 1991.

Great Performances: Dance in America. Television Broadcast. Directed by Judy Kinberg, 60 min., Thirteen/WNET, 1990.

Greenberg, Clement. *Forum Lectures*. Washington, DC: US Information Agency, 1960.

Guilbaut, Serge. *How New York Stole the Idea of Modern Art: Abstract Expressionism, Freedom, and the Cold War*. Translated by Arthur Goldhammer. Chicago: University of Chicago Press, 1983.

Haas, Susan, Drew Margolin, and Monroe Price. "New Technologies and International Broadcasting: Reflections on Adaptations and Transformations." *Annals of the American Academy of Political and Social Science* 616, no. 1 (March 2008): 150–172.

Hallinan, Victoria. "The 1958 Tour of the Moiseyev Dance Company: A Window into American Perception." *Journal of History and Cultures* 1 (2012): 51–64.

Hamera, Judith. *Dancing Communities: Performance, Difference and Connection in the Global City*. London: Routledge, 2007.

Heger, Kenneth. "Race Relations in the United States and American Cultural and Informational Programs in Ghana, 1957-1966." *Prologue* 31, no. 4 (1999): 260–269.

Hubbs, Nadine. *The Queer Composition of America's Sound: Gay Modernists, American Music, and National Identity*. Berkeley: University of California Press, 2004.

Jackson, Shannon. *Social Works: Performing Arts, Supporting Publics*. London, New York: Routledge, 2011.

Jamison, Judith. *Dancing Spirit: An Autobiography.* New York: Doubleday, 1993.

Johnson, David K. *The Lavender Scare: The Cold War Persecution of Gays and Lesbians in the Federal Government.* Chicago: University of Chicago Press, 2004.

Jones, Joni L. "Conversations with History: Sekou Sundiata, Craig Harris, and Elijah." In *The Color of Theater: Race, Culture, and Contemporary Performance,* edited by Roberta Uno and Lucy Mae San Pablo Burns, 410–422. London: Continuum, 2002.

Jones, Joni L. "Performance Ethnography: The Role of Embodiment in Cultural Authenticity." *Theatre Topics* 12, no. 1 (2002): 1–15.

Joo, Jeongsuk. "Transnationalization of Korean Popular Culture and the Rise of 'Pop Nationalism' in Korea." *Journal of Popular Culture* 44, no. 3 (2011): 489–504.

Jordan, Stephanie. *Moving Music: Dialogues with Music in Twentieth-Century Ballet.* London: Dance Books, 2000.

Joseph, Miranda. *Against the Romance of Community.* Minneapolis: University of Minnesota Press, 2002.

Jowitt, Deborah. *Jerome Robbins: His Life, His Theater, His Dance.* New York: Simon & Schuster, 2004.

Karlinsky, Simon. "Russia's Gay Literature and Culture: The Impact of the October Revolution." In *Hidden from History: Reclaiming the Gay and Lesbian Past,* edited by Martin Duberman, Martha Vicinus, and George Chauncey Jr., 347–364. New York: Penguin, 1989.

Kent, Allegra. *Once a Dancer...* New York: St. Martin's Press, 1997.

King, Martin Luther, Jr.. "The Negro Is Your Brother." *Atlantic Monthly* 212, no. 2 (1963): 78–88.

Kirstein, Lincoln. *Thirty Years: Lincoln Kirstein's the New York City Ballet.* New York: Alfred A. Knopf, 1978.

Klein, Christina. *Cold War Orientalism: Asia in the Middlebrow Imagination, 1945–1961.* Berkeley: University of California Press, 2003.

Kodat, Catherine Gunther. "Dancing through the Cold War: The Case of *The Nutcracker.*" *Mosaic* 33, no. 3 (2000): 1–17.

Koikari, Mire. *Pedagogy of Democracy: Feminism and the Cold War in the U.S. Occupation of Japan.* Philadelphia, PA: Temple University Press, 2008.

Koner, Pauline. *Solitary Song.* Durham, NC: Duke University Press, 1989.

Kowal, Rebekah J. "Dance Travels: 'Walking with Pearl,'" *Performance Research* 12, no. 2 (2007): 85–94.

Kowal, Rebekah. *How to Do Things with Dance: Performing Change in Postwar America.* Middletown, CT: Wesleyan University Press, 2010.

Krasovskaya, Vera. *Vaganova: A Dance Journey from Petersburgh to Leningrad.* Gainesville: University Press of Florida, 2005.

Kraut, Anthea. "Between Primitivism and Diaspora: The Dance Performances of Josephine Baker, Zora Neale Hurston, and Katherine Dunham." *Theatre Journal* 55, no. 3 (2003): 433–450.

Kushner, Marilyn S. "Exhibiting Art at the American National Exhibition in Moscow, 1959: Domestic Politics and Cultural Diplomacy." *Journal of Cold War Studies* 4, no. 1 (2002): 6–26.

Leonardi, Susan J., and Rebecca A. Pope. *The Diva's Mouth: Body, Voice, Prima Donna Politics.* New Brunswick, NJ: Rutgers University Press, 1996.

Madison, D. Soyini. *Critical Ethnography: Method, Ethics, and Performance.* Thousand Oaks, CA: SAGE, 2012.

Manning, Susan. *Modern Dance, Negro Dance: Race in Motion*. Minneapolis: University of Minnesota Press, 2004.

Martha Graham Collection. Library of Congress. Washington, DC.

Martha Graham Dance Company's *Dance in America*. Wea Corp: 1987.

Martin, John. "Dance as a Means of Communication." In *What Is Dance? Readings in Theory and Criticism*, edited by Roger Copeland and Marshall Cohen, 22. Oxford: Oxford University Press, 1983.

Martin, John. "Metakinesis." In *What Is Dance? Readings in Theory and Criticism*, edited by Roger Copeland and Marshall Cohen, 23–24. Oxford: Oxford University Press, 1983.

Martin, John. *The Modern Dance*. New York: A. S. Barnes and Co., 1933.

Martin, Michael F. "U.S. Policy Towards Burma: Issues for the 113th Congress." Congressional Research Service. March 12, 2013. http://www.fas.org/sgp/crs/row/R43035.pdf. Accessed November 25, 2013.

Martin, Randy. *Critical Moves: Dance Studies in Theory and Politics*. Durham, NC: Duke University Press, 1998.

Martin, Randy. *Performance as Political Act: The Embodied Self*. New York: Bergin & Garvey, 1990.

May, Elaine Tyler. *Homeward Bound: American Families in the Cold War Era*. New York: Basic Books, 1988.

McConachie, Bruce. *American Theater in the Culture of the Cold War: Producing and Contesting Containment, 1947-1962*. Iowa City: University of Iowa Press, 2003.

Meyer, Richard. "'Have You Heard the One about the Lesbian Who Goes to the Supreme Court?': Holly Hughes and the Case Against Censorship." *Theatre Journal* 52, no. 4 (2000): 543–552.

Morris, Gay. *A Game for Dancers: Performing Modernism in the Postwar Years, 1945-1960*. Middletown, CT: Wesleyan University Press, 2006.

Muñoz, José Esteban. "Feeling Brown: Ethnicity and Affect in Ricardo Bracho's *The Sweetest Hangover and Other STDs*" *Theatre Journal* 52, no. 1 (2000): 67–79.

New York City Ballet. The Archives. Lincoln Center, New York, NY.

Ninkovich, Frank. *The Diplomacy of Ideas: US Foreign Policy and Cultural Relations, 1938-1950*. Cambridge, UK: Cambridge University Press, 1981.

Nye, Joseph. "Public Diplomacy and Soft Power." *Annals of the American Academy of Political and Social Science* 616, no. 1 (March 2008): 94–109.

Obama Biden. "Barack Obama and Joe Biden: Champions for Arts and Culture." The Obama/Biden Arts Platform. Accessed June 2, 2014. http://www.artsdel.org/advocacy/Obama_Arts.pdf.

Obama, Barack. "Remarks by President Barack Obama." Speech in Hradcany Square. Prague, Czech Republic. April 5, 2009. http://www.whitehouse.gov/the_press_office/Remarks-By-President-Barack-Obama-In-Prague-As-Delivered.

Panov, Valery. *To Dance*. New York: Alfred A. Knopf, 1978.

Pascoe, Peggy. "Miscegenation Law, Court Cases, and Ideologies of 'Race' in Twentieth-Century America." *Journal of American History* 83, no. 1 (1996): 44–69.

Pavis, Patrice. Introduction to *The Intercultural Performance Reader*. Edited by Patrice Pavis. New York: Routledge, 1996.

Pew Research Global Attitudes Project. "Global Unease with Major World Powers." Last modified June 27, 2007. http://www.pewglobal.org/files/pdf/2007%20Pew%20Global%20Attitudes%20Report%20-%20June%2027.pdf.

Pew Research Global Attitudes Project. "Views of a Changing World 2003." Last modified June 3, 2003. http://www.pewglobal.org/2003/06/03/views-of-a-changing-world-2003/.

Plisetskaya, Maya. *I, Maya Plisetskaya*. Translated by Antonina W. Bouis. New Haven, CT: Yale University Press, 2001.

Pratt, Mary Louise. "Arts of the Contact Zone." *Profession* 91 (1991): 33–40.

Prevots, Naima. *Dance for Export: Cultural Diplomacy and the Cold War*. Middletown, CT: Wesleyan University Press, 1998.

Records of the United States Information Agency. National Archives II. College Park, MD.

Richmond, Yale. *Cultural Exchange and the Cold War: Raising the Iron Curtain*. University Park: Pennsylvania University Press, 2003.

Robinson, Harlow. *The Last Impresario: The Life, Times, and Legacy of Sol Hurok*. New York: Penguin, 1994.

Román, David. *Performance in America: Contemporary U. S. Culture and the Performing Arts*. Durham, NC: Duke University Press, 2005.

Roslavleva, Natalia. *Era of the Russian Ballet*. London: Da Capo Press, 1979.

Sadlier, Darlene J. *Americans All: Good Neighbor Cultural Diplomacy in World War II*. Austin: University of Texas Press, 2012.

Said, Edward. *Orientalism*. New York: Vintage, 1970.

Saunders, Frances Stonor. *The Cultural Cold War: The CIA and the World of Arts and Letters*. New York: New Press, 1999.

Schechner, Richard. *Performance Theory*. London: Routledge, 2003.

Schneider, Rebecca. *The Explicit Body in Performance*. New York: Routledge, 1997.

Schneider, Rebecca. *Performing Remains: Art and War in Times of Theatrical Reenactment*. New York: Routledge, 2011.

Scholl, Tim. *From Petipa to Balanchine: Classical Revival and the Modernisation of Ballet*. London: Routledge, 1994.

Scholl, Tim. *Sleeping Beauty, a Legend in Progress*. New Haven, CT: Yale University Press, 2004.

Schulzinger, Robert. *A Time for Peace: The Legacy of the Vietnam War*. New York: Oxford University Press, 2006.

Schwoch, James. *Global TV: New Media and the Cold War, 1946-1969*. Urbana: University of Illinois Press, 2009.

Shay, Anthony. *Choreographic Politics: State Folk Dance Companies, Representation and Power*. Middletown, CT: Wesleyan University Press, 2002.

Starr, Alexandra. "Charlotte Beers' Toughest Sell." *Business Week*, December 17, 2001.

Strub, Whitney. "The Clearly Obscene and the Queerly Obscene: Heteronormativity and Obscenity in Cold War Los Angeles." *American Quarterly* 60, no. 2 (2008): 373–398.

Taper, Bernard. *Balanchine: A Biography*. New York: Times Books, 1984.

Taylor, Diana. *The Archive and the Repertoire: Performing Cultural Memory in the Americas*. Durham, NC: Duke University Press, 2003.

Terry, Walter. *Frontiers of Dance: The Life of Martha Graham*. New York: Thomas Y. Crowell, 1975.

Thompson, Robert Farris. *African Art in Motion*. Berkeley: University of California Press, 1974.

Tracy, Robert. *Goddess: Martha Graham's Dancers Remember*. New York: Limelight Editions, 1997.

Trey McIntyre Project. "Gangnam-Style Welcome." Accessed November 18, 2013. http://www.treymcintyre.com/video/gangnam-style-welcome/.

US Congress. "The Message Is America." Hearing Before the Committee on International Relations, 107th Cong. 12 (2001). Statement of Edward Walker Jr., former US ambassador to Egypt, Israel, and the United Arab Emirates.

US House of Representatives. "Winning the Cold War: The U.S. Ideological Offensive." Part 4. Hearings Before the Subcommittee on International Organizations and Movements of the Committee on Foreign Affairs House of Representatives. 88th Cong., 407 (1963).

United States Code. "Mutual Educational and Cultural Exchange Program." Title 22, chapter 33. Government Printing Office. http://www.gpo.gov/fdsys/pkg/USCODE-2012-title22/html/USCODE-2012-title22-chap33.htm.

Urban Bush Women. "Mission & Core Values." Accessed June 4, 2014. http://www.urbanbushwomen.org/mission_values.php.

Valis Hill, Constance. "Katherine Dunham's *Southland: Protest in the Face of Oppression.*" In *Dancing Many Drums: Excavations in African American Dance*, edited by Thomas F. DeFrantz, 289–316. Madison: University of Wisconsin Press, 2002.

Villella, Edward. *Prodigal Son: Dancing for Balanchine in a World of Pain and Magic.* New York: Simon & Schuster, 1992.

Von Eschen, Penny. "Made on Stage: Transnational Performance and the Worlds of Katherine Dunham from London to Dakar." In *Transnational Lives: Biographies of Global Modernity, 1700–Present,* edited by Desley Deacon, Penny Russell, and Angela Woollacott, 156–167. London: Palgrave Macmillan, 2010.

Von Eschen, Penny. *Race against Empire: Black Americans and Anticolonialism, 1937-1957.* Ithaca, NY: Cornell University Press, 1997.

Von Eschen, Penny. *Satchmo Blows Up the World: Jazz Ambassadors Play the Cold War.* Cambridge, MA: Harvard University Press, 2004.

Western Symphony. Film. Directed by Thomas Rowe. 1957. Monitor Productions.

White House. "Remarks by President Obama at the University of Yangon." Last modified November 19, 2012. http://www.whitehouse.gov/the-press-office/2012/11/19/remarks-president-obama-university-yangon.

White House. "Statement by President Obama on Burma." Last modified November 18, 2011. http://www.whitehouse.gov/the-press-office/2011/11/18/statement-president-obama-burma.

White House Central Files. Lyndon B. Johnson Library and Museum. Austin, TX.

Williams, Linda. *Playing the Race Card: Melodramas of Black and White from Uncle Tom to OJ Simpson.* Princeton, NJ: Princeton University Press, 2002.

Williams, Raymond. *Marxism and Literature.* New York: Oxford University Press, 1977.

Wolf, Charles, and Brian Rosen. *Public Diplomacy: How to Think about and Improve It.* Santa Monica, CA: RAND Corporation, 2004. http://www.rand.org/pubs/occasional_papers/OP134. October 1, 2009.

Wong, Yutian. *Choreographing Asian America.* Middletown, CT: Wesleyan University Press, 2010.

Wyszomirski, Margaret. *International Cultural Relations: A Multi-Country Comparison.* Washington, DC: Center for Arts and Culture, 2003.

INDEX

CPSIA information can be obtained at www.ICGtesting.com
Printed in the USA
LVOW11s1203040116

469013LV00002B/4/P